Candidates in Conflict

D1383971

STUDIES IN RHETORIC AND COMMUNICATION
General Editors:
E. Culpepper Clark
Raymie E. McKerrow
David Zarefsky

William L. Benoit and William T. Wells

Candidates in Conflict

Persuasive Attack and Defense in the 1992
Presidential Debates

The University of Alabama Press Tuscaloosa and London

∞

The paper on which this book is printed meets the minimum requirements of
American National Standard for Information Science–Permanence of Paper for
Printed Library Materials, ANSI Z39.48-1984.

Library of Congress Cataloging-in-Publication Data

Benoit, William L.
    Candidates in conflict : persuasive attack and defense in the 1992
presidential debates / William L. Benoit and William T. Wells.
        p.   cm.
    Includes bibliographical references (p.   ) and index.
    ISBN 0-8173-0868-7 (pbk. : alk. paper)
    1. Political oratory—United States. 2. Television broadcasting
of campaign debates. 3. President—United States—Elections—1992.
I. Wells, William T. II. Title.
PN4055.U53B46 1996
    808.53′08835—dc20   96-16792

British Library Cataloguing-in-Publication Data available

Contents

Tables

Preface

The present investigation into persuasive attack and defense in the 1992 presidential debates is part of an established research program into discourse that concerns face, image, or reputation, all terms for the audience's impression of a persuader. Most of this work on image has focused on persuasive defense (*apologiae, accounts*) rather than persuasive attack. A theory of image restoration discourse was sketched in an article (Benoit, Gullifor, and Panici, 1991) and then elaborated and illustrated in a book (Benoit, 1995). Several of the studies in this research program have examined discourse from politicians: President Nixon's Watergate rhetoric (Benoit, 1982), Senator Kennedy's Chappaquiddick address (Benoit, 1982), President Reagan's Iran-Contra discourse (Benoit, Gullifor, and Panici, 1991), and President Nixon's Cambodia address (Benoit, 1995). Other research has investigated corporate image repair efforts: Tylenol (Benoit and Lindsey, 1987b), AT&T (Benoit and Brinson, 1994), Union Carbide (Benoit, 1995), Exxon (Benoit, 1995), Coke and Pepsi (Benoit, 1995), Dow Corning (Brinson and Benoit, in press), and Sears (Benoit, in press). Image repair in entertainment and sports has also been studied: Tonya Harding's defense after the attack on Nancy Kerrigan (Benoit and Hanczor, 1994), Oliver Stone's defense of *JFK* (Benoit and Nill, under review), and Murphy Brown's response to Vice President Dan Quayle's attacks (Benoit and Anderson, under review).

Taken as a whole, this body of work builds a case for the claim that persuasive defense is an important and pervasive communication phenomenon and that a limited range of options are available for image repair regardless of the domain in which the defense occurs. Up to this point, however, this theory has not been applied to political *campaigns* generally (Dan Quayle's attack on Murphy Brown in his speech before the Commonwealth Club, Benoit and Anderson [under review], being the only exception) or to presidential debates specifically. Given the importance of persuasive attack in provoking persuasive defense, and the results of initial research on persuasive attack (Benoit and Dorries, in press), studies of persuasive attack ought to be as fruitful as research on persuasive defense, but much less work has been conducted there to date (mostly to provide a context for understanding and evaluating a particular persuasive defense). Hence we decided that an analysis of persuasive attack and defense in the 1992 presidential debates would be worthwhile, both to extend existing work on persuasive defense to political campaigns and to help articulate a correlative theory of persuasive attack strategies.

Of course, presidential debates merit scholarly attention. Hellweg, Pfau, and Brydon argue that "the public has come to expect" presidential debates (1992, p. 18). More specifically, Carlin (1994, p. 8) explains that "voters apparently place a premium on the importance of these events. A February 1987 Gallup survey indicated that 72 percent of the respondents wanted debates in 1988 (Gallup, 1987, p. 35)." Thus it should come as no surprise that presidential debates are viewed by millions, and the 1992 presidential debates were no exceptions. Owen declared, "With each passing electoral contest, debates have gained in importance. The media have accorded debates a central role in their election coverage, coming as they do at a crucial point late in the campaign" (1995, p. 136). Clearly, the presidential debates are an important political event, with the potential to influence large numbers of voters.

There is also evidence that the debates can influence the outcome of an election. Jamieson and Birdsell argue, "When debates are announced movement in the polls slows; in anticipation, the electorate suspends its willingness to be swayed by ads and polls" (1988, p. 56). Analysis of particular presidential debates suggests that they probably influenced segments of voters, especially those still undecided (see, e.g., Davis, 1979, 1982; Geer, 1988; Kelley, 1983; Middleton, 1962; Pfau, 1988; Roper, 1960; Wayne, 1992; this claim is discussed in more detail in chapter 1). Voters themselves believe the debates are important, as Carlin (1994) explains: "*Times-Mirror* (1992) exit poll results from 1988 and 1992 showed that 48 percent of voters in 1988 and 70 percent in 1992 considered the debates helpful in making a voting decision" (p. 8). Presidential debates are thus important campaign events, clearly worthy of close study.

As the review in the first chapter reveals, many scholars think of the presidential debates as flawed (if not failed) academic debates. This book as a whole makes a case for the alternative view that the debates can usefully be viewed as extended instances of persuasive attack and defense. This perspective is an important departure from current treatments of the debates, because the candidates' speeches attack and defend *both* image (or personality, or character) and issue (or policy) matters. While the candidates in presidential debates may fall short of the standards of evidence and reasoning, they clearly attack one another and defend themselves against such attacks. Incidentally, some forms of persuasive "defense" are quite proactive in their attempts to create a favorable impression of the candidate, and use of the term "defense" must not be taken to imply that these statements are necessarily "defensive" in nature.

Part 1 presents the results of our investigation into the 1992 presidential debates. Chapter 1 reviews the literature on presidential debates and justifies the approach we adopt in this study. We develop five research questions that guided our work. Chapter 2 describes the method used to answer our research questions, investigating persuasive attack and defense. Chapter 3 answers the first two questions, describing the strategies of persuasive attack used by the three candidates in the three 1992 presidential debates and the issues addressed in those attacking utterances. Chapter 4 answers the third and fourth research questions, describing the strategies of persuasive defense used by the three candidates in the 1992 debates and the issues covered in those defensive remarks. Chapter 5 answers the final research question, evaluating the three candidates' use of persuasive attack and defense and discussing implications of the findings. Part 2 (chapters 5, 6, and 7) offers corrected transcripts of the three 1992 presidential debates. Appendix 1 describes the specific procedures used in our analysis, including the computer program (The Ethnograph) used in our analysis of the text of the debates. Appendix 2 reproduces the coding for part of the transcript of one debate to illustrate the coding system used in the analysis.

This particular project began as a research practicum, required of all doctoral candidates at the University of Missouri. The course enables faculty to mentor doctoral students in research, involving them in the design, execution, and reporting of a study. The longer we worked on this project, the longer our manuscript became, until we decided to conceptualize it as a research monograph rather than a journal article. This book is the end product of the process. It is also the first project conducted under the auspices of the Missouri Political Communication Research Center.

We would like to thank several people for their support. First,

Pamela Benoit is always willing to be a sounding board for ideas, and we appreciate her input. Second, Jennifer Benoit is always an inspiration (for at least one of us) and a lot of fun. She was also very helpful in compiling the summary tables on persuasive attack, defense, and the issues addressed in each. Third, Mary Jeannette Smythe, chair of the Communication Department at the University of Missouri, has supported us personally and as chair. Coauthors who have worked with us on various other projects made less direct but still important contributions. Ray McKerrow, one of the editors of the University of Alabama Press series, provided useful comments on an early draft of the manuscript, as did external reviewers for the University of Alabama Press. This research was also supported in part by the University of Missouri Alumni Faculty Development Award, which provided a VCR and monitor used to view the debates. Bill Wells thanks Dr. William L. Benoit for providing the opportunity to work on this project. He also thanks his wife, Stephanie, who provided support and encouragement through the long hours and late nights. Bill Benoit dedicates this work to Pam and Jennifer Benoit.

Part I

Analysis of the 1992 Presidential Debates

We begin part 1 by reviewing the research on presidential debates in chapter 1 and developing two claims: first, that presidential debates are important campaign events and, second, that it is reasonable to study them as persuasive attack and defense. In chapter 2 we present the method used in this investigation: typologies for analyzing the debates into strategies for attack and defense. Chapter 3 on attack and chapter 4 on defense, present the results of this analysis. Finally, in chapter 5, we assess Bush's, Clinton's, and Perot's use of persuasive attack and defense in these debates, and we discuss the implications of our findings.

1

Traditional Approaches to Presidential Debates

Three weeks from now—two—two weeks from tomorrow, America goes to the polls, and you're going to have to decide who you want to lead this country to economic recovery.—Bush, Debate 3

You have to decide whether you want to change or not.—Clinton, Debate 2

Pretty simply—who's the best qualified person up here on the stage to create jobs? Make your decision and vote on November 3.—Perot, Debate 3

Presidential debates—surrounded by hype generated by candidates and media alike—capture America's attention and are extremely important events in the campaign for the presidency. Of course, some voters may have made up their minds before the debates, but the potential influence of these events is staggering. For example, in 1992 debate 1 was watched by 81 million viewers, the second debate by 90 million, and the third debate enjoyed 99 million viewers ("The Aftermath," 1992, p. 3336). While the candidates attack each other, and defend their own character and policy stands, throughout the campaign, the debates thrust them together in a direct and highly publicized confrontation. The drama created in these events is high, and rarely does a debate pass without some fireworks. This book examines the 1992 presidential debates as embodiments of persuasive attack and defense.

Given the amount of attention focused by the media on presidential debates, and the potential for affecting the results of the election, it should not be surprising to discover that scholars of communication have devoted considerable attention to studying them. We need to understand the context of scholarship on the debates, because our analysis grows out of, and contributes to, that literature.

This chapter addresses several topics. First we discuss those who treat these events as "debates." We then examine research concerning the possible effects of political debates on voting decisions. We review specific studies of particular debates to illustrate the work that has been done on presidential debates. With this context, we justify our approach to understanding presidential debates as persuasive attack and defense and describe the purpose of our investigation. Then we describe the discursive context of the 1992 debates as a backdrop for reporting the results of our investigation and as information necessary for our evaluation of the debates. Finally, we briefly describe the remainder of the book.

Swerdlow observed in 1987 that, "given the present ascendency of campaign debates, there is every reason to believe that they will continue to flourish" (p. 14). The last several elections have created an expectation that the candidates of the major parties will engage in presidential debates (see, e.g., Denton and Woodward, 1990; Friedenberg, 1994a). Because the election boils down to a relatively simple choice between two (or three) candidates, there is a certain logic to this expectation: a simple and direct way to make such a choice is to find out how each candidate stands on the same issues and to see how each one "performs" in direct comparison. This is not to ignore the importance of "image" in politics; as we will explain during this book, we conceptualize the debates as attack and defense that address both image or character and policies or issues (see, e.g., Friedenberg, 1994a; Hinck, 1993; Leff and Mohrmann, 1974; Rosenthal, 1966; Stuckey and Antczak, 1995). We believe these concepts are inherently intertwined: one's image is surely shaped by the policies one embraces and rejects; on the other hand, a candidate's image influences perceptions of his or her stands on policy questions. Presidential debates can thus be seen to provide an opportunity for voters to contrast the leading candidates directly (how well they satisfy this expectation is a separate question, of course).

Because all candidates are looking for an "edge" over their opponents, they are unlikely to approach the debates (or the campaign generally) as merely an opportunity to display their own views, accomplishments, and platforms. Rather, they presumably want to put their opponents into an unfavorable light even as they portray themselves positively. In other words, campaigns generally and debates in particular are seen as an opportunity to attack one's opponent(s) persuasively. Although both texts focus on campaigns generally rather than on the debates in particular, both Pfau and Kenski (*Attack Politics*, 1990) and Jamieson (*Dirty Politics*, 1992) provide compelling evidence that attack messages are prevalent in political campaign discourse.

Candidates attacked by their opponent(s) naturally feel compelled to defend themselves, their records, and their proposals. Riley and Hollihan argue that "candidates strive to demonstrate that they perceive the weaknesses of their opponents and that they do not possess the same weaknesses" (1981, p. 51). Martel (1983) identifies five relational strategies for presidential debate, which concern the interaction between candidates, moderator, panelists, and the audience:

> *Attack* means that a candidate's arguments are offensively directed at his opponent's positions, party, character, or campaign. *Defend* is a candidate's response strategy after being attacked by his opponent. *Sell* is the candidate's presentation of credentials that are not clearly related to attack or defense. *Ignore* involves debating on the candidate's own terms, paying little or no heed to his opponent's arguments. "*Me too . . . me better,*" in effect a combination attack/sell strategy, is generally employed against a frontrunner or any candidate who has espoused a popular idea with which the opponent would be ill-advised to disagree. Thus, the candidate identifies with the idea ("me too") but explains that, if elected, he could relate to it more effectively ("me better"). (Pp. 62–63)

Attack and defense are the first two strategies. Sell, as will become clear in chapter 2, is related to bolstering, a form of defense that does not respond to a specific attack but attempts to enhance the candidate's image so as to counterbalance damage from attacks. Thus it— as well as "me too . . . me better," which combines attack and sell— concerns persuasive defense; only Martel's strategy of "ignore" does not embody persuasive attack and defense. Throughout the campaign, but especially in the short, intense clash of the debates, persuasive attack and defense play key roles. In fact, political debates could reasonably be characterized as essentially instances of persuasive attack and defense (taking "defense" to include responses to opponent's specific attacks as well as utterances that bolster the candidate's image). However, current writing on political debates does not adopt this perspective, or else it tends to view debates as shoddy versions of academic debates (while this evaluation may be merited, format and other considerations may make academic debate an unrealistic though laudable standard).

Presidential Debates as Debate

The literature on presidential debates is quite diverse. Some scholars debate the worth of presidential debates (Drucker and Hunold, 1987; Graber and Kim, 1978; Kelley, 1962; Kraus, 1987; Lang, 1987; McClain, 1989; Meadow, 1987). Friedenberg (1979, 1981) identifies conditions necessary for debates to occur (although, as mentioned earlier, he has argued more recently that our country has developed expectations that presidential debates *will* occur; see 1990a). Other essays argue that the meaning or effects of the debates are mediated by journalistic reporting and commentary after the fact (Berquist and Golden, 1981; Condit, 1989; Lemert, Elliott, Bernstein, Rosenberg, and Nestvold, 1991; but cf. McKinnon, Tedesco, and Kaid, 1993) as well as by loaded questions asked during debates (Hogan, 1989). Madsen examines the interpretations of the debates—"spin control"— proposed by the candidates (1991; see also Conrad, 1993, or Martel, 1983). Some research investigates the criteria used by viewers to decide who "won" and "lost" the debates (Vancil and Pendell, 1984; Winkler and Black, 1993) or the effect of audience predispositions on such decisions (Leuthold and Valentine, 1981).

Some authors discuss merits of the various formats of the debates (Carlin, Howard, Stanfield, and Reynolds, 1991; Hellweg and Phillips, 1981a). Other scholars even deliberate about whether we should consider presidential debates to be genuine "debates" at all (Bitzer and Rueter, 1980; Carlin, 1989; Gill, 1986; Weiler, 1989). Auer (1962) characterizes them as counterfeit debates. Zarefsky, for example, writes that:

> Debates have great potential for focusing the audience's attention, for identifying issues, and for inviting deliberation. Sadly, however, this potential is largely unrealized. The [presidential] debates have been formatted for television—the confrontation with reporter-questioners adds dramatic conflict and the short time limits respond to audience's limited attention span. But these same conventions thwart sustained discussion of serious issues; they encourage one-liners and canned mini-speeches. (1992, p. 412)

Presidential campaign debates are thus not generally considered to be optimal examples of the potential inherent in debate.

Jamieson and Birdsell discuss three influences on the nature of presidential debate: debate, press conferences, and television. "The common audience, the presence of opposing candidates, the time limits, the right to rebut, and the established rules are vestiges of traditional debate. From press conferences come the multiple topics, the question-and-answer form and the use of interrogating reporters. The production techniques and the abbreviated answers are residues of television's grammar" (1988, p. 118). Thus it may well be more appropriate to recognize presidential debates as a hybrid form (see Jamieson and Campbell, 1982), drawing on several antecedents, than to dismiss them as flawed or defective academic debates. Swerdlow (1984) argues that "to govern, however, a president indisputably must be skilled in the use of television" (p. 12), and therefore the fact that television influences the format of presidential debates should not be assumed to be pernicious.

The idea that presidential debates should not be considered "pure" instances of academic debate makes our perspective especially valuable. These events *are* debates: they provide candidates with a widely televised opportunity to *clash*—an opportunity they exploit to the best of their abilities. However, they are not *academic* debates. We believe that presidential campaign debates are best considered as instances of persuasive attack (of opposing candidates and their policies/proposals) and persuasive defense (of one's self and one's policies/proposals). Tony Schwartz, a Democratic media consultant, observed that "the presidency is the only job interview in the world for which all of the applicants show up at the interview and attack each other" (quoted in Jamieson and Birdsell, 1988, p. 218). Cursory examination of any presidential debate (and the close examination of the 1992 presidential debates we report in subsequent chapters) clearly shows that the candidates attack their opponents and their opponents' policies and defend themselves and their own policies.

As suggested above, we also reject the distinction between issue (or policy) and image (or character) as a false dichotomy: one cannot and should not attempt to divorce one from the other. A candidate's policy stances (vague as they might be) cannot help but influence that person's image; a candidate's image surely influences voters' beliefs about that candidate's policies. Attacks on your opponent's policies may damage his or her image; articulate defense of your policies surely enhances your image. Damage done to a candidate's image may undermine the policies they support. Furthermore, Cragan and Cutbirth (1984) argue that personal competence and trustworthiness are essential factors in evaluating political candidates and that it is a mistake to assume that all ad hominem ("to the person") arguments are fallacies in political campaigns. Thus we believe that our examination of the presidential debates in the light of persuasive attack and defense (concerning image and issues) is more appropriate, and could potentially provide greater insights into them, than would be viewing presidential debates simply as aberrant academic debates.

The Impact of Political Debates

The effect of the debates has been a popular topic of interest in the literature (see, e.g., Becker, Sobowale, Cobbey, and Eyal, 1978; Bishop, Oldendick, and Tuchfarber, 1978; Desmond and Donohue, 1981; Hagner and Rieselbach, 1978; Lang and Lang, 1978; Lanoue and Schrott, 1989; McLeod, Bybee, and Durall, 1979; Nimmo, Mansfield, and Curry, 1978; and the essays in part 2 of Kraus, 1979). Several studies suggest that the effects of the debates are limited. According to Lubell (1977), interview data reveal that the 1960 Kennedy-Nixon debates did not influence voting intentions (Lang and Lang, 1977, believe that the influence of these debates on voting intentions was slight). Abramowitz (1978) claims that the first 1976 debate increased knowledge of candidates' positions but did not influence voting intentions and brought about little net change in candidate popularity (Miller and MacKuen, 1979, offer similar conclusions). Lanoue (1991) argues that the second 1988 debate provoked only short-lived increases in information and had little effect on voting intentions. Three studies based on interviews, rather than on survey research, found that viewers reported little learning (Bishop, Oldendick, and Tuchfarber, 1978; Graber and Kim, 1978; McLeod, Durall, Ziemke, and Bybee, 1979; however, it is not clear that people remember where they learned information, so their reports may not be the best indicators of actual learning). Jamieson and Birdsell conclude that "debates don't very often convert partisans on one side to the other" (1988, p. 161; see also Swerdlow, 1984). Sigelman and Sigelman (1984) report that prior attitude toward the candidates is a better predictor of perceptions of who won the debate and voting behavior than debate performance (see also Rouner and Perloff, 1988; Wall, Golden, and James, 1988). Party affiliation is another factor in addition to debate performance that is cited as an important influence on voting behavior (Sigelman and Sigelman, 1984).

However, other studies argue that the debates are worthwhile activities (see Kraus and Davis, 1981) and that they do influence voting behavior. Kraus (1988) believes that televised presidential debates "serve the majority of the electorate better than any other single campaign communication device that attempts to present both the candidates' personality and their positions on the issues" (p. 5). We agree with this general assessment and develop several arguments in support of it.

First, Wayne recognized that presidential debates "regularly attract great interest and many viewers, more than any other single event of the entire campaign" (1992, p. 225). More specifically, Jamieson and Birdsell indicate that, "historically, other campaign messages have failed to attract audiences comparable in size to those drawn to the debates. In 1964, for example, no message by either Johnson or Goldwater reached even a quarter of the audience that watched the first of the 1960 Kennedy-Nixon debates" (1988, p. 122). Chaffee (1979) noted that, in the 1960 and 1976 debates, "the viewing audiences have constituted between 70 and 80 percent of all adults in the nation" (p. 19). Carlin (1994, pp. 6–7) reports other examples to illustrate the comparatively huge audiences attracted by presidential debates, compared with other campaign discourse:

> Nielson (1993) reported that the second presidential debate in 1992 attracted 43.1 million television households or 69.9 million viewers . . . (p. 4). Those numbers contrast sharply to the 4.1 million homes or 20.5 million viewers who tuned in for each of the major party conventions. In 1980, nearly 81 million people watched Ronald Reagan and Jimmy Carter in their only debate encounter (p. 4). Miller and MacKuen (1979) noted that 90% of the adult population watched at least one of the Kennedy-Nixon debates, and 83% watched at least one Ford-Carter matchup. These numbers compared favorably to 73 percent who read about the campaigns in the paper, 4 percent who read magazines, and 45 percent who listened to radio reports. (P. 328)

Similarly, Hellweg, Pfau, and Brydon (1992, p. 101) report that "approximately 80 percent of Americans watched at least one debate in 1960 (Katz & Feldman, 1977); 90 percent watched at least one in 1976 (Alexander & Margolis, 1980)." The fact that the audiences for presidential debates are so large—larger than the audiences for other forms of campaign discourse—means the potential for influence from these communication events is huge.

Second, there is quite a bit of evidence that debates *do* further voter learning. Jacoby, Troutman, and Whittler (1986) studied comprehension of the 1980 presidential debates, reporting that viewers achieved comprehension rates of about 80 percent. Studying intraparty debates, Pfau (1988) concluded that political debates can help people learn about issues and about candidates' positions on those issues (see Pfau, Diedrich, Larson, and Van Winkle, 1993). Drew and Weaver reported that more campaign issue learning was attributable to the 1988 Bush-Dukakis debates than to other sources of news (1991). During the 1988 election Lemert (1993) found that exposure to presidential debates predicted knowledge increases. Their review of the literature led Hellweg, Pfau, and Brydon to conclude that "most studies suggest debate viewing contributes to considerable learning about the candidates and their positions" (1992, pp. 106–107). Carlin (1992) further argues that the debates provide a framework for understanding the campaign, influencing perceptions of the candidates. Thus the debates have been found to provide information to the electorate.

Other studies suggest that presidential debates can influence voting decisions. Middleton (1962) found that one of eight registered voters reported that the 1960 presidential debates were "extremely important" in their voting decision. Roper (1960) declared that the 1960 Kennedy-Nixon debates changed the voting intentions of 4 million voters. Davis (1979) declared that the 1976 debates probably had more effect on perceptions of the candidates than any other form of mass media. Chaffee concluded:

> Prior to the [1976] debates, many voters reported that they were undecided, and they looked to the debates for information about the candidates' stands on policy issues. The debates provided issue information, and most voters watched and learned from them. Those who were the most regular viewers changed the most in their voting intentions, were the ones least influenced by dispositional factors, and were the most likely to vote in conformance with policy differences they perceived between themselves and the candidates. (1978, p. 341)

Wayne argued that "Kennedy and Carter might not have won without the debates" and that "Reagan probably would not have won by as much in 1980" (1992, p. 229). Davis (1982) found that, in the 1980 campaign, decisions to vote for Reagan were significantly influenced by perceptions of the debate—but not decisions to vote for Carter. Kelley (1983) reported that almost 20 percent of respondents said they had decided how to vote after watching the Carter-Reagan debate. Geer (1988) argued on the basis of the 1976 and 1984 debates that "a sizable minority of the public altered their preference for president" (p. 498). Thus considerable research on past debates suggests that they can influence voters.

Owen (1995) makes the interesting argument that the effects of the debates have grown in importance over the years: "Increasingly, however, voters rely on debates when evaluating candidates and even when making their vote choices" (p. 136). Perhaps this is why the 1992 presidential debates were so influential. Paul Kirk, co-chair of the Commission on Presidential Debates, reported that "focus groups and exit polls told us that more people based their decision in 1992 on the debates than any other single means of information throughout the course of the campaign" (1995). Pfau and Eveland, while acknowledging that no single source of information dominates, concluded:

The regression analysis of the survey data, subsequent paths computed from beta weights, and the focus group responses reveal that the 1992 presidential debates exerted considerable direct impact on voter knowledge and their perceptions of candidates' competence and persona and as a result, the debates played an important, if indirect, role influencing attitudes and voting disposition during the final weeks of the 1992 campaign. (1994, p. 161)

Thus research suggests that the 1992 presidential debates, our focus in this study, were an important factor in that election.

It has also been argued that while the debates rarely change the vote of committed viewers, they often influence the undecided (Carlin, 1994; Geer, 1988; Kraus and Davis, 1981; Pfau and Kang, 1991). For example, Gallup observed that "presidential debates in all years have tended to reinforce the convictions of voters who were already committed. They have caused few people to change their minds; their main impact appears to have been on undecided or wavering voters" (1987, p. 34). However, this impact is very important, because the number of uncommitted voters can be sizable enough to influence the outcome of an election. Zakahi and Hacker develop a detailed argument on this point:

Several elections have had enough uncommitted voters around the time of the presidential debates to influence the election. In 1960, John Kennedy beat Richard Nixon by about 100,000 popular votes. This is a fraction of a percentage (0.2%) of the total vote. In 1968, Nixon defeated Hubert Humphrey by 500,000 votes (0.7%). In 1976, Jimmy Carter won by less than 2 percent of the popular vote. Polls in late September of 1976 showed an unusually large number of undecided voters (Reinhold, 1976). In 1980, Ronald Reagan beat Carter by less than 10 percent of the popular vote, yet two weeks before the election, 25 percent of the voters were still undecided. (1995, p. 100; see Jamieson and Birdsell, 1988, p. 161)

Similarly, Payne, Golden, Marlier, and Ratzan (1989), studying the 1988 debates, indicate that while some partisans were unaffected, the debates did influence the opinions of others, and that the early debates were more influential than later ones. Summarizing research on effects from 1960 through 1988, Hellweg, Pfau, and Brydon conclude: "For those viewers with weak or no preferences among candidates, debates often shape or even change their attitudes about candidates, often with sufficient force to alter voting intention. Thus, debates tend to exert considerable influence during the candidate selection process and during general elections featuring a substantial undecided and conflicted vote" (1992, p. 124). Thus while the research is somewhat mixed, the weight of evidence through 1988 suggests that presidential campaign debates can influence the attitudes and voting intentions of voters who are conflicted or undecided. Most recently, after analyzing data on the 1992 debates, Pfau and Eveland (1994) concluded: "The debates made an important difference during the 1992 presidential campaign because of more fluid conditions (Stokes & DiIulio, 1993), with many potential voters uninformed about third party challenger Ross Perot, and conflicted over the performance of incumbent George Bush and over the character and capabilities of challenger Bill Clinton" (p. 173). Therefore, even if debates are unlikely to sway large numbers of partisan viewers, they can affect undecided and conflicted voters, which can influence the outcome of an election. This may have been important in the 1992 campaign.

Furthermore, it is certainly conceivable that an important effect of the debates is to solidify existing attitudes—attitudes that could have changed absent the debates. If so, studies of voting shifts could not possibly detect these very real effects of the debates. Hellweg, Pfau, and Brydon (1992), who reviewed research on debate effects from 1960 to 1988, report that, "for those viewers with clearly defined preferences among candidates, presidential debates tend to strengthen those attitudes, thus exerting a reinforcing effect" (p. 124). As Mayer and Carlin recognize, this tendency is important because "reinforcement is an important persuasive function, and, in a voting context, could make the difference as to whether or not voters actually participate at the polls" (1994, p. 137). In other words, while the debates might not *change* the attitudes of partisan viewers, debates might strengthen the attitudes of some viewers' attitudes enough to *increase substantially the likelihood that they will vote.* Swerdlow (1984) asserts that debates did not affect voter turnout in 1960, 1976, or 1980, because voter turnout decreased over time. However, he admitted, "It is possible, of course, that turnout would have declined even *more* without debates" (p. 11; these points are echoed by Gallup, 1987). So watching the debates may increase voter turnout for partisan viewers, affecting the outcome of the campaign without changing their voting preference.

In addition, Hellweg, Pfau, and Brydon recognize that presidential debates are important because they have been the "only opportunity for the American voters to see the nominees side by side for an extended period of time, during which they are forced to deal with the issues of the day" (1992, p. 37; Carlin echoes these sentiments in 1994, p. 3; see also Swerdlow, 1984). Jamieson (1987) explains, "As messages running an hour or longer, debates offer a level of contact with candidates clearly unmatched in spot ads and news segments. . . .

the debates offer the most extensive and serious view of the candidates available to the electorate" (p. 28). Nor are these advantages lost on viewers, as the results of focus group studies indicate: "Many participants claimed they relied on the debates to provide them with what advertising, conventions, stump speeches, and news reports could not—a chance to see the candidates face to face and 'head on without the benefit of a teleprompter, speechwriter, or coach' " (Lamoureaux, Entrekin, and McKinney, 1994, p. 58). While candidates do have advisers who anticipate questions and rehearse answers, the candidates are on their own when the debates begin. As a result voters may have a less distorted view of the candidates than they get from other forms of campaign messages.

Finally, Denton and Woodward argue that political campaign debates have several important benefits for the electorate:

> Debates . . . provide an opportunity to compare the personalities and issue positions of the candidates in a somewhat spontaneous setting. They also invite serious consideration and attention to the campaign and the candidates, thus stimulating voter interest in the election. And finally, they certainly increase candidate accountability. What they say, suggest, and promise becomes a matter of record for future evaluation. (1990, p. 102)

Similarly Trent and Friedenberg (1983) argue that presidential debates create positive political socialization, increase confidence in government, and generally contribute to a healthy democracy (see also Chaffee, 1978; Hinck, 1993; Kraus and Davis, 1981). Thus there is considerable evidence that presidential debates have potentially important effects and merit scholarly attention.

Review of the Literature

A number of studies have examined the presidential debates themselves. Martell (1981) discussed preparations for the 1980 debates. Several studies have explored visual aspects of presidential debates (Hellweg and Phillips, 1981b; Morello, 1988a, 1988b, 1990, 1992; Pfau and Kang, 1991; Tiemens, 1978; Tiemens, Hellweg, Kipper, and Phillips, 1985; see also the discussion in chapter 4 of Hellweg, Pfau, and Brydon, 1992). Some research focuses on the images of the candidates (see also Hellweg, Pfau, and Brydon, 1992, chapter 3). Weiss (1981) examined the relationship between issues and images in the 1980 debates. Simons and Leibowitz (1979) report that there was no evidence in their data from the 1976 debates that the candidates' images related to voting behavior. Bowes and Strentz (1978) surveyed people before the 1976 debates and after each debate. While they contrast different sources of information (e.g., television, friends, and classes) to investigate the impact of the debates generally, they do not analyze the content of the debates themselves. Wall, Golden, and James (1988) report that viewers' perceptions of the strength of arguments influenced who voters thought won more than did image. Pfau and Burgoon (1989) report that attacks on issues affected attitudes toward candidates—among those committed to the opposing candidate—more than attacks on character or image.

Jackson-Beeck and Meadow (1979a) performed content analysis on the 1960 and 1976 debates, focusing on general topics such as government and politics, health, economics, and law (see also Meadow and Jackson-Beeck, 1978a, 1978b; and Riley and Hollihan, 1981). Jackson-Beeck and Meadow (1979b) suggest that candidates' utterances are often not responsive to journalists' questions and that they do not always emphasize the issues considered most important by the public.

Other studies applied content analysis to presidential debates. For example, Samovar (1962) reported the presence of ambiguity in the Nixon-Kennedy debates and noted that "the issues discussed ambiguously were primarily concerned with significant topics" (p. 279). Samovar (1965) examined passages from those debates judged to be ambiguous and unequivocal so as to identify characteristics of ambiguous and unequivocal discourse. Hellweg and Phillips (1981b) compared candidates on such variables as the use of evidence, jargon, and loaded language; the latter study also examined the use of additional elements such as analogy, humor, fear appeals, and inductive and deductive reasoning.

Ellsworth (1965) examined the 1960 debates for analysis, evidence, and declaration (generally, in criticism of the other, or defense of self). He suggested that candidates were more likely to respond to attacks from their opponent in the debates than in other speeches.

Bitzer and Rueter (1980) analyzed the argumentation in the 1976 Carter-Ford debates. They concluded that Carter advanced 45 percent more arguments, including more argument from principle, while Ford committed over 50 percent more errors in evidence and reasoning. Carter was found to have attacked Ford substantially more often than Ford attacked Carter. Riley, Hollihan, and Cooley found Carter to be more critical, while Ford was more defensive (1980).

Riley and Hollihan (1981), in their investigation of the 1980 Reagan-Anderson debates, analyzed both critical and defensive statements and found a significant difference between the critical (but not the defensive) statements of the two candidates (they also analyzed declarative statements, evidence, and analytic statements but found no differences).

Tiemens, Hellweg, Kipper, and Phillips (1985) identified instances of attack and refutation during the 1980 Carter-Reagan debate held in Cleveland. Their analysis tended to focus on utilization of techniques of debate rather than on identification of particular strategies and found that Carter attacked Reagan more than Reagan attacked Carter (21 to 16), while Reagan refuted Carter more than Carter refuted Reagan (14 to 1).

Another analysis of the 1980 Carter-Reagan debates was conducted by Rowland (1986). He focused on substance rather than style and examined three questions: how well did they answer the questions, how well did they support their claims with evidence and reasoning, and, most important, their refutation. He argued that they attacked one another about the same amount (Carter attacking Reagan seventeen times, while Reagan attacked Carter fifteen times, a conclusion somewhat different from the findings of Tiemens, Hellweg, Kipper, and Phillips, 1985). Rowland gave Reagan a decisive edge in all three areas.

Brydon (1985a) analyzed the 1984 Reagan-Mondale debates. He found that Mondale criticized Reagan more than Reagan criticized Mondale in the first debate. He also reported that, appropriately enough, given Reagan's higher frequency of attack, Reagan refuted Mondale more than Mondale responded to Reagan. However, both candidates were less critical in the second debate, and Reagan refuted Mondale less in the second than in the first debate.

Finally, two studies examined the 1988 Bush-Dukakis debates. Morello reported "99 separate statements of attack and defense" in the 1988 debates (1990, p. 4). Hellweg and Verhoye concluded that "Dukakis was more attack-oriented than his counterpart in both debates" (1989, p. 19). They also found that Dukakis attacked Bush in 77 percent of his messages, while Bush attacked in 40 percent of his opportunities. Hellweg and Verhoye reported that Bush offered more refutation in the first than the second debate. Thus several studies find support for the assumption that the debates contain instances of persuasive attack and defense—although their primary purpose is not necessarily to analyze the debates by topoi or strategies of persuasive attack and debate.

Leon (1993) performed a computer content analysis of word occurrence in the 1992 presidential debates. She found no substantial difference in linguistic choices among Bush, Clinton, and Perot that might influence comprehensibility. Perot's word choices indicated that he revealed more human interest than Clinton, who in turn scored higher than Bush on this variable. Perot's utterances conveyed the most powerful language, and Bush's the most powerless language (Clinton's language was neither highly powerful nor highly powerless). Bush was the least concrete and Perot the most concrete. Using Hart's (1984) criteria, Leon's data showed that Perot revealed the most presidential style and Bush the least presidential style. Finally, she reported that Clinton had the most references to the topics considered most important to voters, while Bush had the fewest such references.

A few studies have examined multiple debates. Brydon (1985b) contrasted Jimmy Carter's discourse in the 1976 Carter-Ford debates with his rhetoric in the 1980 Carter-Reagan debates. In 1976, Carter portrayed himself as the outsider, and he attacked the incumbent, Ford, on unemployment and the economy. He also accused Ford of distorting the truth. In 1980, with unemployment and inflation high, and his presidential approval rating at an all-time low, he was forced to defend his incumbency. He attacked Reagan as dangerous. Thus Carter's discourse was dramatically different in the debates in these two campaigns, largely as a result of his shift from the role of challenger to that of incumbent. However, he engaged in persuasive attack against his opponent in both campaigns.

Friedenberg (1994c) edited a collection of studies of the presidential debates from 1960 to 1992. Windt (1994) studied the 1960 Kennedy-Nixon debates. Berquist (1990) examined the Carter-Ford debates of 1976. Ritter and Henry (1990) analyzed the single 1980 debate between Reagan and Carter. Smith and Smith (1994) looked at the 1984 debates featuring Reagan-Mondale. The 1988 debates between Bush and Dukakis were studied by Ryan (1990). Hahn (1994) analyzed the 1992 presidential debates between Bush, Perot, and Clinton. While there are differences between these chapters, they tend to describe the decision to debate, background, goals, strategies, and effects.

Hinck (1993), adopting an Aristotelian perspective, studied presidential and vice-presidential debates from 1960 through 1988. He summarized the rhetorical problems they faced, analyzed how well the candidates enacted the presidency (the extent to which they appeared presidential), and examined their stances on key issues that arose in the debates.

Justification for the Analytical Framework

Thus while some studies have conducted content analyses of presidential debates, and indicate that attack and defense (or criticism and refutation) permeate the debates, existing research does not focus on analyzing strategies of persuasive attack and defense in the debates (Tiemens, Hellweg, Kipper, and Phillips, 1985; Riley and Hollihan, 1981, and Rowland, 1986, come the closest in this regard). Nor do studies of the 1992 debates tend to take this approach (e.g., Leon, 1993; McKinnon, Tedesco, and Kaid, 1993; Winkler and Black, 1993). Windt examined presidential attacks on the news media but not attacks by presidential candidates on each other (1987). Hahn and Gustainis (1987) analyzed defensive tactics in presidential discourse but did not focus on presidential debates in particular or on persuasive attack. Thus persuasive attack and defense in presidential debates have not been studied before, although there are good reasons to undertake such a project.

First, the debates themselves are worthy of attention. Jamieson and Birdsell argue that the audience "is drawn to the event by the prospect of clash" (1988, p. 95). Not surprisingly, given the point made earlier that debates are watched by more people than any other campaign event, the 1992 presidential debates were watched by, and had the opportunity to influence, millions of voters. The same has been true in the past (e.g., about 80 percent watched at least one of the 1960 debates [Katz and Feldman, 1977] and 90 percent watched at least one of the 1976 debates [Alexander and Margolis, 1980]). Clearly, the presidential debates are one of the most popular campaign events, if not the most popular.

Additionally, presidential debates have come to be seen as almost obligatory campaign rituals, as Friedenberg (1994a) demonstrates. Hellweg, Pfau, and Brydon claim that "presidential debates have nearly become an institutionalized part of the campaign landscape. The public has come to expect them" (1992, p. 18). In short, we can reasonably expect to see presidential debates in future campaigns. Findings concerning the 1992 presidential debates—worth examining in their own right—should also be relevant to future campaign debates. Conclusions drawn from analysis of the 1992 debate could also shed light on previous presidential encounters.

Furthermore, although the evidence is not completely clear-cut, and while the debates' importance may well vary from one campaign to another, the evidence reviewed earlier suggests that they are significant events in our presidential campaigns, worthy of extensive study. Jamieson and Birdsell argue that " 'Debate' has become a buzzword for 'serious politics' " and that "when debates are announced movement in the polls slows; in anticipation, the electorate suspends its willingness to be swayed by ads and polls" (1988, p. 56). Thus the presidential debates, even though they constitute only a portion of the entire campaign, clearly merit close scholarly scrutiny.

Second, it makes sense to approach presidential debates as instances of persuasive attack and defense. Looking at presidential campaign ads, Gronbeck writes that they contain "forensic attack upon the personal qualities of opponents" and "epideictic praise or blame of the candidates" (1992, p. 337). A cursory examination of any presidential debate makes it quite obvious that the candidates do attack each other and defend themselves in the debates. Wayne explains that "candidates have viewed presidential debates as a way to improve their image and damage their opponent's image" (1992, p. 224), which is consistent with the claim that the debates can plausibly be viewed as persuasive attack and defense. Studies of earlier debates that most closely resemble our approach (Riley and Hollihan, 1981, Rowland, 1986; Tiemens, Hellweg, Kipper, and Phillips, 1985) indicate that presidential candidates do engage in copious persuasive attack and defense in debates. This finding makes sense, because in the debates (unlike other parts of the campaign), the candidates confront one another face to face, so that it is difficult for them to ignore persuasive attacks from their opponents. Thus we are likely to find that persuasive attack and defense play a significant role in the presidential debates, and research reviewed above shows that the candidates engage in criticism and attack as well as defense and refutation. Accordingly, persuasive attack and defense offer a suitable perspective for viewing the presidential debates.

Of course, because presidential debates are a hybrid form, as suggested earlier, the candidates do not conform to the expectations of academic debate (and arguably should not or could not). They may not always exemplify ideals of rationality, evidence use, or policy deliberation. But they certainly do clash in these debates: they attack one another on both personal and policy grounds, they defend themselves and their policies, and these tasks are accomplished through their discourse. Again, we believe that construing presidential debates as instances of persuasive attack and defense—focusing on both image and policies—can be a very fruitful approach to understanding these important political events.

Analytical Objectives

In 1992, George Bush, Bill Clinton, and Ross Perot gathered to debate on October 11, 15, and 19 (there was also one vice-presidential debate on October 13, which we do not analyze). This book investigates the use of persuasive attack and defense in presidential campaign debates, using the most recent presidential debates as the texts for analysis. We address five research questions as a means of examining and evaluating the persuasive discourse of Bush, Clinton, and Perot in the 1992 presidential debates:

1. What strategies of persuasive attack did the three candidates use in the 1992 presidential debates?

2. Which issues did the three candidates address in their instances of persuasive attack in the 1992 presidential debates?

3. What strategies of persuasive defense did the three candidates use in the 1992 presidential debates?

4. Which issues did the three candidates address in their instances of persuasive defense in the 1992 presidential debates?

5. How well did the three candidates engage in persuasive attack and defense in the 1992 presidential debates?

Our study does not purport to be a complete or exhaustive analysis of the campaign generally or the debates specifically. First, we limit our investigation to the debates. There were many other persuasive discourses (e.g., commercials and speeches) in the campaign—including one vice-presidential debate—that we exclude from this analysis. Second, we focus on the text of the debates. As mentioned earlier, interesting work has included visual analyses of the debates (Hellweg and Phillips, 1981b; Morello, 1988a, 1988b, 1990, 1992; Tiemens, 1978; Tiemens, Hellweg, Kipper, and Phillips, 1985) that we do not attempt to replicate with the 1992 debates. Furthermore, we examine the debates only for attack and defense, not for other utterances (although our analysis revealed that most of the candidates' remarks fell into one of these two categories). Finally, we examined only their persuasive attack on each other and defenses of themselves (e.g., when the candidates attacked Congress, as they did occasionally, we did not code it as persuasive attack, although we frequently construed it as an attempt to shift the blame, a defensive strategy). However, given our belief in the importance of persuasive attack and defense to the debates—which was reaffirmed as we conducted our analysis—we believe that an investigation with this clear and specific focus is worthwhile.

Discursive Context of the Debates

Before turning to an explication of the methods used to investigate the debates, we want to provide a brief description of the discursive context of the debates. How well were the candidates doing in the public opinion polls? What did the voters think about the need for change or the desirability for continuity in government? What were political commentators saying about the candidates and the upcoming debates? This context will be especially useful when we present and discuss the results of our analysis in chapters 3 and 4 and when we evaluate the debates in chapter 5 (see also Trent and Trent, 1995).

It is important to realize that Bush went into the debates as a decided underdog. Apple observed that prior to the debates he was "trailing badly in the national polls and in most big states" (1992, p. A1). More specifically, Balz reported that a CNN/*USA Today* poll "gave Clinton a lead of 50 percent to 34 percent, with Perot at 9 percent as of Wednesday night," October 7 (1992a, p. A35). While not utterly insurmountable, a fifteen-point lead was a huge deficit for Bush to attempt to overcome in the scant time remaining until the election.

Consistent with this evidence, other data revealed that many voters believed that the time was ripe for a change in leadership. For example, Taylor indicated that, according to a recent Harris Poll, about three-fourths of those likely to vote agreed that it was time for "a new generation of leadership" (1992, p. 1). Almost all of Clinton's (94 percent) and Perot's (89 percent) supporters agreed with this statement. Surprisingly, given that Bush was an incumbent, even 39 percent of Bush supporters agreed with this sentiment. Thus there was widespread agreement that we needed to change the direction of our federal government, and Clinton appeared to represent the best chance for change among most voters.

Furthermore, Clinton enjoyed support across a wide spectrum of concerns or topics. Balz reported that, according to a *Washington Post*/ABC News poll, "by last week, Clinton led Bush on all issues [family values, crime, race relations, taxes, the economy, poverty, the deficit, and bringing change to government] except foreign policy" (1992a, p. A35). Nor was the exception especially salient to voters, as Taylor revealed: "Clinton is maintaining his strong lead in the campaign in that the issues at the top of the voters' minds are mainly the issues where he does well. The economy has increased in importance in every Harris Poll since June; 56% of likely voters say it is one of the two most important issues. The president's strong issues, such as trust, character, and foreign policy, are a long way down this list" (1992, p. 1). Yet another poll yielded similar results, as Kelley reported that a *Wall Street Journal*/NBC poll showed that many voters supported Clinton "because they believed he would do a better job in dealing with the issues they most cared about, while retaining doubts about his personal character" (1992, p. A24). Thus, prior to the 1992 presidential debates, Clinton was more popular than Bush (or Perot) on many issues, and particularly on the issues that mattered the most to the majority of voters. On the other hand, Bush's strongest issues—including character and trust—were simply less important to most voters.

Besides Clinton's position on the issues (and in the polls), commentary focused on Bush's recent campaign strategy. Ifill reported that Bush "has done what voters claim to hate—attack, attack, attack" (1992, p. A21). More specifically, an editorial in the *New York Times* observed: "President Bush's attacks on Gov. Bill Clinton have grown more bitter by the day. Now Mr. Bush is impugning Mr. Clinton's patriotism with absurd charges that date back to the Vietnam War. That's not just nasty, its demagogic. It also consumes time that Mr. Bush might better spend telling voters why they should re-elect him" ("Mr. Bush's Campaign," 1992, p. A32). Assuming Bush continued to attack Clinton during the debates, which seemed likely, Ifill recommended that Clinton should "be prepared to counterattack" (1992, p. A21).

Finally, Balz speculated on the impact of Perot in the debates: "To the extent that Perot keeps his focus on the state of the economy, he could hurt Bush more than Clinton" (1992a, p. A35). Thus in the days leading up to the debates, Bush seemed to be attacking Clinton more, although many commentators thought he would be better advised to discuss the economy. Given Perot's interest in the economy generally and the deficit specifically, he was expected to put additional heat on the incumbent.

2

Investigating Persuasive
Attack and Defense

The first chapter provides one context for understanding our investigation of the 1992 presidential debates: prior work on presidential debates. We adopt a new perspective for investigating presidential campaign debates, however, that of persuasive attack and defense. While a few studies discussed in the previous chapter are consistent with this approach (or offer results that suggest this perspective is promising), in understanding the debates as persuasive attack and defense we take an entirely new approach to studying this important political phenomenon. To help clarify the method we used to analyze the debates, we need to review the research on persuasive attack and defense.

In this chapter we first provide a backdrop for understanding our method. We discuss the three key dimensions (or purposes or effects) of communication—one of which is image repair. Next we advance a theory of persuasive attack, a form of discourse that attempts to damage the image, face, or reputation of another person, group, or organization. Then we describe a theory of persuasive defense, or image repair discourse, developed elsewhere, along with research applying it. These two typologies will guide our analysis of the 1992 presidential debates. The first appendix discusses specific procedures we used to analyze the debates.

Dimensions of Communication

Scholars who study communication have long understood that messages have multiple dimensions. For example, several writers have asserted that all messages have content and relational dimensions (see, e.g., Reusch and Bateson, 1951; Watzlawik, Beavin, and Jackson, 1967). We embrace the conceptualization of goals, purposes, or intents advanced by Clark and Delia (1979), who indicate that there are three:

> issues or objectives explicitly or implicitly present for overt or tacit negotiation in every communicative transaction: (1) overtly instrumental objectives, in which a response is required from one's listener(s) related to a specific obstacle or problem defining the task of the communicative situation, (2) interpersonal objectives, involving the establishment or maintenance of a relationship with the other(s), and (3) identity objectives, in which there is management of the communicative situation to the end of presenting a desired self image for the speaker and maintaining a particular sense of self for the other(s). (p. 200)

Thus communication can be usefully understood to have three dimensions: instrumental, relationship (interpersonal), and identity. Research on the third dimension, identity, includes work on face (e.g., Mehrabian, 1967; Tracy, 1990) and on embarrassment (e.g., Cupach and Metts, 1990, 1992; Metts and Cupach, 1989; Modigliani, 1971; Sharkey, 1992; Sharkey and Stafford, 1990).

These three concepts are called dimensions, but they are useful for conceptualizing both purposes and effects of communication.[1] That is, a source may engage in communication in order to accomplish a goal (instrumental: secure a job, sell a product, change a school board policy, etc.), in order to develop or enhance a relationship (relationship: deepen intimacy with a romantic partner, bond with a friend or relative, etc.), or in order to influence an image (identity: injure another's reputation, remedy damage to one's own reputation, establish a new image, or enhance an existing image). A person or organization might want to accomplish two or all three goals or purposes in a given message or in a group of related messages.

However, these dimensions are also a way of looking at the effects (intended and unintended) of messages. For example, a message may be more or less successful at accomplishing the source's instrumental goal, but it could also influence the source's relationship with the audience, and it could affect the speaker's (or someone else's) image. A given message could affect any two or all three of the dimensions.

Our project, investigating the 1992 presidential debates, explicitly acknowledges that communication is multidimensional. The communicators have an obvious instrumental goal: each candidate wants to persuade viewers to vote for him in the election (it is possible that Perot's instrumental objective may have been as much or more to focus or force attention on issues that he considered important than to win the election). It would of course be possible to analyze the relationship between candidate and voter implied or fostered by their discourse (e.g., leader-follower; servant-master; representative-represented). However, we focus primarily on the third, or identity, dimension of communication.

Of course, we believe that these three dimensions are not entirely separable or isolated: one's reputation, for example, surely influences how successful one is at accomplishing one's instrumental goals (i.e., ethos or credibility; see the discussion below on ethos/credibility). Thus we would argue that voters' perceptions of the candidates' images, along with their perceptions of the candidates' stand on issues or policy, both influence voting decisions. We argued in chapter 1 that image and issue exert mutual influence: one's policy stance can shape one's image, and one's image can influence how one's policy stances are interpreted and accepted. Although the three dimensions are interrelated, we believe one's image, identity, or reputation is important enough to warrant focusing on it.

In this book, as previously noted, we are concerned with two aspects of the identity dimension of communication: persuasive attack and defense. "Persuasive attack" means messages that attempt to damage the image (reputation, face, identity) of a person, group, or organization (these attacks may address the character and/or the policies associated with that person, group, or organization). Persuasive defense, on the other hand, attempts to repair an image after persuasive attack.

We might have been well advised to choose a term other than "defense," which may imply that one who attempts to affect his or her image positively is on the *defensive*, only reacting to the criticisms and attacks of others. However, we do not use the term in this sense. While the strategies of persuasive defense are frequently adopted to respond to accusations and suspicions, they can also be employed preemptively to help avoid or reduce potential damage from anticipated attacks, as Benoit's (1995) analysis of Nixon's Cambodia address established. Furthermore, we explicitly acknowledge that a person can proactively attempt to create a favorable image, or to enhance an existing image, without having been provoked by a prior persuasive attack or the threat of an impending attack. Any of the defensive strategies we identify could be utilized in this way, but bolstering and corrective action (plans for solving problems/creating benefits) seem especially useful in this regard. However, in the context of a debate, and with this clarification, we feel justified in employing "defense" as the correlative of "attack."

The identity dimension of communication is important and especially so in political communication. First, in general, face, or reputation, is a crucial commodity because it contributes to a healthy self-image. Snyder, Higgins, and Stucky explain that "achieving and maintaining a positive self-image have been postulated as important motivational variables throughout the history of psychology" (1983, p. 29; see also Schonbach, 1990). The reason is that problematic events (threats to face) have a variety of undesirable consequences, as Schlenker explains: "The more severe a predicament is, the greater the negative repercussions for an actor. The actor should experience greater internal distress such as anxiety and guilt, receive greater negative sanctions from audiences, and produce greater damage to his or her identity—thereby adversely affecting relationships with the audience" (1980, p. 131). Thus the literature establishes that a person's reputation is extremely important for our psychological well-being. While we continually argue that image and policy are interrelated, it should be obvious that a candidate's face, image, or perceived character is especially important in politics, where voters must trust politicians to implement campaign promises and where voters must hope their representatives will take reasonable stances on issues that arise after the campaign.

A second reason for the importance of image or reputation stems from its role in the influence process. For example, in the *Antidosis*, Isocrates makes it clear that he considers the speaker's ethos, or prior reputation, to be important to the effectiveness of discourse:

> The man who wishes to persuade people will not be negligent as to the matter of character; no, on the contrary, he will apply himself above all to establish a most honourable name among his fellow-citizens; for who does not know that words carry a greater conviction when spoken by men of good repute than when spoken by men who live under a cloud, and that the argument which is made by a man's life is of more weight than that which is furnished by words? (1976, p. 278)

In fact, Isocrates goes so far as to argue that a rhetor's prior reputation is a more important factor in persuasion than arguments and evidence: "probabilities and proofs and all forms of persuasion support only the points in a case to which they are severally applied, whereas an honourable reputation not only lends greater persuasiveness to the words of the man who possesses it, but adds greater luster to his deeds, and is, therefore, more zealously to be sought after by men of intelligence than anything else in the world" (p. 280). Thus the assumption that ethos, credibility, or reputation is important pervades the rhetorical literature. Aristotle, for example, writes that "we believe good men more fully and more readily than others; this is true generally whatever the question is, and absolutely where exact certainty is impossible and opinions divided" (1954, 1356a6–8). Thus for classical rhetoricians Isocrates and Aristotle, ethos is extremely important in persuasion. Similarly, attitude change theory and research also support the importance of credibility in facilitating persuasiveness (see, e.g., Andersen and Clevenger, 1963; Benoit, 1991a; Littlejohn, 1971). Therefore, one important goal of discourse is to establish and maintain a positive image or reputation. There is every reason to believe that the same holds true as well in politics generally and presidential debates specifically.

As a result, rhetors have a natural tendency to attempt to repair their image when it is threatened. For example, Brown and Levinson write that "people can be expected to defend their faces if threatened" (1978, p. 66). Goffman concurs in this assessment: "When a face has been threatened, face-work must be done" (1967, p. 27). Schlenker points to consequences of threats to one's image: predicaments "can damage his or her identity . . . , adversely affecting relationships with the audience" (1980, p. 131). Therefore, when our reputation is threatened, we are motivated to develop and present image restoration discourse: explanations, justifications, rationalizations, apologies, or excuses for our behavior. Clearly, political candidates frequently feel compelled to reply to opponents' charges and criticism, a reasonable reaction to accusations.

It should be obvious that in the context of presidential debates, the second reason for the importance of identity is more important than the first. As Nimmo explains, images "can be used to mobilize support for candidates, policies, and institutions; by the same token they are used to oppose political objects" (1974, p. 14). It is essential for a presidential candidate to appear believable or credible in the eyes of the voters (and, it must be said, in the eyes of political commentators as well).

Many writers contrast "image" and "issue." While we agree that, whatever the reason (i.e., the assumption that many voters have a relatively short attention span or that it is easier to secure widespread agreement with vague platitudes than with specific proposals), political candidates are often vague about the policies they will attempt to enact if elected. Furthermore, we personally lament campaigns that degenerate into mud-slinging contests. Nevertheless, as stated before, we believe that candidates' images are intimately tied to their actions, the policies they embrace, and the stand they take (however vague) on the issues. The importance of credibility in persuasion means that one's image ought to influence the acceptance of one's policies. Thus while the "issues" may not be discussed in a political campaign in as much detail as many of us would like to see, issues and images are inextricably intertwined and are not best understood as independent or dichotomous constructs.

Specifically, this study is designed to analyze the 1992 presidential debates rhetorically as discourse that is apparently intended to influence, and presumably affects, the candidates' images, understood as the audience's perception of candidates, their identity or reputation. This aspect embodies past information known about the candidate, as Nimmo explains: "an image is a subjective representation of something previously perceived" (1974, p. 5). However, as Nimmo points out, "political images become public, and thus shared by people, through communication" (1974, p. 22).

Cursory examination of the 1992 presidential debates reveals that most of what was said by the three candidates can readily be seen as attacks on their opponents, their opponents' stands or proposals, and their opponents' past records or as defense of themselves, their own stands or proposals, and their own past records.

The Literature on Persuasive Attack

Despite considerable evidence of interest among scholars in responses to or defenses from persuasive attack (often termed "apologies," or apologiae, in the rhetorical literature, and "accounts" in social science literature), persuasive attack itself, the pervasive form of communication that provokes such responses, has been investigated relatively little. In the realm of rhetoric, Fisher acknowledges the importance of such discourse by identifying subversion, creating a negative image as one of the four motives of communication (1970). Unfortunately, he does not develop his analysis of subversion in detail. Thus far Ryan (1982) has developed the most extensive theory of persuasive attack available in the rhetorical literature.

Ryan observes that accusations may focus on policy, character, or both. He declares, "An accusation always begins with, but is not necessarily limited to, the accusee's policy." Furthermore, he asserts that a policy accusation "always begins with Cicero's stasis of fact, *conjecturalis*, which focuses on whether an action was done or not" (1982, p. 256). Other stases, definition and quality, function optionally to increase the severity of the accusation (and he discusses the stasis of jurisdiction as well). Finally, Ryan suggests that accusations against character—which "must be based on the fact of a policy or practice" (1982, p. 257)—emphasize "ethical materials" (1982, p. 256). However, he offers a more general set of stases, not a more specific list of topoi for persuasive attack. While Ryan's concept of kategoria-apologia as a speech set was amply illustrated in his edited book (1988), development of a theory of persuasive attack in the rhetorical literature has advanced little in the meantime. Notice, though, that Ryan seems to articulate a position similar to the one we embrace on the interdependence of image (character) and issue (policy).

The literature in communication similarly has only a few studies that have some bearing on persuasive attack. Morris (1988) developed a set of six methods for finding fault. Similarly, McLaughlin, Cody, and Rosenstein (1983) identified four types of reproaches (see also McLaughlin, Cody, and O'Hair, 1983). Alberts (1989; cf. 1988) describes five categories of couples' complaints. Vangelisti, Daly, and Rudnick (1991) developed a typology of strategies used to induce feelings of guilt. Sharkey (1992) reports six tactics used to cause embarrassment. However, none of this work is intended to provide either a conceptual understanding of the nature of persuasive attack or a typology of persuasive strategies that can be used as a set of topoi for attacking a political opponent.

In the literature on political communication, two books that consider persuasive attack deserve mention. First, Pfau and Kenski's *Attack Politics* (1990) offers "a theoretical and empirical examination of the role and impact of the attack message approach in modern political campaigns" (p. xv). While Pfau and Kenski provide an interesting and useful analysis of such messages, their goal is not to provide a set of topoi for constructing persuasive attacks. For example, when they mention the "limited number of strategic options available to candidates" (p. xiii), their analysis concerns three very general options: attacking first, counterattacking, and prevention (a refutation strategy).

Second, Jamieson's *Dirty Politics* (1992) has a chapter entitled "Tactics of Attack." She identifies two major approaches, identification (association) and apposition (contrast: "to make their candidate's name a synonym for everything the electorate cherishes and to transform the opponent into an antonym of those treasured values," p. 47). Each process is further divided into verbal and visual aspects. Verbal identification is subdivided into personal (image) and policy identification. She also offers an interesting discussion of the importance of television and highlights inherent differences between television and both print and radio political advertising. However, this analysis, while clearly useful and relevant, is quite general (association and contrast being its two tactics). It does include medium (verbal, visual) but again does not have as its goal the development of a set of topoi or strategies for persuasive attack.

Thus we present a new theory of persuasive attack, designed to fill this void we see in our literature. It should be noted that, because relatively little research has been done on persuasive attack (compared with persuasive defense, or apologiae, or accounts), this theory must be considered embryonic, one that would benefit from further exploration beyond this study (for a preliminary version of the theory of persuasive attack advanced here, see the study by Benoit and Dorries, in press).

A Theory of Persuasive Attack

Fundamentally, a persuasive attack must contain two elements: a negatively perceived act and attribution of responsibility for that act to the agent (see Pomerantz, 1987). First, the accused must believe that this act would be perceived negatively by a salient audience. Only if the target of the attack believes his or her reputation will suffer (though linkage to the act) is there a threat to his or her image. The disgraceful act may be an offensive deed, a word, or even an undesirable cognition (belief, value, attitude, or opinion). Furthermore, this negatively perceived event may be an act of commission or omission: it is possible to attack a person or group for not performing an expected (and/or desirable) act as well as for performing a wrongful deed. It is also possible to accuse someone of performing an act poorly. The event may be an incipient act as well—a cognition, trait, or characteristic that could be thought by the audience to make future undesirable behavior likely. However, if no act (viewed broadly) was identified that is perceived negatively by the audience, there cannot be said to be a persuasive attack. Furthermore, it seems reasonable to assume that the damage to the accused's reputation would be directly related to the perceived offensiveness of the act.

Second, the accused must be perceived as responsible, wholly or partially, for the wrongful deed. Responsibility may appear in a variety of forms. The target of the attack may have actually committed the act, or may have encouraged, provoked, or suggested the act, or may in some way have permitted it to occur—for example, through inaction. The accused may be the sole perpetrator or may be one of several accused. However, if the accused has no apparent responsibility for the act, he or she cannot reasonably be blamed or attacked for that act, and her or his reputation should not suffer because of that act, no matter how heinous.

A persuasive attack may thus focus attention on the offensive act (demonstrating or increasing its perceived offensiveness) or on the responsibility for the act (demonstrating or increasing the target's apparent guilt) or on both. Depending upon the audience's beliefs about the event in question, there may well be circumstances in which either the offensiveness of the act, or the blame for that act, can be assumed in the persuasive attack. However, a variety of discursive strategies are available for embellishing or developing these two essential components of a persuasive attack.

We could not illustrate our typology from rhetorical criticism because so little work has been conducted into persuasive attack. Consequently we chose to illustrate each of the potential strategies for persuasive attack, where possible, with public events of the last several years reported in newspapers. Although our search for examples can hardly be considered conclusive, some strategies (e.g., extent of the damage and inconsistency) occurred rather more frequently than others. Possibly if we had looked beyond newspaper articles, other strategies would have been more prominent (e.g., personal injury suits in the courts might have exhibited various strategies for establishing blame more frequently).

Increasing Negative Perceptions of Act

We identify seven specific discursive strategies for increasing the apparent offensiveness of the act in question. An act should be seen as more reprehensible when its consequences are more extensive (the number of people harmed, the number of trees destroyed, the number of countries attacked, etc.) or more severe (the more an individual suffers, the greater the damage to a tree, the greater the devastation of a country by war). Second, negative effects that persist longer should reflect more negatively on the accused's image than short-lived effects. A third strategy is to stress that the recency of the harmful act, because outrage is more likely to be engendered by wrongs in the immediate past than by old injuries. Also, innocent or helpless victims (for example, children) should evoke more outrage than victims who accepted risk or should have been able to protect themselves from injury. Fifth, revulsion should be greater if the accused had a special duty (e.g., as a scoutmaster, day care provider, doctor/nurse, priest, teacher) to protect the victim. When the behavior in question is inconsistent with the actor's utterances (e.g., if the accused promised not to commit the act, or had attacked others for doing similar acts), then the offensiveness should increase, a sixth way of enhancing offensiveness. Finally, making the effects explicitly relevant to the audience should increase their condemnation of the accused. We will discuss each method separately.

EXTENT OF THE DAMAGE. Images are frequently damaged by the extent of the effects of the offensive act under consideration. For example, Jim and Tammy Bakker were charged with stealing $10 million from their ministry ("TV Ministry," 1988). This was no simple dip into the till but (allegedly) a massive plundering of their ministry. Their alleged theft involved literally millions of dollars. Groups as well as individuals can be the targets of this kind of persuasive attack. The national Bass Anglers Sportsman Society (BASS) was accused of having diverted over $75 million from conservation projects ("BASS and Its Founder," 1992). Similar accusations were leveled at Stanford University, accused of misusing federal grant monies. Characterizing its actions as "outlandish," a newspaper story accused Stanford University of having "overcharged the U.S. $140 million in the last decade" (Houston, 1991, p. A3). Thus the accusations in these cases were developed by discussing the large sums of money involved—literally millions of dollars in these three instances. The astronomical sums attest to the magnitude of their respective wrongdoing. The damage to the accused's image ought to be correspondingly significant.

Of course, the emphasis on the offensive act's severity may extend beyond monetary losses. On March 24, 1989, the Exxon oil tanker *Valdez* struck a reef. After nine days, the oil slick had "spread over an area the size of Rhode Island, more than 1,000 square miles" (Peterson, 1989, p. A17). By likening the oil spill in size to a state, the writer indicates that Exxon's disaster was huge. There can be little doubt that Exxon's oil spill was large and therefore terrible, and the threat to its image should be serious.

To emphasize the severity of effects, an accusation can also detail the human costs of tragedies. For example, after the gas leak at a Union Carbide plant in Bhopal, India, McFadden reported:

> Hundreds died in their beds, most of them children and old people. . . . Thousands more awoke to a nightmare of near suffocation, blindness and chaos. Many would die later. By the thousands, they stumbled into the streets, choking, vomiting, sobbing burning tears, joining human stampedes fleeing the torment of mist that seemed to float everywhere. Some were run down by automobiles and trucks in the panic. Others fell, unable to go on, and died in the gutters. (1984, p. A1)

Those reading this description would surely conclude that Union Carbide's gas leak was a catastrophe. If Carbide is held responsible by the audience, its image should be substantially damaged.

PERSISTENCE OF NEGATIVE EFFECTS. We did not find the persistence of negative effects employed frequently as a strategy in the newspaper articles we consulted. Its absence is hardly surprising, given that newspapers tend to focus more on current events (the "new" in news) than on long-term phenomena. However, Hilts did note that the danger to the environment inflicted by the *Exxon Valdez* oil spill was expected to last at least ten years (1989). Harms that last longer arguably appear more offensive, and probably do more damage to the actor's image, than temporary ones.

RECENCY OF HARMS. Given newspapers' emphasis on covering newsworthy, that is, current, events, the recency of harm runs as a theme through most of the stories we scanned. The more immediate an event, the greater its potential impact on an audience. Generally speaking, newspapers and electronic media offer live coverage of news whenever possible—like the trip of O. J. Simpson's white Ford Bronco through Los Angeles. Given this stress on the "current" in current events, more recent objectionable acts often seem particularly offensive. By the same token, events that are more remote in time often have less impact. For one thing, the direct consequences may be less obvious; for another, people sometimes mend their ways. In line with this reasoning, the statute of limitations in the law prevents offenders from being prosecuted once a certain number of years have passed.

INNOCENCE OR HELPLESSNESS OF VICTIMS. The journalistic passage quoted above on the gas leak in Bhopal, India, mentioned that many of the victims were children or the elderly, people who are less capable of taking care of themselves. This detail heightens our sense of the offensiveness of Union Carbide's negligence. Similarly, many people deplore attempts to increase the use of alcohol or tobacco through advertisements. Joe Camel, the cartoon character used to promote Camel cigarettes, came under especially severe attack for allegedly appealing more to children than to adults (Goodman, 1992). Concerns have also been raised about beer commercials, particularly after a recent study "found 10-year-olds reciting slogans, reeling off brand names and saying they intended to drink frequently later in life." When this finding is coupled with the statistic that 1.1 billion bottles or cans of beer each year are consumed by *teenagers*, the problem seems especially offensive ("Flashy Beer," 1994, p. 12A). As a final example, the transportation system for the handicapped in Columbia, Missouri, came under fire when a married couple was refused access although one was blind and the other confined to a wheelchair ("Riders Lament," 1994). The relative helplessness or vulnerability of victims exacerbates the act's perceived offensiveness and consequently increases damage to the image of the accused.

OBLIGATION TO PROTECT CERTAIN GROUPS. The law and public opinion confer a special duty on certain groups and individuals. For example, church leaders have an obligation to their congregation, scout leaders to their scouts, and doctors/nurses to their patients; a special relationship exists in such cases. We expect these people to exercise extra care. They occupy positions of trust, and when they are accused of injuring people in their charge, their misconduct seems worse. Roman Catholic Cardinal Joseph Bernardin was accused of abusing Steven Cook when Cook was a teen ("Prominent Cardinal," 1993). Similarly, almost 2,000 scoutmasters who were suspected of molesting Boy Scouts were thrown out—"but some simply went elsewhere and continued to abuse scouts" ("Scouts Files," 1993, p. 12A). The scout leaders and their organization are held to a higher standard of conduct than ordinary people would be. Sexual molestation is terrible whenever it occurs. However, when priests and boy scout leaders violate our trust, the accusations can seem particularly reprehensible, and the damage to their image may be greater.

INCONSISTENCY. Another way of intensifying an accusation is through charges of inconsistency. A prostitution sting operation arrested St. Louis prosecutor George Peach, who has been a "strong supporter of sting operations to net prostitution arrests" ("Prostitution Sting," 1992, p. 3A). It is bad enough that he was arrested for committing a crime, but his apparent hypocrisy made things look even worse. Similarly, former Missouri attorney general Bill Webster pled guilty to criminal charges in federal court. As the newspaper put it, "Bill Webster—the former top law enforcement official for Missouri—pleaded guilty yesterday to conspiracy and embezzlement charges" ("Webster Guilty," 1993, p. 1A). The fact that the perpetrator of the crime was the chief law enforcement official of the state adds to intensity of the reproach and presumably increases the damage to his image.

The same principle holds true for alleged ethical as well as criminal misconduct. When FBI director William Sessions was accused of ethical misconduct, the Justice Department's ethics office declared that Sessions's behavior was "inconsistent with that expected of the head of the nation's premier law enforcement agency" ("Justice Department," 1993, p. 7A). Finally, "a federal audit sharply criticized the top brass of the U.S. Environmental Protection Agency for driving gas-guzzling luxury cars, in violation of the agency's own environmental standards" ("EPA Officials Criticized," 1992, p. 9A). In this case, the EPA's actions contradicted its internal rules as well as conflicting with its mission in the government.

EFFECTS ON THE AUDIENCE. It is possible to heighten a persuasive attack by relating the negative effects directly to the audience. For instance, federal officials reported that an important breast cancer study used fraudulent data by reporting that women with cancer were cancer-free, by altering dates of treatment, and by downgrading or misclassifying cancer. The falsification is important, because this study "established the relative safety of the operation known as lumpectomy and made it a common surgical procedure" ("Landmark Breast Cancer Data," 1994, p. 6A). This statement takes the fraudulent research from the realm of abstract science and indicates its effects on women throughout America—and on those who care about women.

In another example, Air Force One was held on the ground at Los Angeles International Airport while Hollywood hairstylist Cristophe trimmed the president's hair. Almost seventy-five local and state police remained on duty, and were paid for that time, throughout the presidential haircut. Reports explained the implications of this event: "President Bill Clinton's image-bruising trim from a $200-a-haircut stylist was also an $1,800 bad hair day for taxpayers" ("Security for President's Haircut," 1993, p. 1A). Similarly, after a GAO report found that prescription drug makers charge 60 percent more for certain "best-selling brand-name" drugs in the United States than in England, Congressman Waxman explained, "These numbers translate into real costs to real people, particularly the elderly, who purchase 34 percent of the drugs" ("Same Drugs," 1994, p. 7A). The message intensifies the attack, and increases damage to the target's image, by bringing the consequences home to members of the audience.

Increasing Perceived Responsibility for the Act

We identify five rhetorical strategies for increasing the actor's apparent responsibility for an act. As noted above, the sources we consulted tended to focus more on the offensiveness of the acts (often seeming to presume the blame or guilt of the accused) and tended to concentrate on sensationalism.

First, injuries that are perceived to have been intended probably damage the accused's reputation more than those that seem to be accidental or unintentional. Second, planned harms likely injure one's reputation more than acts committed on the spur of the moment (this statement is not the same as its predecessor: one can intend harm with, or without, prior planning). Third, one can attempt to increase apparent responsibility by arguing that the person was aware of the probable consequences of their misdeed. If the negative effects were unexpected, we may hold the actor to be less responsible. A fourth strategy is to claim that the accused has performed the act before, thereby increasing suspicion that he or she simply did it again. Finally, the idea that the accused has benefited from the act may make him or her more likely to be held responsible for it.

INTENT TO ACHIEVE THE OUTCOME. We may be willing to forgive those who accidentally do wrong. However, consider the discovery that the Central Intelligence Agency (CIA) had managed to conceal a $310 million office project from Congress. When Congress found out, there was an angry outpouring of invective. However, there was no doubt of the CIA's intent to deceive. As Senator DeConcini put it, the CIA hid the office building "with great pride" ("Stealth Job," 1994, p. 1A). The evidence of deliberate intent (the project wasn't just "lost" in a huge federal budget) adds to the blame assigned to the CIA and quite possibly to the damage done to the agency's image.

Similarly, Judy Moriarty was the first Missouri secretary of state ever to be impeached. She allegedly permitted her son to file for elective office after the legal deadline had passed. This action was no accident, or oversight, according to the article of impeachment, which declared that Moriarty "did purposely cause and direct or did knowingly allow" the late filing ("Interim Secretary of State," 1994, p. 1A). When we intend to commit wrongdoing, the likelihood that we will be held accountable for that action is high and presumably the damage to our reputations more severe.

ADVANCE PLANNING. After the tragic plane crash near Pittsburgh, USAir was accused of "trying to milk more use out of the engines on ill-fated Flight 427 by running them on shorter flights rather than giving them an overhaul." Maintenance was delayed on this plane not through oversight but by a calculated cost-cutting strategy: "By using the older engines solely on short flights instead of more taxing long trips, USAir aimed to save $1 million per plane and gain an extra two years before an overhaul" ("Flight 427," 1994, p. 3A). While it was not immediately clear that the delayed maintenance caused the crash, such practices—which appear quite deliberate—are unlikely to endear USAir to its passengers. It seems likely that such allegations would increase apparent responsibility for the offensive act and concomitant damage to the accused's image.

KNOWLEDGE OF THE ACT'S CONSEQUENCES. At times, actions have unforeseen, and possibly unforeseeable, consequences. Presumably the unpredictability mitigates the apparent responsibility of the accused. On the other hand, when people or organizations are thought to have done wrong *knowing* the consequences, we do not hesitate to blame them. Dow Corning, for instance, came under fire for ignoring potential dangers of silicone breast implants (Gladwell, 1992) as well as for faking research results (Rensberger, 1992). A story concerning the revelation that a safer cigarette had been developed but never marketed asserted that Liggett and Myers Tobacco Company "knew about the dangers of tobacco for more than 30 years, despite industry denials of any proven link between smoking and disease" ("Safer Cigarette," 1992, p. 4A). Thus responsibility for ill effects is heightened when perpetrators know the consequences of their actions, and their images should suffer because of this knowledge.

PRIOR COMMISSION OF THE OFFENSIVE ACT. When Show-Me Furniture had a second "going-out-of-business" sale, Wright suggested it might be false advertising. "This isn't the first time that Show-Me Furniture has told the public it was going out of business" (1993, p. 1A). The fact that the attempt had been made to deceive the public in the same way before places the blame squarely on the store.

BENEFIT FROM THE OFFENSIVE ACT. Some observers were dismayed when President Bush pardoned Casper Weinberger, because they were concerned that without a trial the truth was unlikely to emerge. However, Iran-Contra prosecutor Lawrence Walsh suggested that Bush acted to "avoid being a witness at Weinberger's trial" ("Bush's Motive," 1992, p. 1A). The implication was that Bush had issued the pardon not because Weinberger necessarily deserved it but for selfish reasons. If this implication is accepted by the audience, Bush's apparent blame for impeding the Iran-Contra investigation should increase. The threat to his image should be intensified.

Similarly, Congressman Dan Rostenkowski was accused of paying himself for "a Chicago office that appears to be vacant." His selfish motive was self-evident, and there is little question about whether he appears responsible for this apparent misuse of government funds ("Congressman Paid Self," 1992, p. 5A). He was diverting funds not to help widows but for his personal benefit.

During the great midwestern flood of 1993, James Scott allegedly sabotaged a levee on the Mississippi River. While the consequences of this action were serious, reports focused on his motives. A witness claimed he did it to strand his wife on the other side of the river, "so he could have a party at his house" ("Accused Levee Saboteur," 1994, p. 1A). Thus his actions were subject to harsher criticism because they benefited himself.

A summary of the rhetorical strategies available for persuasive attack is presented in table 1. Again, this list of attacking topoi may not be exhaustive, because work developing a typology of strategies for tarnishing another's reputation is still exploratory.[2]

These strategies can of course function together. In the examples we have given, more than one strategy can at times be identified. For example, the Bakkers allegedly stole a huge amount of money (extent). The fact that they were leaders of a *religious* organization (rather than people who may have embezzled from an ordinary business) may have increased the damage to their reputations (inconsistency). Similarly, it is one thing to learn that some teens drink beer (innocent victims). This information seems worse when we learn that teens consume 1.1 *billion* bottles and cans of beer (extent). Thus the strategies for persuasive attack can work together to intensify charges against the accused and the damage to his or her image.

Some predictions can be made on the basis of attribution theory, which concerns the likelihood that behavior is believed to be caused internally (by the actor) or externally (as a product of forces or people outside the actor). Three rules guide attributions: consensus, distinctiveness, and consistency (see, e.g., Harvey and Weary, 1984; Kelley, 1967; Kelley and Michela, 1980). "Low consensus" means that other people act *differently* in *similar* circumstances; the implication is that the actor, not the situation, is responsible for the act. "Low distinctiveness" means that the actor behaves *similarly* in *different* situations; again, an internal attribution (blaming the actor) rather than a situational one would be likely. "Consistency" concerns the actor's behavior in similar situations. High consistency can lead to internal attributions when it occurs with low consensus and/or low distinctiveness. External attributions mean that the accused is *not* responsible for the offensive act.

Previous Work on Persuasive Defense

Several approaches have emerged for explaining verbal self-defense, some developed in communication/rhetoric and some in sociology. The works of Burke (1970), Ware and Linkugel (1973), and Scott and Lyman (1968) each present several verbal image restoration strategies, but each theory includes options neglected by the others. Benoit (1995) developed a typology of image repair strategies that is more complete than those currently available in the rhetorical literature (see also Benoit, in press; Benoit and Brinson, 1994; Benoit, Gullifor, and Panici, 1991; Benoit and Hanczor, 1994; or Brinson and Benoit, in press).

Table 1. Strategies for Persuasive Attack

Increasing negative perceptions of the act
  Extent of the damage
  Persistence of negative effects
  Recency of harms
  Victims are innocent/helpless
  Obligation to protect certain groups
  Inconsistency
  Effects on audience
Increasing perceived responsibility for the act
  Intended to achieve outcome
  Planned
  Knew consequences of act
  Accused committed offensive act before
  Accused benefited from offensive act

In the realm of political communication, Pfau and Kenski's book *Attack Politics* (1990) applies McGuire's (1964) inoculation theory approach to political advertising. McGuire wanted to develop a theory not of how to create attitude change but of how to create resistance to attitude change (from one's opponents or competitors). He developed an analogy from medical inoculation: to create resistance to a disease ("attack"), one exposes patients to a weakened form of that disease (an inoculating shot). This exposure should be strong enough to provoke the body's defenses (production of antibodies) without creating the disease. It is important to note that one cannot inoculate a person who has already experienced the disease; the disease would have already stimulated production of antibodies, rendering the inoculation treatment worthless.

Accordingly, McGuire developed his inoculation theory on "cultural truism" topics (e.g., people should brush their teeth), ones on which he expected that his "patients" had never been exposed to the attacking "disease" (persuasive messages attacking the beliefs in question). Thus the subjects in McGuire's studies had never heard these beliefs challenged and had never been motivated to develop belief defenses. The basic contrast in McGuire's research is between supportive messages, which reinforce the attitudes favorable to the belief without acknowledging the existence of attacking arguments, and refutative messages, which actively refute attacking arguments.

The refuted arguments in the inoculating message are the weakened form of the attack. Exposing people to a refutative defense should encourage them to produce belief defenses. On cultural truism (non-controversial) topics they have never had their beliefs questioned; hearing refutation of an attacking argument in the inoculating message notifies the audience that previously unchallenged beliefs are at risk; the threat of further possible attacks motivates people to create belief defenses. Supportive messages, in contrast, should not motivate subjects to develop defenses. On such topics, McGuire (1964) consistently found that refutative defenses were superior to supportive ones at creating resistance to persuasive attack.

Pfau and Kenski (1990) clearly recommend the inoculation approach for political candidates. However, political campaigns are inherently controversial, and so auditors can be expected to have heard messages on both sides of the issue. Auditors were long ago exposed to potential attacks on their beliefs and realized that their beliefs were at risk. If such threats were going to motivate the auditors to create defenses, they should have done so back when the auditors first became aware of attacking arguments. Thus the refutative message should provide little or no new motivation to develop a defense. Refutative messages should not be expected to be substantially more effective than supportive ones on controversial topics.[3]

Of course, the competition between candidates to win an election ensures that political discourse occurs on controversial topics. Voters have known ever since they began paying attention to political messages that some people disagree with and attack their beliefs. Hence, a refutative message on a political issue cannot be expected to shock voters out of their complacency and motivate them to create a new belief defense, as such a message would do on a cultural truism topic. On the question of the generalizability of McGuire's inoculation theory to controversial topics, Pfau and Kenski (1990) write: "A number of studies during the 1970s (Burgoon et al., 1976; Burgoon and Chase, 1973; Burgoon, Cohen, Miller, and Montgomery, 1978; Burgoon and King, 1974; Freedman and Steinbruner, 1964; Infante, 1975; McCroskey, 1970; McCroskey, Young, and Scott, 1972; Miller and Burgoon, 1979; Tate and Miller, 1973; Ullman and Bodaken, 1975) applied a number of the basic tenets of inoculation theory to more controversial topics" (p. 81). Unfortunately, most of these studies did not include supportive messages (Burgoon et al., 1976; Freedman and Steinbruner, 1964; Infante, 1975; McCroskey, 1970; Ullman and Bodaken, 1975). Studies by Burgoon, Cohen, Miller, and Montgomery (1978), and Miller and Burgoon (1979), on the other hand, did not use refutative messages. McCroskey, Young, and Scott (1972) report that two-sided (refutative) messages produced more immediate attitude change than one-sided (supportive) ones. They discussed the lack of an interaction, but there was no significant difference on the "raw scores" for sidedness after the counterpersuasion.[4] In fact, only two studies cited by Pfau and Kenski (1990)—Burgoon and Chase (1973) and Burgoon and King (1974)—included both supportive and refutative messages, but they found *no significant difference between them in creation of resistance.* Nor have Pfau's studies on inoculation tested the effects of supportive messages (see Pfau and Burgoon, 1988; Pfau, Kenski, Nitz, and Sorenson, 1990; Pfau and Van Bockern, 1994; or Pfau, Van Bockern, and Kang, 1992). Thus, while they assume the superiority of refutative messages, they never actually provide support for this assumption.

Other evidence suggests that *both* supportive and refutative defenses are effective at creating resistance on controversial topics, that is, that refutative messages do not enjoy the same advantage on controversial topics that they have on cultural truism topics (Beatty and Adams, 1977; Benoit, 1991b; Burgoon and Chase, 1973; Burgoon and King, 1974; Thistlethwaite, Kemenetsky, and Schmidt, 1956). Some studies present mixed evidence (Crane, 1962; Pryor and Steinfatt, 1978; Sawyer, 1973), but where is the evidence to support McGuire's inoculation predictions that inoculating or refutational messages are superior to supportive ones where controversial topics are concerned? Refutative defenses can be useful to political candidates, but we should not assume that refutative defenses are inherently better than supportive ones at creating resistance on controversial campaign topics.

Supporters may argue, citing these studies (Pfau and Burgoon, 1988; Pfau, Kenski, Nitz, and Sorenson, 1990; Pfau and Van Bockern, 1994; or Pfau, Van Bockern, and Kang, 1992), that refutative messages create resistance on political issues. These data do not, however, support the claim that *only* refutative defenses create resistance or that refutative defenses are *best* at creating resistance or even that refutative messages create *more* resistance than supportive ones (because they never tested supportive messages).

Furthermore, Pfau and Kenski clearly focus on prevention rather than on repair: "It is unclear whether refutation messages can do much more than to minimize the damage already done by an attack message, especially in the long term"; "Refutation messages are of no value against an opponent's attack that is launched late in a close campaign, thus simply precluding any response" (1990, p. 84). While the strategies of persuasive defense can be used preemptively (see, e.g., Benoit's [1995] analysis of Nixon's Cambodia address), they are most widely used as responses to prior attack.[5] Thus while Pfau and Kenski's book provides valuable insights into attacking messages, it does not provide a set of topoi for attack or defense and is intended primarily for prevention, not remediation. Nor should we accept uncritically the assumption that refutational messages are superior to supportive ones on controversial topics, like politics.

Jamieson's book *Dirty Politics* (1992) analyzes responses to political attacks that she found in her analysis of political campaigns. She describes ten potential responses: counterattack (responding to one illegitimate attack with a like response); inoculation; forewarning of impending attack; reframing (providing an alternative and more favorable interpretation of the attacking message); taking umbrage (expressing outrage at the attack); humorously reframing the attack; using credible sources to rebut the charges; using the press's credibility to rebut the charges; using disassociation; and admitting mistakes and asking forgiveness. Like other inductively derived lists (see, e.g., Benoit, 1982), this one includes strategies at more than one level of abstraction. For example, some concern the content of the response (e.g., counterattack, inoculation, forewarning, reframing, disassociation, and admission), some relate to the source of evidence used in the response (credible sources, media credibility), and two options seem to have to do with the tone of the response (taking umbrage, using humor). Nevertheless, these are potentially useful strategies, and several of them are quite similar to the categories of persuasive defense discussed next (e.g., "counterattack" is the same as "attacking accuser"; "ask forgiveness" seems to be the same as "mortification"; disassociation seems quite similar to differentiation or denial; some of the illustrations of reframing seem to include denials).

Persuasive Defense: A Theory of Image Restoration

The analysis of persuasive attack developed earlier suggests that there are two key elements in such discourse: (1) the accused must be linked to, or seen as responsible for, an act and (2) the act must be viewed as offensive by the audience. The theory of image restoration keys on this analysis of persuasive attack and offers five broad categories. Denial and evasion of responsibility address the first component of persuasive attack, rejecting or reducing the accused's responsibility for the act in question. Reducing offensiveness and corrective action, the third and fourth broad categories of image restoration, concern the second component of persuasive attack: reducing offensiveness of the act attributed to the accused. The last general strategy, mortification, attempts to restore an image not by disputing the charges but by asking forgiveness. Each strategy will be discussed briefly in this section.

Denial

A person accused of wrongdoing may simply deny committing the offensive action (see Ware and Linkugel, 1973). Goffman (1971) explained that the rhetor may also deny that the act occurred (see also Schlenker, 1980; Schonbach, 1980; Semin and Manstead, 1983; or Tedeschi and Reiss, 1981). Brinson and Benoit (in press) add a third option: the rhetor may admit performing the act but deny that it has any harmful effects. Whether the accused denies that the offensive act occurred, denies that he or she performed it, or denies that the act is harmful, such denial, if accepted by the audience, should help restore the image of the rhetor. So one option for responding to persuasive attack is simply to deny the offensive act.

In 1991, Pepsi-Cola accused its chief competitor, Coca-Cola, of requiring its other accounts to pay higher prices, thereby subsidizing Coke's largest customer, McDonald's (see the example below of attacking accuser). Coke replied by denying Pepsi's charges. A letter from Frenett, senior vice president and general manager, stressed that charges that Coke increased prices for some customers but not all "were absolutely false" and that price increases are "universally applied; there were no exceptions" (1991, p. 24). Here, Coca-Cola directly and unequivocally rejects Pepsi-Cola's charges as false: Coke simply did not do what Pepsi had alleged.

A related option is for the rhetor to attempt to shift the blame. Burke (1970) labeled this option victimage (see also Schonbach, 1980). This strategy can have advantages over simple denial. First, it provides a target that the audience can blame for the wrongful deed. Second, it answers an important question: "Well, if you didn't do it, who did?" So another form of denial generally is shifting the blame.

After the *Exxon Valdez* oil spill, Rawl, chair of Exxon, attempted to shift blame for delays in the cleanup. He "blamed state officials and the Coast Guard for the delay, charging . . . that the company could not obtain immediate authorization on the scene to begin cleaning up the oil or applying a chemical dispersant" (Mathews and Peterson, 1989, pp. A1–6). If people accepted this version of events, it could absolve Exxon of guilt for delays in the cleanup (although not for the spill itself).

Evasion of Responsibility

Another general image repair strategy is attempting to evade or reduce responsibility for the offensive act, which had four versions. Scott and Lyman (1968) suggest that the accused can claim that his or her action was merely a response to another's offensive act and that their own behavior can be seen as a reasonable reaction to the provocation (they called this strategy "scapegoating," but we rename it "provocation" to avoid confusing it with shifting the blame). If accepted, this rhetorical strategy may shift some or all of the responsibility from the rhetor, helping to repair his or her image. Schonbach (1980) and Semin and Manstead (1983) also discussed provocation as a strategic option. To illustrate, a child might respond to the charge that he or she broke another's toy by explaining, "You spilled milk on my picture, so I broke your toy." While this response is unlikely to guarantee forgiveness, it may reduce the rhetor's apparent blame for the offensive act.

Another form of evading responsibility is defeasibility (Scott and Lyman, 1968). Here the accused alleges a lack of information about or control over important elements of the situation (see also Schonbach, 1980; Semin and Manstead, 1983; Tedeschi and Reiss, 1981). The rhetor claims that because of a lack of information or control, he or she should not be held completely responsible for the offensive act. If this claim is accepted, it should reduce the responsibility of the accused for the offensive act and help repair the damaged reputation. For instance, a busy executive who missed an important meeting could attempt to justify his or her behavior by claiming, "I was never told that the meeting had been moved up a day." If it is true that the meeting was changed and the executive wasn't informed, he or she lacked crucial information that excuses the absence.

A third option is to claim that the offensive action occurred by accident (Scott and Lyman, 1968; Semin and Manstead, 1983; or Tedeschi and Reiss, 1981). We have a tendency to hold people responsible for factors that may reasonably be regarded as under their control. If the accused can convince the audience that the act in question happened accidentally, he or she should be held less accountable, and the damage to his or her image should be reduced. In 1992, Sears was accused of overcharging its auto repair customers in California. Sears issued two letters, first denying all charges and then (while still denying any wrongdoing) changing wage policies that encouraged unneeded repairs. Chairman Brennan characterized the mistakes as "inadvertent" rather than intentional ("Sears to Drop," 1992, p. 5B). Inadvertent or accidental wrongdoing may be less offensive than intentional harms.

Fourth, the rhetor can suggest that the offensive behavior was done with good intentions (discussed by Ware and Linkugel, 1973, as part of denial). Those who perform improper actions are usually not held as accountable as those who intend to do bad. In his first letter Brennan avowed that "Sears wants you to know that we would never intentionally violate the trust customers have shown in our company for 105 years" (1992, p. A56). In the second letter, Brennan reiterated his assurances that Sears had good intentions: "I do not believe there were any willful overcharges in California" ("Sears to Drop," 1992, p. 5B). Thus Sears repeatedly cited its good intentions in its persuasive defense.

Reducing the Act's Offensiveness

Rather than deny or reduce his or her accountability, a rhetor who is accused of wrongful actions can try to reduce the perceived offensiveness of the act. This general image repair strategy has six versions: bolstering, minimization, differentiation, transcendence, attacking one's accuser, and compensation.

First, a rhetor may use bolstering to strengthen the audience's positive feelings toward the accused, in order to offset the negative feelings connected with the wrongful act (Ware and Linkugel, 1973). Rhetors may describe positive characteristics they have or positive acts they have performed in the past. While the amount of negative affect from the accusation remains the same here, increased positive feelings for the accused may help offset the negative feelings associated with the act, creating a net improvement in reputation.

Following the *Valdez* oil spill, Exxon attempted to use bolstering as part of its image repair effort. Chairman Rawl declared, "Exxon has moved swiftly and competently to minimize the effect this oil will have on the environment, fish, and other wildlife." He declared that this incident "has been receiving our full attention" and expressed his sympathy for "the residents of Valdez and the people of the State of Alaska" (1989, p. A12). By characterizing the company's actions as "swift" and "competent," its attentions as focused on the incident, and its attitude as sympathetic (*if* accepted by the audience), Exxon sought to bolster its image and help offset damage to its reputation from the oil spill.

A second possibility is to try to minimize the negative feelings associated with the wrongful act. If the audience comes to believe that the act is less offensive than it first appeared, the amount of damage to the rhetor's reputation should be reduced. Sykes and Matza (1957), Scott and Lyman (1968), Schonbach (1980), Schlenker (1980), Tedeschi and Reiss (1981), and Semin and Manstead (1983) all discuss denial or minimization of injury and/or victim.

After the *Valdez* oil spill, Exxon officials tried to downplay the extent of the damage. For example, Baker explained, "On May 19, when Alaska retrieved corpses of tens of thousands of sea birds, hundreds of otters, and dozens of bald eagles, an Exxon official told National Public Radio that Exxon had counted just 300 birds and 70 otters" (1989, p. 8). In so doing the company evidently sought to portray the damage as less serious than it appeared to be (and possibly less than it actually was).

Third, the accused can employ differentiation (Ware and Linkugel, 1973). Here the rhetor attempts to distinguish the act he or she performed from other similar but more offensive actions. In comparison, the act performed by the rhetor may seem less offensive, so that the audience has fewer negative feelings toward the rhetor.

President Nixon decided to order troops into Cambodia during the Vietnam War. He attempted to differentiate his *military offensive* from an *invasion of another country:* "This is not an invasion of Cambodia. The areas in which these attacks will be launched are completely occupied by North Vietnamese forces (1970, p. 451). He referred to a map of Southeast Asia in which the North Vietnamese strongholds were marked, saying, "The sanctuaries are in red, and you will note that they are on both sides of the border" (p. 450). Thus he attempted to describe his use of military troops as a continuation of existing policy (attacking the North Vietnamese), *not* as a new offensive or invasion.

A fourth way of reducing offensiveness is transcendence (Ware and Linkugel, 1973), which attempts to view the act in a more favorable light. Ware and Linkugel specifically discuss placing the action in a broader context, but transcendence can also involve simply suggesting a different frame of reference. For example, a rhetor could attempt to shift the audience's attention to other allegedly higher values in order to justify the behavior in question (Schlenker, 1980; Schonbach, 1980; Scott and Lyman, 1968; Semin and Manstead, 1983; Sykes and Matza, 1957; and Tedeschi and Reiss, 1981). A positive context may lessen the apparent offensiveness of the act and improve the accused's image.

Nixon attempted to justify his military offensive in Cambodia by using transcendence. He declared, "We take this action not for the purpose of expanding the war into Cambodia but for the purpose of ending the war in Vietnam, and winning the just peace we desire" (1970, p. 451). Here the president justified his action on the basis of higher goals ("ending the war," "winning a just peace").

Fifth, those accused of wrongdoing may decide to attack their accusers (see Rosenfield, 1968; Schonbach, 1980; Scott and Lyman, 1968; Semin and Manstead, 1983; Sykes and Matza, 1957; and Tedeschi and Reiss, 1981). If the rhetor can damage the credibility of the source of allegations, damage to the rhetor's image may be limited.

Pepsi-Cola attacked Coca-Cola in advertisements aimed at retail outlets (*Nation's Restaurant News*). One advertisement claimed that Coke's pricing policies treated other accounts differently (and worse) than McDonald's: "This year, while Coke required national accounts like you to absorb a per-gallon price increase, we hear *there was no change to McDonald's net price.*" To make sure the implications were clear, the ad stressed that "Coke's pricing policy is requiring you to subsidize the operations of your largest competitor" (1991, p. 34). Here the persuasive attack on Coke is quite clear.

Compensation is the final form of reducing the offensiveness (Schonbach, 1980). Here the rhetor offers to reimburse the victim to help mitigate the negative feeling arising from the act. This payment can be goods or services as well as monetary reimbursement. If the compensation is acceptable to the victim, the negative affect produced by the wrongful act should be eliminated or reduced, improving the rhetor's image. For example, a group of disabled people were denied admission to a movie theater. An official later apologized and offered them free passes to a future movie ("Rebuffed Moviegoers," 1992). Clearly the passes were intended to help compensate them for the offensive act.

Corrective Action

Another general strategy for image restoration is the promise of corrective action. Such action can take the form of restoring the state of affairs existing before the offensive action and/or promising to prevent recurrences. Goffman (1971) mentions this strategy as a component of an apology, although it can occur without one (e.g., Tylenol introduced tamper-resistant packaging after the first episode of poisoning while denying responsibility for the deaths [Benoit and Lindsey, 1987b]). A willingness to correct and/or prevent recurrence of the problem can improve the accused's image (this strategy differs from compensation, because corrective action offers to correct/prevent the problem, while compensation seeks to pay for it).

On September 17, 1993, AT&T experienced a breakdown in long distance service to and from New York City. In his attempt to repair AT&T's image, Chairman Allen also relied heavily on corrective action. For example, he announced that "we have already taken corrective and preventive action at the affected facility" in New York City, including "a thorough examination of all of our facilities and practices, from the ground up." He also announced that AT&T plans "to spend billions more over the next few years to make them even more reliable" (1993, p. C3). Thus he promised not only to correct the prob-

lem at the New York City switching plant but also to prevent its recurrence in the future.

Mortification

Another general strategy for image restoration is to confess and beg
forgiveness, which Burke labels mortification (1970, 1973). If the audience believes the apology is sincere, it may pardon the wrongful
act. Schonbach (1980) discusses concessions, in which one may admit guilt and express regret.

AT&T used this strategy as part of its response. Allen accepted
responsibility for the disruption: "I am deeply disturbed that AT&T
was responsible for a disruption in communications service." Not
only does he explicitly accept full responsibility for the incident, but
he makes no attempt to minimize the impact of the service outage.
The first paragraph ends with an explicit apology: "I apologize to all
of you who were affected, directly or indirectly" (Allen, 1993, p. C3).

Of the five basic strategies available to the rhetor who engages in
image repair discourse—denial, evasion of responsibility, reducing
offensiveness, correction, and mortification—several have variants.
Table 2 outlines the strategies. We made one change in the list used
in this analysis for purposes of coding: because we coded each instance of persuasive attack according to the strategies discussed
above (and displayed in table 1), we did not include attacking one's
accuser in our analysis and tabulation of persuasive defense strategies.

Previous Research on Image Restoration Discourse

The theory of persuasive attack is a new development, and although it shows promise, thus far nothing has been published using
this method. However, the theory of persuasive defense, or image restoration strategies, has been developed and applied in several studies,
undertaken in three contexts: political rhetoric, corporate discourse,
and sports/entertainment rhetoric.[6] This body of work has examined
discursive image repair efforts by politicians (Nixon's Watergate rhetoric, Kennedy's Chappaquiddick speech, Reagan's Iran-Contra rhetoric, and Nixon's Cambodia address); corporations (Tylenol's response
to the first poisoning episode, AT&T's apology for its New York City
long distance interruption, Exxon's discourse on the *Valdez* oil spill,
Union Carbide's response to the Bhopal gas leak, advertisements by
Coca-Cola and Pepsi-Cola in a trade journal, and Sears's defense

Table 2. Strategies for Persuasive Defense

Denial
  Simple denial
  Shift blame
Evade responsibility
  Provocation
  Defeasibility/biological
  Accident
  Good intentions
Reduce offensiveness of event
  Bolstering
  Minimization
  Attack accuser[a]
  Differentiation
  Transcendence
  Compensation
Corrective action
Mortification

[a]This category was not used in this analysis because persuasive attack was coded separately.

Source: W. L. Benoit (1995), *Accounts, Excuses, and Apologies: A Theory of Image Restoration Strategies* (Albany: State University of New York Press), p. 95.

against charges of fraud in auto repair); and sports and entertainment (Tonya Harding's defense against accusations that she was involved in the attack on Nancy Kerrigan, Murphy Brown's response to Dan Quayle's charges, and Oliver Stone's defense of his film *JFK*). Of course, a great deal of other research on apologiae and image restoration has been conducted prior to and independent of this research program, and this work is reviewed in Benoit (1995).

Political Image Repair Studies

Benoit (1982) analyzed President Nixon's speeches and press conferences on the Watergate affair. He identified a variety of strategies that developed through three stages (principally shifts occurred as demands for tapes and documents grew and as he was forced to turn them over). Nixon used corrective action (ordering investigations), bolstering (emphasizing his cooperation, emphasizing his electoral "mandate"), shifting the blame to subordinates, minimization, attacking one of his principal accusers (John Dean), and transcendence (by stressing the allegedly more important need for confidentiality and the principle of executive privilege).[7] These strategies were judged to be ineffectual. For example, internal investigations lack the credibility of independent inquiries. Shifting the blame to his subordinates (Dean, Haldeman, and Ehrlichman) was risky, because it could exonerate him from Watergate only by calling into question his judgment in selecting such people as his key subordinates. An emphasis on his "mandate" was irrelevant to the charges in Watergate. Furthermore, his attempt at bolstering (emphasizing his cooperation) was contradicted by his actions: attempts to conceal materials via the principles of confidentiality or executive privilege.

Senator Edward Kennedy's Chappaquiddick speech has also been analyzed for image repair strategies (Benoit, 1988). Suspicions concerned both his responsibility for the accident and his failure to report it promptly to the police. He attempted to shift the blame for the accident to situational features (a narrow bridge, without guardrails, built at an angle to the road, etc.). Kennedy also attempted to shift the blame for failing to report the accident to the trauma he suffered (exhaustion, a concussion). These strategies were effective in preserving his Senate seat but probably were not sufficient to resurrect his presidential hopes (especially because portraying himself as at the mercy of the scene, in shifting the blame, may have created the impression that Kennedy was not in control of his actions, an attribute that is not favorable for a presidential candidate). An argument could be made that, because Kennedy is shifting the blame to situational features rather than to other people, these might be better considered to be instances of defeasibility.

A preliminary version of the theory of image restoration discourse was developed for a study of Reagan's speeches and press conferences on the Iran-Contra affair (Benoit, Gullifor, and Panici, 1991). This analysis found that Reagan's defense developed through several stages as the situation changed. His defensive discourse included instances of denial, evasion of responsibility, minimization, mortification, and plans to correct the problem. His defense was judged to be more acceptable when he shifted from an overall posture of denial to one of mortification.

A final application of this theory to political discourse is Benoit's (1995) critical analysis of Nixon's Cambodia address. This speech was designed to preempt charges that Nixon was widening the war in Vietnam by invading another country. He used three strategies: bolstering, differentiation, and transcendence. Nixon bolstered himself and his decision by pointing out that previous presidents had made successful military decisions in the very same room. He differentiated his *military offensive* from the more offensive label of *invasion of another country*, arguing that he was simply continuing the past policy of attacking Viet Cong strongholds (not undertaking a new action, like invading another country). The only difference was the location of the Viet Cong strongholds. Nixon also attempted to transcend this action by placing his decision in the broader context of a new action necessary to end the war. These strategies are not implemented very well in the speech. The fact that prior presidents had made successful military decisions in the same room is exceptionally weak evidence of the wisdom of his action. Nixon failed to provide a strong rationale for his claim that military action in Cambodia would in fact end the war. Furthermore, his depiction of the war as business as usual (still just attacking Viet Cong as we always have, differentiating his offensive from an invasion of another country) clashed with his description of the offensive as a new action that will win the war (in transcendence). Thus Nixon's strategies were individually weak and collectively inconsistent.

Corporate Image Repair Studies

This perspective on image restoration discourse also has been applied to corporate apologiae. Benoit and Lindsey (1987b) examined Tylenol's response to the poisonings of September 1992, in which seven people died. Tylenol (through Johnson & Johnson, Tylenol's parent company) denied that it had introduced cyanide into the capsules, and it shifted the blame to a madman. This denial was reinforced with the report of a Food and Drug (FDA) inspection of the manufacturing plants and the argument that, because other products (products not made by Johnson & Johnson) had been adulterated, it was the work of someone not connected with Tylenol. Second, Johnson & Johnson bolstered its image. Several commercials featured women who expressed their trust in Tylenol. In addition, Tylenol introduced tamper-resistant packaging, an action designed to prevent recurrence of tampering. Tylenol would henceforth use three safety seals to prevent further episodes of poisoning.[8] Finally, Tylenol used differentiation, pointing out that most of its products were not capsules and hence were not susceptible to tampering. These strategies were appropriate and remarkably effective in restoring Tylenol's image, which several observers had wrongly concluded was irrevocably tarnished.

AT&T's defense following an interruption of its long distance service in New York was critically analyzed by Benoit and Brinson (1994). In September of 1991, AT&T's long distance service in New York City was interrupted. Not only did the interruption block literally millions of telephone calls, but it also stopped airline transportation, because air traffic control uses long distance telephone lines. Initially, AT&T tried to blame low-level workers. However, as the complete story emerged, AT&T apologized for the interruption (mortification), then bolstered its image (e.g., stressing its commitment to excellence, reporting billions invested in service, and citing skilled workers). Finally, AT&T promised several forms of corrective action. The factors that led to this interruption of long distance service were corrected. AT&T promised a comprehensive review of its operations to anticipate and prevent other problems. It also stressed its commitment to providing excellent service and promised to spend billions of dollars to do so. After the initial fumbling attempt to shift the blame, these strategies were well conceived and should have helped restore AT&T's image.

Exxon's response to the *Valdez* oil spill was analyzed by Benoit (1995). Exxon shifted the blame for the accident to Captain Hazelwood and for the delay in the cleanup to slow authorization from Alaska and the Coast Guard. It attempted to minimize the size of the problem, bolstered its image as a concerned company, and promised corrective action to alleviate any damage. Shifting the blame to Hazelwood may have been helpful (especially after it became known that he had been drinking before the accident). However, the state of Alaska and the Coast Guard were unlikely targets for blame. Exxon's attempts to minimize the extent of the problem were graphically denied by television and newspaper coverage. Similarly, the characterization of the cleanup as slow and apparently inept undermined both the company's attempts to bolster its image and the credibility of its promised corrective action. Thus Exxon's image restoration campaign was relatively ineffectual. It would have been preferable for Exxon to discuss policies to prevent the recurrence of this oil spill (it is possible that Exxon's attorneys advised against this option because it could create or exacerbate legal difficulties).

Union Carbide's response to the Bhopal, India, gas leak that killed thousands and injured hundreds of thousands was analyzed in Benoit (1995). Carbide's primary strategies were bolstering and corrective action. Four specific actions were described: establishing a relief fund, establishing an orphanage, sending medical supplies, and sending medical personnel. While these strategies were appropriate, they failed to address a very important question: what, if anything, would Union Carbide do to prevent another tragedy?

Another application of the theory of image restoration to corporate discourse can be found in Benoit's (1995) examination of persuasive attack and defense in three years of advertising (1990–1992) by Coca-Cola and Pepsi-Cola in a trade publication, *Nation's Restaurant News*. That each used bolstering in a variety of advertisements is hardly surprising. However, Pepsi declared that Coke charged McDonald's less than other customers, in effect subsidizing its largest customer. Coke expressly (and effectively) denied these charges. Furthermore, Coke revealed that Pepsi ran its allegations a second time after Coke notified them that the charges were false. Then Coke turned the tables on Pepsi, pointing out that Pepsi used the profits it made from its customers to buy fast food restaurants. Coke pointed out that Pepsi owned 19,500 Taco Bells, Kentucky Fried Chickens, and Pizza Huts. Surely Pepsi's interest in the restaurants it actually owned is far greater than Coke's interest in its largest customer (McDonald's). Thus, Coke and Pepsi both used bolstering and attack accuser, and Coke used simple denial. Pepsi probably should have apologized for its (apparently) false accusations but did not. Coke's persuasive attack and its persuasive defense were each superior to Pepsi's.

Dow Corning was subjected to harsh criticism over the dangers of its breast implants (Brinson and Benoit, in press). Its defense went through three phases. Initially, Corning used denial, minimization, bolstering, and attacking one's accuser. As its own damaging internal documents became public, it attempted transcendence. Finally, Corning engaged in mortification and corrective action.

A final case in point concerns Sears's response to allegations by the California Department of Consumer Affairs that its repair shops had defrauded consumers by making unneeded repairs (Benoit, in press). Sears's defense went through two stages. In both, it employed denial, differentiation, bolstering, and minimization. In the first stage, these were coupled with an attack on its accuser. In the second stage, they were used with corrective action. Sears's use of denial and minimization were unpersuasive. Its attempts at bolstering were unrelated to the accusations. Its attack on its accuser was unconvincing. Corrective action was a good idea, but it was simply too little too late.

Sports/Entertainment Image Repair Studies

After she was accused of involvement in the attack on fellow skater Nancy Kerrigan, Tonya Harding appeared on *Eye-to-Eye with Connie Chung* to defend her reputation. Benoit and Hanczor (1994) found that her defense consisted primarily of denial, bolstering, and attacking her accusers. While these were plausible strategies, her development of them was ineffectual. She had lied about when she first learned of the attack, which damaged her credibility. The image of her as a passive recipient of abuse was inconsistent with her public image and (regardless of whether it was true) was ineffectual. She also provided no support for her assertions, even though several other people contradicted her claims.

The theory of image restoration discourse has been used to analyze Oliver Stone's defense of his film *JFK* (Benoit and Nill, under review). He relied primarily on bolstering and denial to defend his film and his sources. He also attacked his accusers, and his defense was generally well crafted. Stone's critics were unsuccessful at keeping people from seeing his film, which renewed interest in declassifying secret documents from the investigation.

A third illustration of this theory in the realm of sports and entertainment examined Murphy Brown's response to persuasive attack by Dan Quayle (Benoit and Anderson, under review). This television show denied Quayle's charges (visually and verbally), bolstered its image, and attacked its accuser, Dan Quayle. This defense was well designed (much more so than Quayle's attack) and was judged a success.

The studies suggest that those who desire to restore a tarnished image must choose from a limited number of discursive strategies to achieve this goal. Political, corporate, and sports/entertainment rhetors used denial, bolstering, shifting the blame, corrective action, and attacking one's accuser relatively frequently. Minimization, differentiation, transcendence, and mortification were also used. These strategies were operationalized in many different ways, with varying degrees of success. Thus it appears that the basic repertoire of image repair strategies is limited, that the theory of image restoration discourse identifies those strategies, and that these options are available to rhetors across different domains.

Summary

This investigation thus advances a theory of persuasive attack, takes a well-established theory of image repair discourse, and applies them to analysis of the 1992 presidential debates. Although the theory of image restoration discourse has been applied to political discourse (as well as corporate and sports/entertainment), it has for the most part ignored political campaign discourse (one exception is Benoit and Anderson, under review). Specific details of our procedure can be found in appendix 1. We turn now to the results of our analysis.

Notes

1. We assume that communication is goal directed. Others have made this point previously. For example, O'Keefe and Delia conceptualize "messages as ways of carrying out communicative intentions" (1982, p. 48). Any such broad assumption deserves qualification, and this one is no exception. First, communicators may well have multiple goals that are not completely compatible. In such circumstances, behavior that functions to further one goal may well mean that other goals remain partially or completely unmet. It is even possible that utterances intended to further one goal may impair attainment of another. However, we contend that people try to achieve the goals that seem most important to them at the time they act or to achieve the best mix of the goals that appears possible (considering the perceived costs of the behavior enacted in pursuit of the goals, and the importance of those goals to the actors).

Second, at times a person's goals, motives, or purposes are vague, ill formed, or unclear. Nevertheless, to the extent a person's goals are clear, he or she will try to behave in ways that help to accomplish them. Furthermore, even when a communicator has a clear conception of a particular goal, that does not necessarily mean that he or she is aware of (and/or is willing or able to use) the most effective means for achieving the goal. However, to the extent a particular goal is salient to a communicator, he or she will pursue it by enacting the behavior that the communicator believes is likely to achieve the goal at a tolerable cost.

Third, we do not claim that people devote the same amount of attention to each and every communicative encounter, micromanaging all utterances and all characteristics of an utterance, constantly identifying goals and unceasingly planning behavior to accomplish them. Some behavior is automatic rather than controlled (see, e.g., Hample, 1992; Kellermann, 1992; Schneider and Shiffrin, 1977; or Shiffrin and Schneider, 1977). In situations that are particularly important to us, however, we do plan aspects of our utterances carefully. In other situations, we devote as much cognitive effort to the task at hand as seems reasonable to us.

It can be difficult to identify communicators' goal(s) because people sometimes attempt to deceive or mislead others about their goals. Furthermore, certain artifacts (e.g., television shows, films, and artwork) may not have readily identifiable persuasive goals, purposes, or intents for the critic to discover. Despite these reservations, communication generally is best understood as an intentional activity. Communicators attempt to devise utterances that they believe will best achieve the goals that are most salient to them when they communicate.

Von Wright's idea of the practical syllogism is a useful way to view communication. He explains the relationship between goals and action in this way:

> A intends to bring about p.
> A considers that he cannot bring about p unless he does a.
> Therefore, A sets himself to do a.

> A scheme of this kind is sometimes called a *practical inference* (or syllogism) (1971, p. 96).

Thus people have goals or desires (that they believe communication can help accomplish), symbolized by Von Wright as p. People present the message(s) (a) that they think will be instrumental in obtaining their goal (p).

Of course, if there is more than one means of accomplishing a goal, people will choose the utterance that (they believe) maximizes the likelihood of success, or the utterance that (they believe) has the fewest costs, or the utterance that (they believe) also facilitates another goal. Furthermore, if people believe more than one utterance is required to accomplish their goal, they will offer several messages. They must believe that any utterance they produce is one they are capable of performing, one that is likely to help accomplish their goal, and one that does not have unreasonable costs. When these circumstances obtain, then speaker A will say utterance a in an attempt to accomplish goal p (see von Wright's chapter 3, "Intentionality and Teleological Explanation," pp. 83–131).

2. This discussion could create the impression that persuasive attack should be considered a negative or vindictive form of discourse. Of course, that is a possibility, and thoughts of "yellow journalism" or worse may come to mind. However, the strategies of persuasive attack as we envision it can also be used to expose wrongdoing and to call malefactors to account for misdeeds. In the case of political discourse persuasive attack can falsely accuse and smear, and it can expose a politician's weaknesses and/or unfitness for office.

3. The importance of motivation to create the defense was shown in other ways. For example, McGuire (1964) studied threat, operationalized as telling (or not telling) subjects that they would be exposed to an attacking message. Threat enhanced the effectiveness of the defensive messages, but it helped the supportive messages significantly more than the refutative ones. While those in the refutative condition may not have known they would soon hear a persuasive attack, the act of refuting opposing arguments puts them on notice that their beliefs are at risk. However, on a cultural truism topic, notification that they will read an attack is the first time that subjects in the supportive condition become aware of the possibility of an attack. Indeed, supportive messages with threat are nearly the equal of refutative messages (without threat) in creating resistance.

Similarly, McGuire (1964) studied reassurance, in which subjects were told (or not told) that others do not question these cultural truisms. Reassurance reduced the motivation of those in the refutative condition to create a defense. Thus the key element in McGuire's inoculation theory is motivation to develop a belief defense *where no such motivation has existed before.*

4. We now believe Benoit (1991b) erroneously concluded that this study found the two-sided message created more resistance than the one-sided message.

5. We do not share the assumption that persuasive defense can be expected to work only preemptively. First, the work on image repair discourse, including some political (although not campaign) discourse, shows that rhetors are capable of restoring their image by effectively using the strategies of persuasive defense (e.g., Kennedy: Benoit, 1988; Reagan: Benoit, Gullifor, and Panici, 1991; Tylenol: Benoit and Lindsey, 1987b; AT&T: Benoit and Brinson, 1994; Coca-Cola: Benoit, 1995). Second, if they were correct in their assumption (that it is nearly impossible to counter an attack after the attack and that an inoculating message can be expected to prevent damage from a subsequent attack), then attitude change research would find primacy effects but no recency effects. However, work on the question of primacy-recency does not reveal a clear and consistent advantage to the first message. As O'Keefe (1992) observes, "The research evidence quite clearly shows that there is no *general* advantage to either position" (p. 183). Ironically, McGuire's (1961) research found that immunization (defense before attack) and restoration (defense following attack) "were equally effective" (p. 196). Tannenbaum, Maccaulay, and Norris (1966), promoting congruity theory as an alternative to McGuire's inoculation theory, found that refutative messages were effective in both immunization and restoration sequences (although more effective in the former). Thus it is a mistake to assume that the defense *must* precede the attack: both critical analyses and experimental research show restoration can be effective.

6. Hahn and Gustainis (1987) analyze presidential discourse to illustrate defensive tactics. They argue that three myths predominate: problems are caused by "outgroups," leaders are "benevolent heroes," and citizens should "sacrifice" and obey the leader (p. 44). They do not focus on presidential debates or rely on the typologies accepted in the literature (e.g., Ware and Linkugel, 1973), however.

7. Benoit (1982) conducted an inductive analysis, identifying recurrent themes in Nixon's discourse. He also included "Quoting the White House Tapes" (after they were released) as a defensive strategy, which is a form of evidence and not a distinct image restoration strategy. The categories discussed here are labels taken from the theory of image restoration, which was actually developed later.

8. Benoit and Lindsey (1987b) applied the theory of apologia developed by Ware and Linkugel (1973), which is subsumed in the theory of image restoration. Corrective action is not discussed as a separate strategy by Ware and Linkugel, and therefore Benoit and Lindsey include it with bolstering in their analysis.

3

Persuasive Attack
Bush the Primary Target,
Perot Relatively Unscathed

My argument with Governor Clinton—you can call it mud wrestling, but I think it's fair to put it in focus—is I am deeply troubled by someone who demonstrates and organizes demonstrations in a foreign land when his country's at war. Probably a lot of kids here disagree with me, but that's what I feel. That's what I feel passionately about. I'm thinking of Ross Perot's running mate, sitting in the jail; how would he feel about it? —Bush, Debate 2

We have gone from first to thirteenth in the world in wages in the last twelve years, since Mr. Bush and Mr. Reagan have been in. Personal income has dropped while people have worked harder. In the last four years there have been twice as many bankruptcies as new jobs created. We need a new approach.—Clinton, Debate 1

I don't like to see the people in a deteriorating economy, in a deteriorating country, because our government has lost touch with the people. The people in Washington are good people. We just have a bad system. We've got to change the system. It's time to do it, because we have run up so much debt that time is no longer our friend. We've got to put our house in order.—Perot, Debate 1

Presidential candidates frequently engage in persuasive attack. Furthermore, as will become clear, they can and do attack both other candidates' character (personal invective) and other candidates' policies (issues). That some attacks concerned character while others addressed policy was especially important in 1992, because President Bush relied heavily on personal attack against Governor Clinton—and the audience in debate 2 demanded a stop to mud-slinging. The audience's objection to personal attack severely handicapped Mr. Bush in this debate.

This chapter describes and discusses the results of our analysis of persuasive attack in the 1992 presidential debates. The data for the first research question—"What strategies of persuasive attack did the three candidates use in the three 1992 presidential debates?"—are summarized in table 3. The discussion of these results will begin by considering the nature of persuasive attack in the debates generally. Next each candidate's use of the specific strategies of persuasive attack in the debates will be discussed separately and then contrasted. We conducted an additional analysis of the target of persuasive attack, reported in table 4. Finally, the candidates' treatment of issues in their persuasive attacks will be addressed at the end of this chapter. The results of our analysis of the issues addressed in these attacking utterances are displayed in table 5, answering the second research question—"Which issues did the three candidates address in their instances of persuasive attack in three 1992 presidential debates?" We hope that our description of the discursive context of the debates in chapter 1 provides useful background material for appreciating the results of our analysis.

Persuasive Attack in the Debates

The data presented in table 3 reveal that there are several differences in use of the strategies of persuasive attack over the three debates.[1] Our analysis suggests that there are four important differences in the persuasive attack during the three debates. After describing these differences across the debates, we will discuss contrasts between the three candidates' use of persuasive attack.

First, the three candidates engaged in the least amount of persuasive attack in the second debate. Debate 1 contained almost 50 percent more persuasive attacks than debate 2, and the last debate contained well over twice as many as the middle debate (debate 1: 74, debate 2: 51, and debate 3: 132). In the second debate, audience members repeatedly made it quite clear that they did *not* want to hear personal attacks (when we contrast the three candidates, we shall see that Bush was affected most by this sentiment). For example, one audience member observed, "The amount of time the candidates have spent on this campaign trashing their opponents' character and their programs is depressingly large." Another questioner asked, "Can we

Table 3. Persuasive Attack in the 1992 Presidential Debates

Strategy	Bush				Clinton				Perot			
	D1	D2	D3	T	D1	D2	D3	T	D1	D2	D3	T
Negative general	12	5	12	29	11	8	30	*49*	10	4	25	39
Extent	2	1	9	12	7	8	3	*18*	3	7	7	17
Effect on audience	2	1	4	7	6	4	6	16	5	6	5	16
Inconsistency	2	1	15	*18*	6	1	9	16	—	—	2	2
Planned	6	1	1	*8*	—	—	—	—	—	—	—	—
Responsible	—	—	—	—	—	1	1	2	1	1	1	*3*
Persistence	—	—	—	—	1	2	2	*5*	—	—	—	—
Total	24	9	41	74	31	24	51	106	19	18	40	77

Note: Italics indicate the largest numbers in each category.

focus on the issues and not the personalities and the mud?" These complaints about mud-slinging indicate two things. First, it appears that a large proportion of the candidates' persuasive attacks (in the first and third debates and very likely elsewhere) are *personal* attacks. While all persuasive attack is not personal (i.e., some is aimed at policies or actions), character attack is a large part of persuasive attack generally. Second, the format of the debates—and in particular when audience members are able to clearly express their desires to the candidates—can affect the nature of persuasive attack produced by the rhetors.

A second difference is that all three of the candidates engaged in the largest number of persuasive attacks in the last debate. Each of the three candidates made considerably more persuasive attacks in the third debate than in the first (Bush, 70 percent more; Clinton, 65 percent more; Perot, 110 percent more). The increase was more than 100 percent from the second debate to the third for all three candidates (Bush, 355 percent more; Clinton, 113 percent more; Perot, 122 percent more). This last debate, one of three, accounted for 55 percent of Bush's, 48 percent of Clinton's, and 53 percent of Perot's persuasive attacks. The fact that this was the last chance for the candidates to "get in their licks" in the debates probably accounts for much of the sharp increase in the number of persuasive attacks in the final debate.

Furthermore, the candidates, and especially Bush (who increased the most between debates 2 and 3), perhaps feeling particularly frustrated by the constraints the audience imposed on persuasive attacks in the second debate, may have attempted in the last debate to make up for lost opportunities. Comparison of the incidence of persuasive attack in debates 2 and 3 indicates that the increase may also have been caused in large part by the format of these debates, which (given the audience's stated preference in this case) tended to stifle personal attacks in the second debate. Our reading of the debates reveals that Bush tended to rely more on personal attack (and less on policy or issue attacks) than the other two candidates; if so, audience demands affected his persuasive attack the most.

Third, each candidate reveals a marked proclivity to general persuasive attacks. This category accounted for 40 percent of the persuasive attacks in the three debates (39 percent of Bush's attacks, 46 percent of Clinton's attacks, and 51 percent of Perot's attacks). In fact, general negative attacks were the single most frequent form of attack used by each candidate in each debate, with the single exception of Bush in the third debate (when charges of inconsistency were slightly more numerous). Their frequency may reflect the fact that it easier or quicker simply to make a general attack than to intensify it by, for example, providing statistics (severity) or by relating the consequences to the viewers (effects on audience).

Fourth, there is a marked absence of attempts to demonstrate responsibility for offensive action: only 15 utterances out of 222 persuasive attacks coded concerned responsibility (see the items labeled planned and responsible). Fully 208 of the attacks, almost 94 percent, concerned the offensiveness, rather than the causes, of problems. The analysis of persuasive attack in chapter 2, and the strategies of persuasive attack outlined in table 1, indicate that there are several strategies for attributing responsibility as well as for increasing offensiveness of the act (at least in this preliminary theory of persuasive attack). Why would there be such an imbalance (208 to 15) in utterances between those attempting to show offensiveness of actions and those attempting to ascribe responsibility?

We believe the fact that all three men were candidates for president means that they would all be unlikely to diminish the importance of the power of the agent in these matters. They were all trying to persuade voters to elect them because of what they would *accomplish* as president. If the presidential candidate has no power to solve (or prevent) problems or to create benefits, then there is no reason to elect him. For example, Bush claimed that, to the extent that the economy is in trouble, he would improve it (as Clinton and Perot also claimed). Thus when Clinton and Perot argued that the economy is weak, they didn't have to establish that Bush is responsible for the state of the economy. President Bush cannot be expected to deny that he has the responsibility or power to have solved these alleged economic problems: if he didn't tacitly admit that he is at least partly in control of the economy, he could hardly claim to be able to improve it in a second term.[2] Similarly, if Arkansas's economy is troubled, Bush did not need to attempt to prove that Clinton was responsible for those problems. Governor Clinton wanted voters to believe he had the power to affect the state's economy, which permits him to take credit for alleged successes in Arkansas. This assumption of an agent's power is also consistent with the notion that the audience should accept the claim that he would have the ability as president to affect the national economy if he were elected. Thus, as presidential candidates, Bush, Clinton, and Perot were more likely to dispute, for example, whether the economy was troubled or the extent of economic problems than whether the president was responsible for our country's economic woes.

It is also possible that persuasive attack generally is more likely to address offensiveness than responsibility, but of course these data on persuasive attack in the 1992 presidential debates are insufficient to test that speculation. We might add, though, that our reading of newspaper accounts to illustrate the theory of persuasive attack advanced in chapter 2 seemed to find more instances of discourse that stressed offensiveness than responsibility (but we made no attempt to test this speculation systematically).

Thus our analysis shows that the least persuasive attack occurred in the second debate, indicating the influence of format and audience on persuasive attack and revealing that the candidates (especially Bush) tended to rely heavily on personal attack (when audience demands do not restrict their utterances). The most persuasive attack happened in the last debate, possibly because it was the candidates' last chance to attack their opponents in the debates and in part to make up for the audience's constraints on persuasive attack (especially personal) in the second debate. The most common form of persuasive attack was a general negative attack, possibly indicating that the methods of intensifying attacks are more difficult and/or more time consuming to develop. Finally, the great preponderance of persuasive attack strategies concerned offensiveness, not responsibility.

Bush

Bush used five different strategies of persuasive attack during the debates. He relied most heavily on general negative attacks, which accounted for 39 percent of his attacks. He also repeatedly charged Clinton with inconsistencies, almost one-quarter of his attacks, and he used this strategy more often than either of the other candidates. Especially in the third debate, he attacked on grounds of severity of problems. A fourth strategy was to stress the effects on the audience. He also argued that Clinton had planned acts that were wrongful. Each of these strategies will be described, but more attention will be devoted to the strategies Bush used most frequently.

Bush used general negative attacks in all three debates. In the first debate, Bush discusses the fact that Clinton had demonstrated against the Vietnam War: "I questioned his judgment and his character." Also in the first debate, Bush explained, "I don't think we need to tax more and spend more. . . . And I'm afraid that's what I think I'm hearing from Governor Clinton." He even criticized Clinton's complaints, declaring, "I would hate to be running for president and think that the only way I could win would be to convince everybody how horrible things are." In the second debate, Bush continued to accuse Clinton of wanting to tax and spend: "Governor Clinton's program wants to tax more and spend more." Bush also declared that "I don't believe that's the way to do it." He also declared in the second debate, in reference to Clinton's policies, "I don't see how you can grow the deficit down by raising people's taxes." In the third debate Bush declared, "Arkansas is doing very, very badly against any standard—environment, support for police officers, whatever it is." In the third debate he explained, "We got a big philosophical difference here tonight between one who thinks the government can do all these things through tax and spend and one who thinks it ought to go the other way." These statements clearly functioned as general attacks on Clinton.

Bush also stressed the extent or severity of the problem attributed to one's opponent. In the first debate, the president attacked Clinton's tax policy, suggesting that the effects would not be trivial: "You end up socking it to the workingman." Bush attacked Clinton's record as governor of Arkansas in debate 3, declaring that "on all these categories Arkansas is right near the very bottom." Nothing is worse than being at the bottom, and the clear implication is that Clinton could run the entire country into the ground, based on his allegedly abysmal record in Arkansas.

Bush also emphasized effects on the audience to intensify some of his attacks. For example, in the first debate Bush stressed the effects on the audience. "That old adage that they use—we're going to soak the rich, we're going to soak the rich—it always ends up being the poor cab driver or the workingman that ends up paying the bill." He also argued that Clinton's defense cuts would "throw another 50,000 kids on the street because of cutting recklessly in troop levels." Referring to Clinton in the third debate, Bush warned, "Mr. and Mrs. America, when you hear him say, 'We're going to tax only the rich,' watch your wallet. Because his figures don't add up, and he's going to sock it right to the middle-class taxpayer and lower." He reiterated this argument later in the third debate, advising taxpayers to "lock your wallet; he's coming right after you." These instances of Bush's persuasive attack stress effects on his audience.

Bush also employed charges of inconsistency in his attacks on Clinton. For instance, in debate 2, he explained: "The big argument I have with the governor on this is this taking different positions on different issues, trying to be one thing to one person here that's opposing the NAFTA agreement and then for it—what we call waffling. And I do think that you can't turn the White House into the Waffle House." Similarly, he exclaimed in debate 3 that Clinton takes conflicting positions on issues: "My problem with Governor Clinton, once again, is that one time he's going to make up his mind he will see some merit in it, but then he sees a lot of things wrong with it. And then the other day he says he's for it, however, then we've got to pass other legislation. When you're the president of the United States, you cannot have this pattern of saying, well, I'm for it, but I'm on the other side of it." Thus in the debates Bush repeatedly accused Clinton of taking inconsistent positions.

In the first debate, Bush repeatedly harped on Clinton's demonstrations against the war in Vietnam. Bush emphasized in three places that Clinton planned or organized them: "What I don't accept is demonstrating and organizing demonstrations." These charges were repeated in the second debate: "I am deeply troubled by someone who demonstrates and organizes demonstrations in a foreign land when his country's at war." It would have been bad enough had Clinton simply participated in antiwar protests. However, planning requires forethought and indicates that the act was not accidental or a spur-of-the-moment action but deliberate and intentional. Thus if one shares Bush's assumption that demonstrating against the war was a wrongful deed, there is little question that Clinton should be blamed for this act.

In the 1992 presidential debates, Bush relied on five different strategies of persuasive attack. First, general negative attacks constituted about 40 percent of his attacks. Second, approximately 25 percent of his attacks alleged inconsistencies (Bush employed this strategy more than either of the other two candidates). A third strategy used by Bush is severity. Fourth, he mentioned effects on the audience. Finally, Bush claimed that Clinton had planned acts that were offensive.

Clinton used six of the persuasive attack strategies in the debates. Negative general attacks accounted for 46 percent of his attacks, and he used this strategy more frequently than Bush or Perot. This was followed by three strategies with about the same frequency: severity, effects on the audience, and inconsistency (Clinton used severity more than any other candidate, and he was tied with Perot for frequency of use of effects on audience). Finally, Clinton argued that Bush was responsible for offensive acts and that the problems persisted for years. Each of these forms of persuasive attack will be discussed, with the greatest emphasis on the most frequent ones.

Like Bush, Clinton made general attacks in the presidential debate. For example, in the first debate, Clinton rebuked Bush because he vetoed "a bill that has an investment tax credit, middle-class tax relief, research-and-development tax credits." In the next debate, Clinton lamented the fact that "I did not want my child to grow up to be part of the first generation of Americans to do worse than their parents." Elsewhere in that debate, he charged that the bill established enterprise zones "by asking the wealthiest Americans to pay a little more, which is why he wants to veto it." In the last debate he asserted that "Mr. Bush said for a long time there was no recession and then said it would be better to do nothing than to have a compromise effort with the Congress." Elsewhere in that debate, he charged that Bush was wrong to promise not to raise taxes in the previous election: "The mistake that was made was making the 'read my lips' promise in the first place, just to get elected . . . , knowing what the size of the deficit was, knowing there was no plan to control health care costs, and knowing that we did not have a strategy to get real economic growth back into this economy." Both of these gibes are clearly aimed at President Bush, and they function as a general attack on his policies and actions.

Another strategy Clinton used was to discuss the extent or severity of the problem attributed to one's opponent. Clinton observed in the first debate, "We have gone from first to thirteenth in the world in wages in the last twelve years, since Mr. Bush and Mr. Reagan have been in." In the first debate Clinton reported, "There are 200,000 people unemployed in California alone because we have cut defense without planning to retrain them." Similarly, Clinton complained about China's "$15 billion trade surplus with the United States under Mr. Bush." In the second debate he declared, "A hundred thousand Americans a month have lost their health insurance just in the last four years." In the second debate Clinton argued, "We've had four years where we've produced no private-sector jobs." In the third debate, Clinton charged that, "under this administration, spending has increased more than it has in the last twenty years, and he asked Congress to spend more money than it actually spent. Now, it's hard to outspend Congress, but he tried to for the last three years." These utterances stress the claim that these charges against Bush are not simply minor concerns but extremely serious problems.

Clinton's attacks at times stressed effects on the audience. In the first debate Clinton declared that: "People are working harder for less money than they were making ten years ago, two-thirds of our people. A $1,600 drop in average income in just the last two years." In the second debate he reminded the audience of "six increases in the payroll tax—that means people with incomes of $51,000 a year or less pay a disproportionately high share of the federal tax burden, which is why I want some middle-class tax relief." He also discussed the problems of obtaining health insurance, declaring, "All across America, you know, people that lost their jobs, lost their businesses, had to give up their jobs because of sick children." In the third debate Clinton lamented the fact that "middle-class Americans are working harder for less money than they were making ten years ago." Clinton also suggested in debate 3 that "most people looking at us tonight would like it if we had more jobs and a lower spending burden on the government." These instances of persuasive attack all stress the effects of Bush's policies on the audience, potential voters.

Clinton also attacked Bush with charges of inconsistency. In the first debate, Clinton declared that "Mr. Bush talked about taxes. He didn't tell you that he vetoed a middle-class tax cut because it would be paid for by raising taxes on the wealthy." Near the end of that debate, Clinton pointed out inconsistencies between Bush's words and deeds: "Mr. Bush has said some very compelling things tonight that don't quite square with the record." In debate 3 he declared, "I can't believe he is accusing me of getting on both sides. He said trickle-down economics is voodoo economics. Now he's its biggest practitioner." Not surprisingly, Bush's broken campaign promise from his first presidential campaign figured prominently in the third debate: "I really can't believe Mr. Bush is still trying to make trust an issue after 'Read my lips' and 15 million new jobs and embracing what he called voodoo economics and embracing an export enhancement program for farmers he threatened to veto and going all around the country giving out money in programs that he once opposed." Clearly, Clinton's persuasive attack on Bush included multiple accusations of inconsistency.

Clinton also suggested that the problems that Bush had created were persistent. Clinton in the second debate argued that this was a persistent problem: "It is because we've had twelve years of trickle-down economics." In the last debate he argued, "The truth is that middle-class Americans are basically the only group of Americans who have been taxed more in the 1980s and during the last twelve years even though their incomes have gone down." Of course, this twelve-year period encompassed Bush's tenure as vice president (eight years) and as president (four years). Thus Clinton employed persistence as a strategy for persuasive attack.

Finally, Clinton occasionally argued that the administration was responsible for our economic problems. In the last debate he charged, "We don't have a national economic strategy that will build the industrial base of this country." This utterance pretty clearly impugns Bush's leadership, assigning him blame for our country's difficulties and accusing him of lacking an economic plan.

So Clinton employed six strategies for persuasive attack in these debates. First, he relied most heavily on negative general attacks, which accounted for about 45 percent of his attacks. While all three candidates used this form of attack, Clinton did so more than either Bush or Perot. He used three strategies about 15 percent of the time: severity, effects on audience, and inconsistency (Clinton used severity more than the other candidates, and he and Perot used effects on audience an equal number of times). Two strategies that occurred only a few times were claims that Bush was responsible for offensive acts and that the problems that plagued the economy persisted for years (during the Reagan and Bush administrations).

Perot

Like the other two candidates, Perot used general negative attacks more often than any other strategy. He used severity and effects on the audience fairly frequently (and tied with Clinton for the most frequent use of effects on audience as an attacking strategy). He also made infrequent use of the charges of inconsistency and responsibility. The strategies Perot used most frequently will be discussed in this section.

Perot engaged in general negative attacks in the debates. For example, in debate 1, Perot asserted, "We are sitting on a ticking bomb, folks, because we have totally mismanaged our country." He also criticized Bush's staff (and by implication the president): "We have someone who I'm sure regrets having said it, in the president's staff, said he didn't care whether we made potato chips or computer chips. Well, anybody who thinks about it cares a great deal." In debate 2 Perot accused the present administration of shipping jobs "to China" because of "diplomatic deals." In the third debate he focused on foreign policy: "If you create Noriega, using taxpayer money, step up to the plate and say, 'It was a mistake.' " Elsewhere Perot leveled an attack concerning domestic issues, especially the budget deficit. These general attacks function to implicate the incumbent, President Bush.

A strategy used to intensify Perot's attack was to stress the extent or severity of the problem attributed to one's opponent. In the first debate Perot argued, "We've got the most expensive health care system in the world. It ranks behind fifteen other nations in—when we come to life expectancy and twenty-two other nations when we come to infant mortality. So we don't have the best." In debate 2 he stressed the severity of the national debt: "We're $4 trillion in debt. We're going into debt an additional $1 billion—a little more than a billion dollars every working day of the year." In the second debate he also decried the fact that "we've shipped millions of jobs overseas" and we're "ranked at the bottom of the industrialized world in terms of education achievement," clearly serious problems. In debate 3, Perot predicted that if NAFTA is passed, "you're going to hear a giant sucking sound of jobs being pulled out of this country right at the time when we need the tax base to pay the debt." Also in debate 3, on the savings-and-loan debacle, Perot said, "The whole problem came up in 1984. The president of the United States was told officially it was a $20 billion problem. . . . I believe the vice president [Bush] was in charge of deregulation." Thus at times Perot argued for the severity of the problems he identified in the debates.

Perot also employed the strategy of stressing effects on the audience. In the first debate Perot discussed the effects of inflation: "A lot of folks on Medicare are out there every day, making the choice between food and medicine—not poor enough for Medicare, Medicaid, not wealthy enough to buy their medicine. I've met them." In the second debate, he claimed that "the facts are, the American people are hurting." He pointed out in that debate that "the eighteen- to twenty-four-year-old high school graduates ten years ago were making more than they are now." In discussing the question of foreign lobbyists who serve as campaign consultants, Perot declared in debate 3, "I don't believe that's in the American people's interest." In each of these persuasive attacks, Perot stressed the unpleasant effects on the audience.

Finally, Perot assigned responsibility for our country's woes. For example, in the first debate, he asserted, "We have totally mismanaged our country, and we had better get it back under control." This remark seems to suggest that the current administration can be faulted for not properly managing our nation. In the third debate, discussing the huge federal deficit, he declared, "Both parties carry a huge blame for that on their shoulders. . . . That's not leadership."

These utterances function to direct blame for the problems facing our country.

Perot used general negative attacks about 50 percent of the time, which made it his most frequent strategy. Perot employed severity and effects on the audience about 20 percent of the time (he tied with Clinton for the most frequent use of effects on audience as an attacking strategy). Perot also occasionally used the charges of inconsistency and responsibility.

Comparison of the Candidates

A comparison of the three candidates' persuasive attack strategies revealed four differences. One marked contrast is that, while the number of persuasive attacks generally in debate 2 was less than in debates 1 or 3, Bush initiated by far the least persuasive attack in debate 2. In fact, this figure was half or less of any of the other figures for number of persuasive attacks for any of the three candidates in any of the three debates. As mentioned in the first section of this chapter, the audience demanded that the candidates refrain from personal attack. While this depressed the amount of persuasive attack generally in debate 2, it hit Bush especially hard. Because a sizable proportion of Bush's attacks were personal in nature (in the first debate, for example, Bush repeatedly said that he questioned Clinton's "character"), he was left with much less ground for attack than either Clinton or Perot in the second debate. Thus the audience demand that candidates stick to issues took away much of the basis for Bush's persuasive attack in the second debate. Clinton also reduced the number of attacks he made from the first to the second debate, but the drop was less precipitous for Clinton than for Bush; Perot presented one less persuasive attack in debate 2 than in debate 1 (Bush: 24 to 9; Clinton: 31 to 24; Perot: 19 to 18).

A second difference in the candidates' use of persuasive attack is that Clinton (106) engaged in considerably more persuasive attack than Bush (74) or Perot (77). Clinton is the challenger and Bush the incumbent, so it is reasonable to see Clinton attack Bush's record (of course, Perot was a challenger too but in a less traditional role than Clinton). The disparity might have been greater if Clinton had not been governor of Arkansas, because just as Clinton attacked the state of the national economy, Bush claimed that Arkansas had troubles that were Clinton's fault and thereby attacked Clinton's record as chief executive of Arkansas. We believe that Perot's purpose in the debates was more to call attention to the federal deficit—and other problems salient to Perot—than to serve as a viable candidate, and while he attacked Bush, we see Clinton more as the challenger than Perot.

Third, both Clinton and Perot more frequently increased the offensiveness of their attacks by pointing to severity and effects of problems that occurred during the Reagan/Bush years on the audience than Bush (Clinton: 34; Perot: 33; Bush, 19). Again, we see this as a reflection of the fact that Bush was the incumbent, and it was relatively easy to lay perceived problems at his doorstep.

Our reading of the debates led us to believe that a fourth difference between the three candidates is that Bush was the primary target of persuasive attack in these debates. We conducted an additional content analysis to test this suspicion. We returned to the instances of persuasive attack and identified the target of each attack. In this case, one author did the initial coding for all three debates, the other author checked the coding, and differences were resolved through discussion. We agreed on the apparent target of each attack. The results of this analysis are presented in table 4.

First, neither Bush nor Clinton really attempted to savage Perot. Across the three debates, Bush and Clinton each attacked Perot twice. In other passages, they expressed agreement with Perot. For example, in the second debate, Clinton, speaking of the need for investment tax credits, explained, "Mr. Perot wants to do the same thing. I agree with him. I mean we agree with that." Similarly, during the third debate, Bush carefully explained, "My argument is not with Ross Perot. It is more with Governor Clinton." Elsewhere he refers to "all this extra spending that concerns Mr. Perot and me," which seems to be a clear attempt to associate himself favorably with Perot and, by implication, with Perot's followers. It seems likely that neither major party candidate considered Perot an actual threat to win the election. Thus there was no need to attack Perot. Furthermore, he commanded the loyalty of a sizable minority of voters, who might be persuaded to vote for either Clinton or Bush (as more viable candidates than Perot) in the election. Thus not only were attacks on Perot probably unnecessary, but they could have alienated potential swing votes. There were a few exceptions (e.g., in the third debate Bush suggested that Perot had employed a foreign lobbyist, which was probably a tactical error), but in general neither Bush nor Clinton attacked Perot.

Furthermore, Perot's discourse appeared to attack Bush, but not, in general, Clinton. In the first debate, Perot aimed no attacks at Clinton: all of his attacks were aimed at President Bush or the status quo (especially the economy), over which Bush presides. In debate 2, three of Perot's eighteen attacks were aimed at both Bush and Clinton, while the remainder attacked Bush or the status quo. In the

Table 4. Target of Persuasive Attack by Candidate

Source	Target Bush	Target Clinton	Target Perot
		Debate 1	
Bush	—	23	1
Clinton	31	—	0
Perot	19	0	—
Total	50	23	1
		Debate 2	
Bush	—	9	0
Clinton	23	—	1
Perot	18	3[a]	—
Total	41	12	1
		Debate 3	
Bush	—	40	1
Clinton	50	—	1
Perot	40	11[a]	—
Total	90	51	2

[a]In each instance, Perot attacked both Bush and Clinton together.

last debate, eleven of Perot's forty attacks struck at both Bush and Clinton, while the rest targeted Bush or the status quo. For example, in debate 3, Perot stated, "You look at a *Who's Who* in these campaigns, around the two candidates, they're foreign lobbyists taking leaves." He also declared, "Both parties have foreign lobbyists on leaves and key roles in the campaigns. And if there's anything more unwise than that, I don't know what it is." On his opponents' economic plans, Perot declared in the last debate that "both have plans that will not work. The *Wall Street Journal* said your numbers don't add up."

In contrast, Perot often attacks Bush alone. For example, in the final debate, he said, "Now guess who's on the president's campaign big-time? A guy from Northwest" Airlines. Elsewhere, Perot reprimanded the president: "If you create Saddam Hussein over a ten-year period, using billions of dollars of U.S. taxpayer money, step up to the plate and say, 'It was a mistake.'" Perot attacked Bush on the savings-and-loan deregulation debacle in debate 3: "The vice president was in charge of deregulation." Perot did not tend to single out Clinton for harsh attacks of this sort.

In our opinion, Perot did not seem to favor or oppose either of his opponents as individuals: his purpose in the campaign generally and in the debates in particular seemed to be to direct public attention to problems facing the nation (especially economic ones) that concerned him in the hope that whoever won the election would be forced to deal with those problems. However, because President Bush was an incumbent, the consequence was that Perot's discourse (lamenting our nation's economic woes) had the *effect* of (or appeared to be) attacking Bush. Perot tended to dismiss Clinton, the governor of a small state, as more or less irrelevant. In the third debate, Perot explained, "I could say that I ran a small grocery store on the corner, therefore I extrapolate that into the fact that I could run Wal-Mart; that's not true," suggesting that Clinton's experience as governor of a small state like Arkansas was not a good basis for judging his potential as president. While this comment may not reflect favorably on Clinton, the fact remains that the majority of Perot's attacks functioned to indict Bush, not Clinton.

The cumulative effect of these factors was that there was little attack directed to Perot. One candidate, Bush, attacked Clinton. However, both Clinton and Perot attacked Bush. Thus, Bush was the target for more persuasive attack than Clinton, and Perot received the smallest amount of persuasive attack.

In summary, Bush engaged in the least persuasive attack during debate 2. Clinton, the challenger, engaged in more persuasive attack than Bush, the incumbent, or Perot, the third party candidate. Clinton and Perot tended to intensify their attacks with severity and effects on audience than Bush. Bush was more of a target of persuasive attack than either Clinton or (especially) Perot.

Issues Addressed

The second research question investigates the issues covered in the candidates' persuasive attacks. This analysis has limitations, of course. First, the survey that served as the basis for this analysis asked respondents to indicate the single most important issue they wanted the candidates to address in the debates. If viewers were keenly interested in the candidates' stances on several issues, the responses to this question might not necessarily reflect those additional issues. However, another poll that asked respondents to report the two most important issues produced generally similar results (Taylor, 1992). Second, it is possible that over the course of the de-

Table 5. Issues Addressed in Persuasive Attack

Issue	Bush D1	D2	D3	T	Clinton D1	D2	D3	T	Perot D1	D2	D3	T	Survey (%)
Economy	1	—	5	6	12	5	11	*28*	5	3	6	14	34
Deficit/tax/spend	4	3	8	15	7	6	25	*38*	5	6	7	18	15
Unemployment	1	—	4	5	2	4	6	*12*	—	2	4	6	13
Health care	1	—	—	1	3	3	2	*8*	1	1	—	2	7
Education	—	—	1	1	—	—	—		1	1	—	2	4
Domestic policy	1	—	2	3	2	1	1	4	5	1	3	*9*	3
Abortion	—	—	—		—	—	—		—	—	—		3
Environment	—	—	1	*1*	—	—	—		—	—	—		2
Defense/foreign	4	—	—	4	1	1	2	4	1	1	9	*11*	2
Poverty/welfare/ homeless	—	—	—		—	—	—		—	—	—		2
Elderly	—	—	—		1	—	—	1	—	—	1	1	1
Honesty/integrity	7	4	15	*26*	—	3	7	10	1	—	—	1	1
Family values	—	—	—		—	—	—		—	—	—		—
Rebuilding of inner cities	—	—	—		—	1	—	1	—	3	—	*3*	—
Race relations	1	—	—	*1*	—	—	—		—	—	—		—
AIDS	—	—	—		2	—	—	2	—	—	—		—
Crime	—	—	—		—	—	—		—	—	—		—
Child care	—	—	—		—	—	—		—	—	—		—

Note: Italics indicate the largest numbers in each category.

bates, the issues perceived to be most important shifted. For example, prior to the first debate, only 1 percent of the respondents listed honesty/integrity as the topic they most wanted the candidates to discuss. However, Bush's insistence on addressing this question could have led viewers to see this issue as more important as the debates progressed. Indeed, Bush may well have wanted to increase the perceived importance of this particular issue. Third, the candidates' utterances were influenced by the questions asked. However, closing statements (and the opening question of debate 1, which asked what issue separated the candidates) allowed candidates to decide which issues to address. Furthermore, candidates often left the topic of the question to address another, often previously discussed, topic.

Finally, and most important, this analysis addressed only the issues the candidates talked about, not what they said on those issues or how persuasively they said it. Nevertheless, the question of the extent to which the candidates addressed the issues considered most important is worth answering as a gauge of audience adaptation. The data on the second research question are summarized in table 5.

In this analysis of persuasive attack, Clinton had the largest number (as well as the largest percentage) of remarks of the three candidates in the top four categories (those rated most important for the candidates to address by over 5 percent in the opinion poll). In the seven bottom categories (each rated most important by 2 percent or less of the public) that were addressed by at least one candidate, Bush had the largest number (and the largest percentage) of remarks three times (Perot had the largest number of references to two of the categories of little importance to voters in his attacks, and Clinton the largest in one such category).

Thus it is clear that Clinton devoted more (than the other candidates) of his attacking remarks to the issues that were rated as more important by the public just prior to the debates. Conversely, Bush devoted the largest number of attacking utterances of the three candidates to the issues that the public rated as less important than either Clinton or Perot. It appeared that Clinton devoted more of his persuasive attacks to the issues that were thought to be most important to the public than Bush or Perot. Leon (1993) performed a word count to determine the amount of time each candidate devoted in the debates to various topics. She arrived at a similar conclusion (that Clinton spent more time on the issues that were most important to voters), although she did not separate her analysis into persuasive attack and defense as we did.

Notes

1. A chi-square was computed on the data in table 3. Two categories were omitted from the analysis ("responsible," "persistence") because this statistic assumes that the expected frequency in each cell is at least 2. The chi-square computed was 36.54, and a value of 20.09 is required for significance at the .01 level. Thus statistical analysis confirms that there are significant differences in the candidates' use of persuasive attack strategies.

2. Bush does attempt to shift the blame (to Congress) and argue defeasibility, as will be seen in the next chapter. However, the more he relies on these defenses, the less the audience is likely to believe that he can improve matters if he is reelected.

4

Persuasive Defense
Bush on the Defensive

Governor Clinton . . . said that the country is coming apart at the seams.
Now, I know that the only way he can win is to make everybody believe
the economy is worse than it is. But this country's not coming apart at the
seams, for heaven's sakes. We're the United States of America. We—in
spite of the economic problems, we are the most respected economy
around the world. Many would trade for it. We've been caught up in a
global slowdown.—Bush, Debate 1

What about the honor of my state? We rank first in the country in job
growth. We got the lowest spending state and local in the country and the
second lowest tax burden, and the difference between Arkansas and the
United States is that we're going in the right direction and this country is
going in the wrong direction, and I have to defend the honor of my state.
—Clinton, Debate 3

Well, they got a point. I don't have any experience in running up a $4 tril-
lion debt. I don't have any experience in gridlock government, where nobody takes responsibility for anything and everybody blames everyone
else. I don't have any experience in creating the worst public school system
in the industrialized world. But I do have experience in getting things
done.—Perot, Debate 1

As much time as the presidential candidates spent on attacking one
another (chapter 3), they spent even more time defending themselves.
Not surprisingly, a good deal of their time was spent bolstering their
own image and proposing solutions to perceived problems (corrective

action). As we found in our analysis of persuasive attack, image and policy are both important in persuasive defense.

The results of our analysis of the 1992 presidential debates for instances of persuasive defense are presented and discussed in this chapter. These results respond to the third research question—"What strategies of persuasive defense did the three candidates use in the three 1992 presidential debates?"—and are summarized in table 6. This discussion of these results will commence with consideration of persuasive defense, or of image repair strategies, generally. Then each candidate's use of the specific strategies of persuasive defense in the debates will be discussed separately, and then contrasted. Finally, the candidates' discussion of issues will be addressed. Table 7 displays the results of our analysis of the issues addressed in these defensive utterances and answers the fourth research question: "Which issues did the three candidates address in their instances of persuasive defense in three 1992 presidential debates?" As with the previous chapter, the material in chapter 1 on the discursive context of the debates serves as a useful backdrop for this discussion.

Persuasive Defense in the Debates

Examination of table 6 indicates that the candidates differed substantially in their use of the strategies of persuasive defense.[1] We identify three general patterns in the data on persuasive defense, or image repair discourse. First, the candidates spent a substantial amount of their time engaged in self-defense. Comparison of tables 3 (from the previous chapter) and 6 reveals that in almost every case the candidates enacted substantially more strategies of persuasive defense than of persuasive attack. In the three debates, Bush engaged in over twice as much defense as attack, Clinton employed about 75 percent more defense than attack, and Perot performed about 55 percent more persuasive defense than attack (the only exception is debate 3, in which Perot employed virtually the same number of defensive as attacking strategies). Thus the candidates engaged in a great deal of self-defensive discourse in these debates.

Second, in general, more persuasive defense occurred in the first and last debates than in the middle one: the three candidates totaled 185 instances of persuasive defense in debate 1, 156 in debate 2, and 191 in debate 3 (Clinton had more instances of persuasive defense in the third but used the same number in the first and second debates). As discussed in chapter 3, the amount of persuasive attack was smallest in the second debate (particularly for Bush, who tended toward personal attack), and thus the candidates had correspondingly

Table 6. Persuasive Defense in the 1992 Presidential Debates

Strategy	Bush				Clinton				Perot			
	D1	D2	D3	T	D1	D2	D3	T	D1	D2	D3	T
Bolstering	53	29	26	*108*	21	13	30	64	14	16	25	55
Corrective action	17	23	18	58	33	41	27	*101*	27	17	8	52
Simple denial	6	4	17	*27*	1	2	9	12	—	1	6	7
Shift blame	5	5	4	*14*	1	—	—	1	—	—	—	—
Differentiate	2	1	2	*5*	—	—	4	4	1	—	2	3
Defeasibility	2	4	4	*10*	—	—	1	1	—	—	—	—
Mortification	—	—	5	*5*	—	—	1	1	—	—	—	—
Good intentions	—	—	4	*4*	—	—	1	1	—	—	1	1
Minimization	—	—	—	—	—	—	—	—	1	—	—	*1*
Total	85	66	80	231	56	56	73	185	43	34	42	119

Note: The largest numbers in each category are in italics.

less to defend in that debate. Similarly, chapter 3 revealed that the greatest amount of persuasive attack occurred in the last debate, and that is where the most persuasive defense can be found. The fact that the least persuasive defense occurred in debate 2, and the most in debate 3, and the fact that this corresponds roughly to the incidence of persuasive attack in the debates, seems logical, for persuasive attack and defense are related phenomena.

A third general finding is that the two largest categories of persuasive defense are bolstering and corrective action. This result should not be surprising, because candidates want both to make themselves look good (bolstering) and to promise to improve things once elected (corrective action). The use of corrective action seems especially appropriate for challengers (and two of the candidates were challengers), and for an incumbent, if many voters perceived problems, as seemed to be the case in 1992. As noted earlier, although we classify these remarks as persuasive defense, they are not necessarily "defensive" in tone. They can be quite proud and boastful and may initiate new topics where they claim to be worthy of praise (they do not always respond directly to a prior attack).

Thus the three candidates engaged in considerable persuasive defense; in fact, in general they enacted more persuasive defense than attack. Second, the smallest amount of persuasive defense occurred in the second debate, and the largest amount in the third debate, indicating that persuasive attack and defense are interrelated. Finally, the candidates relied most heavily on bolstering and corrective action as defensive strategies.

Bush

Bush employed eight defense strategies. He relied most heavily on bolstering (over 100 instances) and proposed quite a bit of corrective action (almost 60 utterances). Simple denial (27), shifting the blame (14), and defeasibility (10) were also used on his behalf. Finally, differentiation (5), mortification (5), and good intentions (4) occurred rarely in his defense. This discussion will illustrate the defenses that occurred most commonly in Bush's discourse.

Bolstering is an important part of Bush's rhetorical defense. In the first debate, Bush stressed his experience and, in particular, his foreign policy experience: "Well, I think one thing that distinguishes me is experience—I think we've dramatically changed the world. I'll talk about that a little bit later, but the changes are mind-boggling for world peace. Kids go to bed at night without the same fear of nuclear war." This theme emerged in the second debate as well: "Since I became president, forty-three, forty-four countries have gone democratic—no longer totalitarian, no longer living under dictatorship or Communist rule." In the first debate, Bush reported that "I was nineteen or twenty, flying off an aircraft carrier, and that shaped me to be commander in chief of the armed forces." In the third debate, Bush touted his success in Desert Storm to the audience: "And when he crossed the line, I stood up and looked into the camera, and I said, 'This aggression will not stand.' And we formed a historic coalition, and we brought him down. And we destroyed the . . . fourth largest army." Bush emphasized his foreign policy triumphs throughout the debates.

Bush boasted of his past economic accomplishments as well. In debate 1, Bush argued, "We're the envy of the world in terms of our economy." In the third debate he explained that in "the Reagan-Bush years . . . we created 15 million jobs." He also indicated in the third debate that "productivity in this country is up. It is way up. Productivity is up, and that's a good thing." These statements all function to bolster Bush's image.

The president also stressed other domestic achievements. In debate 1, Bush asserted, "The use of cocaine, for example, by teenagers is dramatically down." In the second debate, he reported, "We're making some progress, doing a little better on interdiction." In the first debate, Bush explained, "I've tried to use the White House as the bully pulpit, speaking out against discrimination. We've passed two very forward-looking civil rights bills." In debate 2, Bush declared, "I've submitted, what, four different budgets to the United States Congress? In great detail. They're so heavy they'd give you, you know, a broken back." Thus bolstering was a recurrent strategy used to defend Bush's image.

At times Bush discussed plans to improve our country (corrective action). In the first debate, Bush repeatedly referred to his "agenda for American renewal," although often without elaborating it. He also mentioned his education program, America 2000, but again often without providing details. In the second debate, Bush provided some insight into his education reforms: "It's called America 2000. And it literally says to the communities: reinvent the schools, not just the bricks and mortar but the curriculum and everything else. Think anew." In debate 1, Bush declared that he wanted to change the capital gains laws and to encourage investment, including first-time home ownership. In the second debate Bush asked for a balanced budget amendment, an income tax check-off system (the taxpayer could earmark 10 percent of the tax paid for reducing the deficit), and term limits for Congress. In the third debate he reiterated his support for a balanced budget amendment and term limits for Congress. Bush also suggested in the last debate that we adopt term limits for members of Congress, that they should be sequestered until they control spending, and that there be "a line item veto." Taking a more general approach to domestic and economic reform, Bush reported in the first debate: "What I'm going to do is say to Jim Baker when this campaign is over: 'All right, let's sit down now. You do in domestic affairs what you've done in foreign affairs. Be the kind of economic coordinator of all the domestic side of the house, and that includes all the economic side, all the training side, and bring this program together.' " Thus many of Bush's utterances throughout the three debates propose solutions to problems facing our country.

Bush also had plans in the realm of foreign policy. In the second debate, Bush declared, "I want to continue work after we get this NAFTA agreement ratified this coming year; I want to get one with Eastern Europe. I want to get one with Chile, and free and fair trade is the answer." Thus Bush had plans for improving our foreign trade.

Bush sometimes employed simple denial to respond to charges against him and his policies. In the first debate, he declared in two places, "We are not coming apart at the seams." In response to concerns raised by Perot about the war on drugs, he exclaimed, "Please don't say to the D.E.A. agents on the street that we don't have the will to fight drugs. Please—I have watched these people." In the second debate he rejected charges that NAFTA would cause jobs to move out of the United States. In the last debate Bush was asked about the absence of women in high positions. He replied, "You don't see Margaret Tutwiler sitting out there with me today?" Similarly, he declared in debate 3, "I don't think in racial, ah, racial harmony that I'm a laggard on that." Bush was also sensitive to the charge that he used foreign lobbyists in the third debate: "What you're assuming is that that makes the recipient of the lobbying corrupt, or the lobbyist himself corrupt. I don't agree with that." These are all instances of simple denial.

In several places Bush tried to shift the blame. For example, several times in the first debate, Bush argued, "We can get it done now, whereas we didn't in the past, because you're going to have a whole brand new bunch of people in the Congress." Clearly, the Congress is being blamed for the lack of needed legislation. Similarly, in the second debate he characterized Congress as "a reckless spending Congress." Discussing the need for enterprise zones, he explained in the second debate, that it's "very difficult to get it through the Congress." In the third debate he referred to the tax increase as Democratic: "Let me remind you it was a Democratic tax increase, and I didn't want to do it, and I went along with it." Clearly, he wanted Congress to share in the blame for this tax. He also referred repeatedly in the third debate to pork barrel amendments to legislation: "The House and the Senate can't send it down without loading it up with a lot of, you know, these Christmas tree ornaments they put on the legislation." Shifting the blame helps to exonerate Bush, completely or at least in part, for some of the problems laid at his door.

A similar strategy used by Bush is defeasibility, suggesting that factors beyond one's control are responsible for problems. In the first debate the president twice explained that America has been "caught up in a global slowdown." In the second debate he referred once to "this global economic slowdown" and once to our "rough economic times." He also argued that part of the budget cannot be cut: "two-thirds of the budget I, as president, never get to look at, never get to touch." Bush explained in debate 3 that "the whole world has had economic problems" and adds, "We're living in an interconnected world. The whole world is having economic difficulties." Surely the president of the United States cannot be held responsible for economic woes of international origin. Similarly, if there are items in the budget he cannot "touch," he cannot be held accountable for the corresponding portion of the deficit.

So Bush used eight different defensive strategies in the debates. Most often, he utilized bolstering (over 100 times) and corrective action (about 60 times). Bush also relied on simple denial (27 instances), shifting the blame (14 times), and defeasibility (10 examples). Three defensive strategies occurred fairly infrequently: differentiation (5 times), mortification (5 examples), and good intentions (4 instances).

Clinton

Clinton's defense employed eight defensive strategies. He relied most heavily on corrective action (101) in his defense. Bolstering also occurred quite frequently (64). Simple denial was used occasionally (12), and Clinton rarely used differentiation (4), shift blame (1), defeasibility (1), mortification (1), and good intentions (1). The major components of Clinton's defensive discourse will be described in this section.

Bolstering was an important component of Clinton's defensive utterances. In debate 1 Clinton described his upbringing: "I grew up in the segregated South, thankfully raised by a grandfather with almost no formal education but with a heart of gold, who taught me early that all people were equal in the eyes of God. I saw the winds of hatred divide people and keep the people of my state poorer than they should have been, spiritually and economically." This statement seems designed to enhance Clinton's image.

In the first debate, Clinton recounted his accomplishments: "I've worked hard to create good jobs and to educate people. My state now ranks first in the country in job growth this year, fourth in income growth, fourth in the reduction of poverty, third in overall economic performance." In the second debate, he reported, "I was really honored when *Time* magazine said that our schools had shown more improvement than any other state in the country except one." In debate 3 he noted: "We rank first in the country in job growth. We got the lowest spending state . . . in the country, and the second lowest tax burden, and the difference between Arkansas and the United States is that we're going in the right direction and this country is going in the wrong direction." He also bragged more than once that he had balanced a governmental budget twelve times. The clear implication is that what Clinton has done for Arkansas he can do for the United States.

Clinton also relied on endorsements of others to bolster his image. In the first debate, Clinton reported, "Nine Nobel Prize–winning economists and 500 others, including numerous Republican and Democratic business executives, have endorsed this approach because it offers the best hope to put America back to work and to get our incomes rising instead of falling." Similar statements occurred in the other two debates. In the third debate, Clinton mentioned an award he received and stressed his past, laudable actions: "The National Women's Political Caucus gave me an award, one of their good guy awards for my involvement of women in high levels of government. And I've appointed more minorities to positions of high level in government than all the governors in the history of my state combined." Thus Clinton made numerous statements that functioned to bolster his image in the third debate.

Corrective action is another strategy frequently used by Clinton. In the first debate, Clinton discussed his plans for tax reform. "My plan triggers in at gross incomes—family incomes—of $200,000 and above. Then we want to give modest middle-class tax relief to restore some fairness." He also mentioned his commitment to investment and research-and-development tax credits and capital gains reform. In the third debate, Clinton reported that he wanted to increase "taxes on families with incomes above $200,000" and ask "foreign corporations . . . to pay the same . . . taxes . . . that American corporations [do]." In the same debate, he promised to "provide over $100 billion in tax relief in terms of incentives for new plants, new small businesses, new technologies, new housing, and for middle-class families." He also indicated in debate 3 that "we have $140 billion of spending cuts." Thus Clinton repeatedly stressed his plans to improve our economy.

Clinton also had suggestions for improvements in other domestic affairs. In debate 1 Clinton discussed his commitment to health care coverage for all Americans. In the first and second debates, Clinton explained that he wanted to invest in transportation, communications, and environmental cleanup. In debate 1 Clinton revealed that he would provide money to teach everyone with a job to read, to help people get high school diplomas, and to fund Head Start completely. In the second debate, Clinton said that he supports the Brady bill, restrictions on assault weapons, and more police. Also in the second debate, Clinton reported that he wants controls on insurance companies, pharmaceutical companies, doctors, and retirement programs. Thus Clinton indicated a variety of policies and reforms he would pursue to improve the state of affairs in America.

Clinton also offered corrective action in foreign trade. In the second debate, he declared, "Number 1, make sure that other countries are as open to our markets as our markets are to them. And if they're not, have measures on the books that don't take forever and a day to implement." Thus Clinton also had plans for improving foreign affairs.

Another defensive strategy employed by Clinton is simple denial. In the second debate Clinton quoted third parties to reject charges from Bush. "Mr. Bush said once again tonight I was going to have a $150 billion tax increase. When Mr. Quayle said that, all the networks said, 'That's not true. He's got over $100 billion of tax cuts and incentives.' " Clinton responded in debate 3 to accusations that he wanted to legislate impossible environmental standards: "I never said, and I defy you to find where I said—I gave an extensive environmental speech in April, and I said that we ought to have a goal of raising the fuel efficiency standards to forty miles a gallon. I think that should be a goal. I've never said we should write it into law if there is evidence that that goal cannot be achieved." Clearly Clinton is engaging in simple denial here. If the charges leveled at him are untrue, he should appear to be a more viable candidate.

Another defensive strategy is to differentiate what one has done (or said) from something more objectionable. Clinton distanced himself from Washington politics in the third debate by stating, "I'd also like to point out that I haven't been part of what we're criticizing in Washington tonight."

Thus in the 1992 presidential debates Clinton used eight defensive strategies. He reversed the rank ordering of Bush's most frequently used strategies. Clinton offered corrective action (101 examples) most frequently, followed by bolstering (64 times). Simple denial appeared occasionally (12 instances). Clinton infrequently utilized differentiation (4 times), and four other strategies were used but once each: shift blame, defeasibility, mortification, and good intentions.

Perot

Perot used six strategies of persuasive defense. He relied most heavily on bolstering (55) and corrective action (52). He used simple denial occasionally (7) and rarely used differentiation (3), good intentions (1), and minimization (1). We will illustrate the strategies that constitute the bulk of Perot's defense.

One defensive strategy used by Perot is bolstering. In the first debate, Perot tried to bolster his credibility by stressing his independence: "I was not put on the ballot by any PAC money, by any foreign lobbyist money, by any special interest money. This is a movement that came from the people. This is the way the framers of the Constitution intended our government to be, a government that comes from the people." Comparable statements can be found in both of the other debates. Similarly, in the second debate, Perot declared that "I don't have any spin doctors. I don't have any speechwriters. Probably shows. . . . But you don't have to wonder if it's me talking." These statements portray Perot as honest and genuine.

Perot also took advantage of his success in the business world. In the first debate, Perot argued, "I've got a lot of experience in figuring out how to solve problems, making the solutions work, and then moving on to the next." In the second debate, Perot observed, "I spent my life creating jobs—it's something I know how to do." In debate 3, Perot stressed, "I do understand businesses. I do understand creating jobs. I do understand how to make things work. And I got a long history of doing that." No one could deny that Perot was an extremely successful entrepreneur, and he used this fact to bolster his reputation during the debates.

In the first debate, he promised, "The day after election, I get with the congressional—we won't even wait until inauguration. . . . And we will start putting together teams to put together, to take all the plans that exist and do something with them." In the second debate, speaking of jobs in the inner city, he asserted, "I could go to Washington in a week and get everybody holding hands and get this bill signed." Thus he promised to take immediate action if elected.

At the end of the third debate, Perot offered a more comprehensive view of the choice facing voters in the election, asking: "Pretty simply—who's the best qualified person up here on the stage to create jobs? Make your decision and vote on November 3. I suggest you might consider somebody who's created jobs. Second, who's the best person to manage money? I suggest you pick the person who's successfully managed money. Who's the best person to get results and not talk? . . . And finally, who would you give your pension fund and your savings account to—to manage?" These utterances all seem designed to foster a favorable image of Perot.

Perot also offered plans for correcting problems in America. In the first debate, Perot stressed his commitment to "a growing, expanding job base to give us a growing, expanding tax base." In debate 1 Perot also proposed task forces on small businesses, big companies that are in trouble, and new industries of the future, as well as on crime and the deficit. In the second debate, Perot reminded viewers that "I've already taken the pledge on cutting the deficit in half." In debate 3 he argued that "our principal need now is to stabilize the tax base, which is the job base, and create a growing dynamic base." He also mentioned in the third debate a plan that "balances the budget within six years."

Perot discussed other issues besides economic reforms. He suggested that the FDA needed to reform its drug approval process. Perot went on record in the second debate as supporting smaller schools and "early childhood education for disadvantaged low-income children." He promised to "do everything I can, if I get up there, to make dirty tricks a thing of the past." Perot also offered a new attitude in the third debate: "We will figure out what to do and you won't tolerate gridlock, you won't tolerate endless meandering and wandering around, and you won't tolerate nonperformance." Thus Perot indicated that he would take action to improve conditions in the country.

At times Perot denied charges that had been made against him. In response to Bush's charge in the third debate that Perot employed a foreign lobbyist, he asserted that "as soon as I found it out, he went out the door. Truth, yes!" This is a clear instance of denial.

So Perot's persuasive defense relied on six strategies. Like Bush, Perot's most frequent strategy was bolstering (55 instances), followed by a fair amount of corrective action (52 examples). Perot employed simple denial occasionally (7 times). He infrequently relied on differentiation (3 times), and two strategies—good intentions and minimization—appeared once each.

Comparison of the Candidates

Our comparison of the use of image repair strategies by the three candidates reveals four differences in their persuasive defenses. Each of these differences will be discussed separately in this section.

First, as table 6 reveals, in each of the three debates, President Bush employed substantially more defensive utterances than either Governor Clinton or Mr. Perot. In fact, Bush, as only one of three participants, accounted for 46 percent of all defensive utterances in the first debate, 43 percent in debate 2, and 42 percent in the third debate. The most marked differences were between Bush and Perot. This pattern probably occurred for two reasons.

As seen in chapter 3, both Bush and Clinton shied away from attacking Perot. Furthermore, Perot's discourse appeared to attack Bush but not Clinton. This means that both Clinton (on purpose) and Perot (in effect) attacked Bush, while only Bush attacked Clinton, and there were few attacks on Perot. This distribution of the attacks can be used to account for the pattern of defensive utterances, in which Bush was on the defensive more than Clinton, while Perot engaged in the smallest amount of persuasive defense. It is important to note that two prominent defensive strategies, bolstering and corrective action, need not necessarily respond to a specific attack, so the fact that Perot engaged in 119 instances of persuasive defense (107 of which were bolstering or corrective action) is not inconsistent with the claim that relatively few attacks were aimed at him.

A second general difference between the three candidates' use of persuasive defense is that Bush engaged in more bolstering than Clinton or Perot (Bush: 108; Clinton: 64; Perot: 55). As the incumbent,

Bush wanted to create the impression that he was doing fine (bolstering), not that he was failing (proposing plans for corrective action suggests that there are problems).

Third, Clinton used more corrective action (101) than either Bush (58) or Perot (52). As the challenger, Clinton (again, Perot did not fit the traditional role of a challenger as well) wanted to portray the status quo as in need of many reforms, and he claimed to have the answers. Not surprisingly, Bush didn't offer nearly as many solutions as Clinton: for Bush to propose a solution would mean acknowledging a problem that he had been unable to solve as the incumbent. Perot tended to focus on fewer topics than either of the other candidates, which meant that he had fewer plans for corrective action than Clinton. This inference is also consistent with the view that his role in the campaign was more to draw voters', and the other candidates', attention to problems that concerned him.

A fourth difference between the candidates was that Bush made very frequent use of simple denial, to deny the existence of problems. Furthermore, he attempted to mitigate his responsibility by shifting the blame to Congress and arguing defeasibility (a global slowdown). However, the more he suggested that things were beyond his control in his first term, the less likely voters would believe that he would be able to correct things in a second term. Chapter 3 discussed the fact that candidates have a reason to assume the power of the president as agent.

Thus Bush engaged in more persuasive defense than either Clinton or Perot—which is readily understandable, given that he tended to receive more persuasive attack than either of his opponents. Second, the incumbent (Bush) relied most heavily on bolstering, touting his accomplishments during the first term in office. Third, the principal challenger (Clinton) used corrective action most extensively. Fourth, Bush uses simple denial, shifting the blame, and defeasibility more than the other candidates.

Issues Addressed

The fourth research question investigates the issues covered in the candidates' persuasive defenses. As with the second research question addressed in chapter 3, this analysis has certain limitations. First, the survey used as the basis for this analysis asked respondents to identify the most important issue they hoped the candidates would discuss in the debates. If viewers were concerned about several issues, the results of this survey might not reflect those other issues. Second, during the debates, the issues regarded as most important might have changed. Third, the questions asked influenced the topics addressed, but candidates could decide which issues to discuss in their closing statements (and in response to the broad question that started debate 1). Also, candidates frequently addressed topics unrelated to the question in part of their utterance. Last, and most important, this analysis only describes the topics that were addressed by the three candidates, not what they said about those topics or how effectively they said it. Despite these limitations, the extent to which the candidates addressed the issues considered most significant is an important consideration and an indication of the extent to which candidates were responsive to audience expectations. These data are displayed in table 7.

Of the top four issues (rated by over 5 percent as the most important issue), Bush made the largest number of remarks on two and Clinton on two. Perot engaged in less persuasive defense than the other two candidates, but a respectable proportion of his remarks were devoted to three of the four top-rated issues (he had little to say in his defenses concerning health care). Of the eight issues at the bottom (2 percent or less rating it as the most important issue) addressed by at least one candidate, four were addressed most often by Bush (and one of these accounted for over one-quarter of his remarks), two were addressed most frequently by Clinton, and one by Perot (Bush and Clinton were tied on one topic). Thus, in contrast to the results for the second research question, Clinton and Bush (and Perot) tended to address the topics considered most important to the public in their persuasive defense.

Of course, portions of one's defense are presumably influenced to a large extent by the attack. In other words, if Clinton and Perot attacked Bush on the issues considered most important to the public, Bush's defense is likely to center on those same issues (but not necessarily because he chose to focus on them). Bush's defense can be faulted in that he devoted over one-quarter of his defensive remarks to an issue rated most important by only 2 percent of the public (national defense/foreign policy) and almost 10 percent to an issue rated most important by only 1 percent of the public (honesty/integrity). In fact, Bush devoted more defensive utterances than his opponents to three issues rated as less important by viewers.

As mentioned in the previous chapter, Leon (1993) conducted a content analysis of words used by the candidates in the 1992 debates and reported that Clinton used more words related to topics considered important by the audience than did Bush. However, she did not divide analysis into persuasive attack and defense, as we did, and thus our conclusion (both Clinton and Bush devoted many defensive re-

Table 7. Issues Addressed In Persuasive Defense

Issue	Bush D1	D2	D3	T	Clinton D1	D2	D3	T	Perot D1	D2	D3	T	Survey (%)
Economy	11	7	17	*35*	6	6	15	27	6	—	2	8	34
Deficit/tax/spend	11	14	21	*46*	7	7	18	32	5	5	2	12	15
Unemployment	4	3	2	9	6	4	9	*19*	6	5	3	14	13
Health care	2	4	—	6	7	12	3	*22*	1	—	—	1	7
Education	2	10	—	12	1	13	2	*16*	—	3	—	3	4
Domestic policy	11	6	1	*18*	6	4	—	10	4	1	—	5	3
Abortion	—	—	—		—	—	—		—	—	—		3
Environment	—	—	—		—	—	7	*7*	—	—	—		2
Defense/foreign	31	15	11	*57*	9	5	6	20	8	2	3	13	2
Poverty/welfare/ homeless	—	—	—		—	—	—		—	—	—		2
Elderly	1	—	1	2	—	2	1	*3*	1	—	—	1	1
Honesty/integrity	8	4	8	*20*	5	3	1	9	4	4	—	8	1
Family values	2	1	—	3	3	—	—	3	4	1	—	*5*	—
Rebuilding of inner cities	—	—	—		—	—	—		—	—	—		—
Race relations	1	—	3	*4*	2	—	1	3	—	—	—		—
AIDS	4	—	—	4	4	—	—	4	1	—	—	1	—
Crime	1	5	—	*6*	3	4	—	7	1	—	1	2	—
Child care	—	—	—		—	—	—		—	—	—		—

Note: Italics indicate the highest numbers in each category.

marks to topics of importance; Bush devoted many such comments to topics not considered important) is more specific than hers.

Summary

The three candidates engaged in considerably more persuasive defense than attack. More persuasive attack occurred in debates 1 and 3, which, not surprisingly, also had the most persuasive attack. The most common defensive strategies were bolstering and corrective action. However, Bush, the incumbent, tended to use bolstering, while

Clinton, one of the challengers, used corrective action the most. Bush also used denial and shifting the blame more than the other two candidates, largely to respond to charges of problems with the status quo. Bush, who was the target of most persuasive attack, as indicated in the previous chapter, produced the most persuasive defense. Perot, least frequently the target, produced the least persuasive defense. Bush and Clinton both addressed issues important to voters in their defense—but Bush also frequently addressed topics less important to voters.

Note

1. A chi-square statistic was computed on the data in table 6. Three categories were omitted from the analysis (mortification, good intentions, and minimization) because this statistic assumes that the expected frequency in each cell is at least 2. The chi-square computed was 58.37, and a value of 23.21 is required for significance at the .01 level. Thus statistical analysis confirms that there are significant differences in the candidates' use of persuasive attack strategies.

5

Evaluation
How Do the Candidates Stack Up?

You can't do that as president. You can't do it on war, where he says, well, I was with the minor—minority, but I guess I would have voted with the majority. This is my point tonight. We're talking about two weeks from now you've got to decide who's going to be president. And there is this pattern that has plagued him in the primaries and now about trying to have it both ways on all these issues. You can't do that.—Bush, Debate 3

That's what's wrong with Mr. Bush. His whole deal is you've got to be for it or against it. You can't make it better. I believe we can be better. I think the American people are sick and tired of either-or solutions, people being pushed in the corner, polarized to extremes. I think they want somebody with common sense who can do what's best for the American people. And I'd be happy to discuss these other issues. But I can't believe he is accusing me of getting on both sides. He said trickle-down economics is voodoo economics. Now he's its biggest practitioner.—Clinton, Debate 3

Certainly anyone in the White House should have the character to be there. But I think it's very important to measure when and where things occurred. Did they occur when you were a young person in your formative years? Or did they occur while you were a senior official in the federal government? When you're a senior official in the federal government spending billions of dollars of taxpayers' money and you're a mature individual and you make a mistake, then that was on our ticket. If you make it as a young man, time passes.—Perot, Debate 1

We have seen that the candidates did not use persuasive attack and defense in the same ways. For example, Perot's concern with our budget deficit (and other matters) meant that his discourse had the effect of attacking Bush the incumbent more than Clinton the challenger. Neither Bush nor Clinton directed much persuasive attack to Perot. Furthermore, because Bush was the most frequent target of persuasive attack, he tended to produce more persuasive defense than either of his two opponents. Nor did the candidates use the same mix of either attack or defense strategies. The obvious question is: if the candidates differed in their use of persuasive attack and defense, which candidate was most effective?

This chapter will take up several topics as it evaluates the persuasive attack and defense by the three candidates, so as to answer the last research question ("How well did the three candidates engage in persuasive attack and defense in the three 1992 presidential debates?"). It will also discuss implications of the analysis. First we evaluate the effectiveness of the candidates' persuasive attacks. Then we sketch the context of political commentary surrounding the debates and providing interpretations of them. Next, we assess the effectiveness of their persuasive defenses. These considerations lead to a brief general assessment of their performance based in part on the election results and public opinion poll data. We primarily contrast Clinton and Bush. We are convinced that Perot's presence significantly influenced the debates (primarily by focusing attention on certain issues and because his discourse had the effect of attacking Bush much more than Clinton), but we do not consider his role as one of a viable candidate. As Hahn observed, Perot "was less a candidate than a critic" (1994, p. 207). After this contrast, we will evaluate Perot's use of persuasive attack. Finally, we consider implications of this analysis.

Evaluation of Persuasive Attack

We evaluate Clinton's performance in the area of persuasive attack as noticeably superior to Bush's showing for several reasons. Clinton attacked more than Bush. Clinton focused more on issues, while Bush tended to attack Clinton personally. Furthermore, Clinton focused more on issues important to voters than did Bush. Clinton's attacks tended to be more specific than Bush's. Finally, the forms of attack most frequently used by Clinton were more damaging than the forms of attacks used most often by Bush.

First, Clinton attacked Bush more. Chapter 3 demonstrated this point quite clearly: Clinton made 106 total persuasive attacks, while Bush made 74. Furthermore, Clinton made the largest number of attacks in each debate. Candidates do not always differ in their attacks.

Rowland (1986) found that Reagan and Carter both made multiple attacks (Reagan attacked Carter fifteen times; Carter attacked Reagan seventeen times; but compare Tiemens, Hellweg, Kipper, and Phillips, 1985). However, differences in amount of attack were found in three other presidential debates. Riley and Hollihan (1981), for example, reported that Reagan and Anderson differed in their use of critical statements, which we take to be similar to persuasive attack. Bitzer and Rueter (1980) report that Carter more frequently than Ford moved from answering a question to attacking his opponent, and Carter's rejoinders were also more likely than Ford's to attack his opponent. Hellweg and Verhoye found that "Dukakis attacked his opponent in 77 percent of the message opportunities, while Bush did so only 40% of the time" (1989, p. 19). Thus presidential debaters frequently do not engage in relatively equal amounts of persuasive attack.

We see this discrepancy in the amount of persuasive attack as important for several reasons. Persuasive attack affords the candidate an opportunity to place his or her opponent in an unfavorable light. Some instances of persuasive defense (e.g., bolstering, corrective action) can be viewed as more proactive utterances that directly improve one's image, but others merely respond to attacks initiated by others. To make an analogy, while it is often said in sports that good defense wins games, the team with the most points (best offense) is the one that wins. We do not want to push this comparison too far (e.g., in football the defense can score points), but in general, one must score points, on the offense, to be effective in presidential debates.

Furthermore, the rhetor who attacks chooses the grounds of clash, while the rhetor who defends responds on grounds chosen by one's opponent (again, bolstering and corrective action can be exceptions). As Bitzer and Rueter write: "In all likelihood, the speaker who initiates—who takes the lead in defining the debate terms and issues, capturing the most favorable argumentative ground and throwing his opponent on the defensive—will gain some advantage" (1980, pp. 79–80). They also indicate something about the nature of this advantage, explaining that the candidate who takes the initiative "can control the focus of debate by placing *his* issues on the agenda; he can attack with greater frequency and put his adversary on the defensive" (p. 86). Thus the candidate who engages in more persuasive attack may gain a tactical advantage in presidential debates.

In the 1992 debates, some might dispute the claim that Clinton should be evaluated favorably simply because he attacked more frequently than Bush. He was the challenger, and Bush the incumbent, so the situation could be said to favor Clinton (especially in light of fairly widespread dissatisfaction with the economy among voters that we mentioned earlier). Martel (1983) explains that "under most circumstances, it is advisable for a challenger to attack an incumbent" (p. 63). Hellweg, Pfau, and Brydon (1992) concluded that, while incumbency is not necessarily a handicap, "if the incumbent administration has serious problems, as Ford did in 1976 and Carter did in 1980, the debates provide an opportunity for challengers" (p. 127). Similarly, Bitzer and Rueter observed that, "as the incumbent with a record to defend, he [Ford] was a large target for panelists' questions and Carter's attacks" (1980, p. 144). Furthermore, the fact that Perot's treatment of the problems important to him functioned to attack Bush, not Clinton, also favored Clinton. However, Clinton had a record in Arkansas, and although Bush did attack Clinton on his record as governor, he could have done so more often and more forcefully. Thus Clinton made the most of the situation facing the candidates, while Bush did not.

Second, while both candidates engaged in personal invective, we believe Clinton chose to direct his persuasive attack more on the issues (e.g., the economy, health care), while Bush tended to attack more on personality (e.g., inconsistency, Clinton's protests against the war in Vietnam).[1] For example, in the first debate, Bush declared, "I questioned his judgment and his character." This contrast was revealed most markedly in the second debate, when audience demands that the candidates eschew personality attacks and stick to the issues reduced Bush to a mere nine instances of persuasive attack. Clinton decreased the number of attacks he made from thirty-one to twenty-four, but Bush's persuasive attack fell much more sharply from twenty-four to nine. Given the stated preference of audience in debate 2—which probably reflected the sentiment of many voters—Clinton had a clear advantage. Respondents to focus group studies on the 1992 debates "seemed to welcome the fact that the questions asked early [in the second debate] forced the candidates to spend more time on issues rather than on character attacks" (Depoe and Short-Thompson, 1994, p. 91). An important second consequence was that Clinton could remain on the offensive in the second debate, where Bush floundered.

Third, our findings for research question 2 in the second chapter indicate that Clinton's persuasive attacks tended to focus more on the issues important to voters than did Bush's attacks. Viewers thought the economy was important, and Clinton stressed it. Analysis of a focus group study of the 1992 debate revealed: "As far as the issues participants desired, a male voter from Portsmouth, NH, spoke for many [focus group members] when he replied, 'I think that first and foremost is the economy!' Issues surrounding the deficit and other related topics were by far the most commonly referenced. . . . The next most frequently mentioned issue was that of health care" (Lamoureaux, Entrekin, and McKinney, 1994, p. 65). Table 5 reveals that Clinton's persuasive attack led all three candidates in the categories of economy, deficit/tax/spend, unemployment, and health care. Thus Clinton's persuasive attack, aimed primarily at Bush, focused most on the issues that were most important to viewers.

Clinton's persuasive attacks also tended to be more specific than Bush's. For example, in the third debate Bush declared, "Arkansas is doing very, very badly against any standard—environment, support for police officers, whatever it is." Elsewhere in that debate, he attacked Clinton's record as governor of Arkansas, declaring that "on all these categories Arkansas is right near the very bottom." Contrast these rather vague attacks with ones advanced by Clinton. Clinton asserted in the first debate, "We have gone from first to thirteenth in the world in wages in the last twelve years, since Mr. Bush and Mr. Reagan have been in." In the first debate Clinton reported, "There are 200,000 people unemployed in California alone because we have cut defense without planning to retrain them." In the second debate he observed, "A hundred thousand Americans a month have lost their health insurance just in the last four years." Of course, Bush did employ some specifics, and Clinton was general in some places. However, our reading of the debates gives a clear advantage to Clinton in this regard, and more specific attacks can be much more damaging than vague ones.

All candidates relied heavily on negative general attacks. However, Bush led in frequency of use in the categories of inconsistency and planned the offensive act (demonstrations on Vietnam). Clinton, on the other hand, used severity and effects on audience more than Bush. We believe that the strategies on which Clinton tended to rely most were more damaging than the ones Bush chose to emphasize—and Clinton often had good responses to Bush's attacks. We develop this claim with several examples of persuasive attack in the debates.

One form of persuasive attack upon which Bush relied heavily was charges of inconsistency in his attacks on Clinton. For instance, in debate 3 Bush charged that Clinton takes conflicting positions on issues: "My problem with Governor Clinton, once again, is that one time he's going to make up his mind he will see some merit in it, but then he sees a lot of things wrong with it." Frankly, we don't believe that the world is best (most realistically) viewed as digital, black or white, good or bad. Nor do we suspect that most voters saw things this way, especially when Clinton made this kind of response: "That's what's wrong with Mr. Bush. His whole deal is you've got to be for it or against it. You can't make it better. I believe we can be better. I think the American people are sick and tired of either-or solutions, people being pushed in the corner, polarized to extremes." Thus one form of persuasive attack to which Bush frequently returned does not seem particularly persuasive.

Another strategy of persuasive attack that Bush used extensively was charges that Clinton committed an offensive act (demonstrating against the war in Vietnam), and in fact Clinton planned this action. In the first debate, Bush emphasized in three places that Clinton planned or organized them: "What I don't accept is demonstrating and organizing demonstrations." These charges were repeated in the second debate: "I am deeply troubled by someone who demonstrates and organizes demonstrations in a foreign land when his country's at war." Many voters may have opposed the war, and to others Clinton may simply have been exercising his constitutional right of freedom of speech. Furthermore, Ross Perot's comment in the first debate may well have defused this issue to a large extent. Perot asserted that the "American people . . . need to clearly understand the backgrounds of each person." He then continued to explain his views on the question:

> Certainly anyone in the White House should have the character to be there. But I think it's very important to measure when and where things occurred. Did they occur when you were a young person in your formative years? Or did they occur while you were a senior official in the federal government? When you're a senior official in the federal government spending billions of dollars of taxpayers' money, and you're a mature individual and you make a mistake, then that was on our ticket. If you make it as a young man, time passes.

It is difficult to interpret this passage other than as a rejection of Bush's attack on Clinton coupled with an attack on Bush's responsibility for our country's economic woes. Again, one of the forms of persuasive attack employed frequently by Bush does not seem to be particularly telling (and this excerpt also illustrates how Perot often seemed to attack Bush).

Furthermore, Clinton specifically counterattacked Bush's charges of inconsistency. In the third debate, Clinton charged that Bush was wrong to promise not to raise taxes in the previous election: "The mistake that was made was making the 'read my lips' promise in the first place, just to get elected . . . , knowing what the size of the deficit was, knowing there was no plan to control health care costs, and knowing that we did not have a strategy to get real economic growth back into this economy." In the first debate, Clinton declared, "Mr. Bush talked about taxes. He didn't tell you that he vetoed a middle-class tax cut because it would be paid for by raising taxes on the wealthy." In debate 3 he declared, "I can't believe he is accusing me of getting on both sides. He said trickle-down economics is voodoo economics. Now he's its biggest practitioner." Not surprisingly, Bush's broken campaign promise from his first presidential campaign figured prominently in the third debate: "I really can't believe Mr. Bush is still trying to make trust an issue after 'Read my lips' and 15 million new jobs and embracing what he called voodoo economics and embracing an export enhancement program for farmers he threatened to veto and going all around the country giving out money in programs that he once opposed." Clearly, Clinton's persuasive attack on Bush included accusations of inconsistency. Which seems worse, to have mixed feelings about legislation rather than to be completely for it or against it or to emphatically promise not to raise taxes and then to raise them? Thus in our opinion, Clinton counterattacked with one of Bush's characteristic forms of persuasive attack, and he used it considerably more effectively than did Bush.

In contrast to Bush, Clinton's frequently used forms of persuasive attack are relatively more damaging. For example, Clinton's persuasive attacks often stressed effects on the audience. In the first debate Clinton declared, "People are working harder for less money than they were making ten years ago, two-thirds of our people. A $1,600 drop in average income in just the last two years." In the second debate he reminded the audience of "six increases in the payroll tax— that means people with incomes of $51,000 a year or less pay a disproportionately high share of the federal tax burden." In the third debate Clinton lamented the fact that "most people are working harder for less money than they were making ten years ago." We feel that these sorts of attacks, common in Clinton's discourse, are simply more persuasive than many of Bush's frequent accusations.

Thus we identify four reasons why Clinton's use of persuasive attack was more effective in the 1992 presidential debates than Bush's. Clinton used persuasive attack more than Bush, allowing Clinton to choose much of the grounds for the debate and putting Bush on the defensive. Clinton tended to focus his attacks more on the issues, while Bush's tendency was to attack Clinton personally, which was unwise (although our analysis is much more detailed, it is generally consistent here with the reactions of political commentators). Clinton's attacks tended to be more specific than Bush's attacks. Finally, the forms of attack that Clinton employed most often were more damaging than the forms of attacks used most frequently by Bush. Although we developed this argument in chapter 3, we would like to mention here that Clinton's persuasive attack was also better developed than Bush's, because Clinton tended to address the issues that were important to the voters, while Bush spent more time on issues of less importance (again, the commentators noted this as well). Clinton also had generally effective responses to many of Bush's attacks.

Perot engaged in a considerable amount of persuasive attack in the debates: 77 instances, compared with 106 by Clinton and 74 by Bush. He relied primarily on general negative attacks, as well as severity and effects on the audience. These are wise choices. In his defensive remarks, he primarily used bolstering and corrective action, again reasonable choices. He focused on the topics of deficit/taxation/ spending and unemployment in both his attacking and defending utterances, which were appropriate choices (given voter concerns and his background as a successful businessman).

Many of his comments were delivered in his folksy style (e.g., asserting in the third debate that, if NAFTA is passed, we will hear a "giant sucking sound of jobs being pulled out of this country"). He stressed that he was open to other ideas by declaring that he was "all ears" and indicated his rather prominent ones. This style may have made a generally favorable impression on many in the audience—which explains his favorable shifts in the public opinion polls—but it is not a *presidential* impression, which may account for his performance at the election polls.

Evaluation of Persuasive Defense

As with persuasive attack, we found Clinton's use of persuasive defense to be better developed than that of Bush. We offer several reasons for this claim. Bush was on the defensive more than Clinton. Bush's use of bolstering emphasized foreign affairs too much. Clinton's reliance on corrective action was beneficial. Bush's reliance on certain defense forms (and on Baker) suggested that he was not in control. Bush's discourse created the impression that he was not cognizant of problems facing our country.

First, Bush's discourse indicates that he was on the defensive more than Clinton. Bush made 231 defensive remarks, while Clinton engaged in persuasive defense 185 times in the debates. This contrast is readily understandable, given our analysis of the target of the persuasive attacks in chapter 3, which indicated that more persuasive attacks were aimed at Bush than at Clinton (and virtually none at Perot).

Other debates have also found differences in defensive utterances, or refutation. Rowland (1986) found that in 1980 Reagan produced more refutation than Carter (see also Tiemens, Hellweg, Kipper, and Phillips, 1985)—although Rowland argued that the quality of Reagan's refutation meant he did a better job than Carter. Similarly, Morello (1990) reported that in 1988 Bush engaged in more refutation than Dukakis. On the other hand, Riley and Hollihan (1981) found no difference in defensive remarks in the Reagan-Anderson debate they analyzed, but of course, that was a different debate. Still, these findings indicate that candidates do not always spend the same amount of time on defensive, or refutative, remarks.

The fact that Bush tended to be on the defensive more, responding to attacks by Clinton and Perot, indicates that Bush was less in control of the debates and his utterances (the correlative of our claim that the candidate who attacks the most tends to control the grounds of the debate). Of course, some of the utterances coded as defensive (i.e., corrective action, bolstering) can be on topics of the candidate's choosing. Still, in general, the fact that Bush made so many more defensive utterances means that he was less in control of the grounds of the debate than Clinton.

A second reason why Clinton's persuasive defense was more effective than Bush's concerns the topics the two men tended to address when bolstering. Most of Bush's (apparent) successes came in foreign policy. Accordingly, much of his bolstering concerned foreign affairs. Clinton had been a governor, so that his successes tended to be domestic and concerned the economy. Given that many voters were more concerned about domestic affairs, one could argue that the situation favored Clinton. As mentioned earlier, however, Clinton took full advantage of the situation. Bush should have spent more time bolstering domestic successes (Bush and his staff would possibly have had to look long and hard to find more domestic successes to tout, but they should have invested that time). Limbaugh observed that Bush could have argued, "Inflation has been whipped, inventories are lean, interest rates have been wrestled to 20-year lows. Housing starts, retail and car sales have been posting gains" (1992, p. A27). Bush tended to bolster with accomplishments that may have appeared more dramatic to him but were less important to voters. Perhaps Bush decided to try to persuade the voters to see foreign affairs as more important than the economy and other domestic issues. If so, he failed.

Third, Clinton relied much more heavily on corrective action than Bush (101 to 58). As the incumbent, Bush may have been reluctant to propose corrective action because recognizing the need for it would implicitly concede that he had failed in his first term. However, many people felt there was a need for a change: Cook reported, "Polling throughout the year found that nearly 80% of the nation believed the country was on the wrong track" (1992, p. 3548). Accordingly, Bush should probably have offered more solutions regardless of this risk. Corrective action helped Clinton in two ways. First, one proposes solutions to *problems*, so each time Clinton proposed a solution, it implied a failure on Bush's part. Second, proposing corrective action suggests that Clinton had answers to our problems and would improve conditions if elected. At least he recognized problems and was willing to try to fix them.

Fourth, Bush in several places portrayed himself as unable to control events or as not responsible. First, shifting the blame to Congress and citing defeasibility (slowdown in the global economy) may have deflected blame from Bush, but it also created doubt that he could solve the problems. In several places Bush tried to shift the blame. For example, Bush argued repeatedly in the first debate that "we can get it done now, whereas we didn't in the past, because you're going to have a whole brand new bunch of people in the Congress." Clearly, the Congress is being blamed for the lack of needed legislation. He assumes there will be a new, cooperative Congress after the election, but would his listeners agree? Similarly, on the question of enterprise zones, he declared in debate 2 that it's "very difficult to get it through the Congress." Here Bush was portraying himself as relatively powerless. While Congress may in fact have prevented Bush from solving some of America's problems, the impression created of powerlessness is not presidential in nature.

Similarly, Bush used defeasibility, suggesting that factors beyond one's control are responsible for problems. In the first debate the president twice explained that America has been "caught up in a global slowdown." In the second debate he referred once to "this global economic slowdown" and once to our "rough economic times." He also argued that part of the budget cannot be cut: "two-thirds of the budget I, as President, never get to look at, never get to touch." Bush explained in debate three that "the whole world has had economic problems" and adds, "We're living in an interconnected world. The whole world is having economic difficulties." While these factors may excuse him from responsibility for past (and current) difficulties, he does not create the impression that he will be able to correct matters in a second term.

One might argue that Clinton would fare no better against these forces, so Bush is not at a comparative disadvantage here. However, it looked like whoever won the election would have a democratic majority in Congress, so in point of fact Clinton could probably work somewhat better with Congress than Bush. More subtly, Bush was probably also at a disadvantage here because he, not Clinton, used these strategies, and the appearance of lack of control/ability was probably more closely associated with Bush than with Clinton.

Furthermore, in the first debate Bush trotted out Jim Baker, who had been an important part of Bush's foreign policy team: "What I'm going to do is say to Jim Baker when this campaign is over: 'All right, let's sit down now. You do in domestic affairs what you've done in foreign affairs. Be the kind of economic coordinator of all the domestic side of the house, and that includes all the economic side, all the training side, and bring this program together.' " This statement implied that Baker (not Bush) was largely responsible for America's foreign policy success (one of Bush's major "selling points") and that Baker would be in charge of America's domestic policy—where many Americans had concerns—in Bush's second term. The voters may have wanted to vote for Baker instead of Bush. Clinton picked up on this in debate 3 (although it wouldn't have hurt for him to have done so earlier) and declared: "Because you know, in that first debate, Mr. Bush made some news. He had just said Jim Baker was going to be secretary of state, but in the first debate he said, 'No, now he's going to be responsible for domestic economic policy.' Well, I'll tell you. I'll make some news in the third debate. The person responsible for domestic economic policy in my administration will be Bill Clinton. I'm going to make those decisions." Thus Bush's discourse suggested that he was not in control and could not be expected to accomplish much in his second term. At least one of the commentators (Apple, 1992) recognized that Bush's use of Baker was problematic (although he did not draw the additional inference that perhaps Bush was not really responsible for his foreign policy successes). Clinton, on the other hand, declared that he would be in control of his administration (Bush did respond to this jibe by declaring that Clinton's acceptance of responsibility was what worried Bush, but this was not a strong response). There is more than a hint of inconsistency in this attack, as well (first Bush says Baker will be secretary of state, then he turns around and says Baker will be an economic coordinator).

Fifth, Bush's use of denial—and other parts of the debates as well—suggested that he was not in touch with the country's problems. In the first debate, for example, he declared in two places that "we are not coming apart at the seams." Many Americans perceived serious problems, as noted before, but Bush does not. Another indication that he may have appeared out of touch with America's problems occurred in the second debate, when an audience member posed a question about how the nation's economic problems affected the candidates' personal lives. Here is the question:

Q: Yes. How has the national debt personally affected each of your lives? And if it hasn't, how can you honestly find a cure for the economic problems of the common people if you have no experience in what's ailing them?

Perot takes first crack at this question, but contrast Bush's and Clinton's answers.

BUSH: Well, I think the national debt affects everybody. Obviously it has a lot to do with interest rates. It has—

Q: She's saying you personally.

Q: On a personal basis, how has it affected you—has it affected you personally?

BUSH: Well, I'm sure it has. I love my grandchildren and I want to think that—

Q: How?

BUSH: I want to think that they're going to be able to afford an education. I think that that's an important part of being a parent. I—if the question—if you're—maybe I get it wrong. Are you suggesting that if somebody has means that the national debt doesn't affect them?

Q: Well, what I'm saying—

BUSH: I'm not sure I get it. Help me with the question, and I'll try to answer it.

Q: Well, I've had friends that have been laid off from jobs. I know people who cannot afford to pay the mortgage on their homes, their car payment. I have personal problems with the national debt. But how has it affected you? And if you have no experience in it, how can you help us if you don't know what we're feeling?

Q: I think she means more the recession, the economic problems today the country faces, rather than the deficit.

BUSH: Well, listen, you ought to—you ought to be in the White House for a day and hear what I hear and see what I see and read the mail I read and touch the people that I touch from time to time. I was in the Lomax A.M.E. Church. It's a black church just outside of Washington, D.C. And I read in the—in the bulletin about teenage pregnancies, about the difficulty that families are having to meet ends—to make ends meet. I talk to parents. I mean, you've got to care. Everybody cares if people aren't doing well. But I don't think—I don't think it's fair to say, You haven't had cancer, therefore you don't know what it's like. I don't think it's fair to say, you know, whatever it is, that if you haven't been hit by it personally—but everybody's affected by the debt because of the tremendous interest that goes into paying on that debt, everything's more expensive. Everything comes out of your pocket and my pocket.

So it's, it's sad, but I think in terms of the recession, of course you feel it when you're president of the United States. And that's why I'm trying to do something about it by stimulating the exports, investing more, better education system. Thank you. I'm glad to clarify it.

Contrast Bush's answer above with this first part of Clinton's response to the same question:

> CLINTON: Well, I've been governor of a small state for twelve years. I'll tell you how it's affected me. Every year, Congress and the president sign laws that makes us—make us do more things and gives us less money to do it with. I see people in my state, middle-class people, their taxes have gone up in Washington and their services have gone down while the wealthy have gotten tax cuts. I have seen what's happened in this last four years when in my state, when people lose their jobs, there's a good chance I'll know them by their names. When a factory closes I know the people who ran it. When the businesses go bankrupt, I know them. And I've been out here for thirteen months meeting in meetings just like this ever since October with people like you all over America, people that have lost their jobs, lost their livelihood, lost their health insurance.

Bush seems to have difficulty even grasping the notion that he might be affected by the United States's economic problems. A participant in a focus group study, commenting on the second debate, suggested that "President Bush did not understand the woman's question 'because he's never been there' " (Depoe and Short-Thompson, 1994, p. 95). When Bush does figure out the question, his answer simply seems much less compelling than Clinton's response. He even suggests that the question is unfair and draws an analogy to cancer (fair question or not, this stance may well have alienated many voters). It may not be the case that if he can't understand our economic problems on a personal level, he can't solve them. However, the audience member asking the question clearly thought so.

Thus we conclude that Clinton's development of his persuasive defense was superior to Bush's. Bush's bolstering accentuated foreign affairs too much, which was less important than domestic (economic) concerns to voters. Clinton was wise to rely so heavily on corrective action. Bush's reliance on shifting the blame and defeasibility (and on Baker) suggested that he was not in control of events. Bush's use of denial (and other aspects of his rhetoric) created the impression that he was out of touch with our country's domestic problems. Furthermore, as discussed in chapter 4, both Clinton and Bush tended to focus on issues important to voters in their persuasive defense (although Bush devoted more of his utterances to issues of less importance). However, we are reluctant to credit either candidate for this, because the defense is in large part a response to attacks made by one's opponents.

Perot engaged in the least amount of persuasive defense in the 1992 contest by a wide margin: 119 defensive utterances, contrasted with 185 by Clinton and 231 by Bush. As discussed in chapter 3, Clinton and Bush tended to handle Perot with kid gloves for the most part, attacking him directly only twice each during all three debates. Furthermore, although all three candidates relied heavily on bolstering and corrective action, these two forms of persuasive defense—which need not respond to a specific attack from an opponent—accounted for 90 percent of Perot's defensive utterances. This configuration of defensive utterances (i.e., relative absence of strategies like shifting blame, minimization, and transcendence) is also due in large part to the fact that Bush and Clinton rarely aimed specific attacks at Perot. Thus he could afford to devote most of his defensive efforts to bolstering and corrective action.

General Assessment

We conclude that Clinton's use of both persuasive attack and defense in the 1992 presidential debates was substantially more effective than Bush's. Perot was also fairly effective in his use of persuasive attack and defense. How did their use of attack and defense strategies influence perceptions of the candidates?

While it is obvious to all that Clinton won the election, we would like to begin to address this question by reviewing some of the statistics to show the size, as well as the direction, of his victory. Clinton carried 43 percent of the popular vote and Bush won 38 percent, while Perot received 19 percent of it. This outcome translated into thirty-two states and 370 electoral votes for Clinton, eighteen states and 168 electoral votes for Bush, and no states or electoral votes for Perot (see table 8). Clinton's margin of victory over Bush in the popular vote was over 5.5 million votes (43 percent to 28 percent), his margin in states was 14 percent (or 64 percent to 36 percent), and his margin of electoral votes was 202 percent (69 percent to 31 percent). Cook (1992) reported that analysis of the voting data revealed that Clinton led with independents and moderates; with blacks and Hispanics; with both women and men; with those under thirty and those sixty and over (double-digit lead); and with those thirty to fifty-nine (single-digit lead), those without a high school diploma, and those who had postgraduate education. Bush and Clinton were virtually tied with whites and those who were married (Clinton led with those who were single). Cook placed Clinton's victory in historical perspective as he explained, "It was the most sweeping triumph for any Democrat since President Lyndon B. Johnson in 1964 and the best showing for any Democratic challenger since Franklin D. Roosevelt ousted Republican Herbert Hoover from the White House in 1932"

Table 8. Results of the 1992 Presidential Election

Item	Bush	Clinton	Perot
Popular Vote %	27.7	43.2	19.0
States Carried	18	32	0
Electoral Votes	168	370	0

Source: Cook, R. (1992, November 7). "Clinton Picks the GOP Lock on the Electoral College: He Was Favored by the Youngest and Oldest, the Best- and the Least-Educated, the Suburbs and Cities." *Congressional Quarterly* 50:3549.

(1992, p. 3548). Thus not only did Clinton win, but he won decisively in the 1992 election.

Perot won no states or electoral votes. However, he did win almost one-fifth of the popular vote, and he also won a fair measure of respect (especially given the suspicion that arose after he dropped out of the race for a time). Zhu, Milavasky, and Biswas's (1994) study found that the debates positively influenced Perot's image. Frankovic reported: "Before the first debate, and on his re-entry into the race, Perot was viewed favorably by only 7 percent of the voters. By the time the debates ended, that percentage had more than quadrupled" (1993, p. 119). Furthermore, if it was an objective for Perot to focus the voters' and the candidates' attention on issues he considered important (i.e., the federal deficit), it appears that he was fairly successful on that basis as well. Thus his performance was, on some measures, a victory.

There is little question that Clinton was at the right place at the right time. Cook reported that "polling throughout the year found that nearly 80% of the nation believed the country was on the wrong track. Exit polls found the majority of voters favoring a change in government" (1992, p. 3548). However, even if conditions were favorable for the challenger, Clinton took full advantage of them, attacking Bush on the state of the economy (with Perot) and defending the changes he supported. Bush, on the other hand, tried to bolster with foreign policy success and unsuccessfully attempted to minimize economic problems, shift the blame to Congress (and the international economy), tout a rather vague agenda for "renewal," and hope that the voters would assume that Baker would revitalize the economy.

The next consideration we would like to address is who the viewers thought won the debates. Gallup polls show that, in answer to the question of who did the best job, Perot was ranked first in debate 1 and Bush last (Gallup, 1994a). In the second debate, Clinton was

Table 9. "Regardless of which candidate you happen to support, who do you think did the best job in the debate—George Bush, Bill Clinton, or Ross Perot?" (percent)

Candidate	Debate 1	Debate 2	Debate 3
Bush	16	16	28
Clinton	30	58	28
Perot	47	15	37
None	5	7	7
No Opinion	2	4	—

Source: Gallup Opinion Polls (1994a, October 12; October 16–18; October 19). Roper Center, University of Connecticut, *Public Opinion Online.*

ranked first, and Bush and Perot virtually tied (Gallup, 1994b). In the last debate, Perot again was ranked first, with Bush and Clinton tied (Gallup, 1994c). Thus Perot clearly came out ahead (first in two debates), but Clinton was never ranked below Bush and twice was put above him, including being ranked first in the second debate. These data are displayed in table 9.

Data are also available on the change in favorable and unfavorable opinions toward the three candidates after the first and third debates. The results are most decisive after debate 1. Perot enjoyed the largest net gain (more favorable minus less favorable) at 57 percent. Clinton followed with a more modest net gain of 15 percent. Bush suffered a net loss (less favorable minus more favorable) of 11 percent. After debate 3, Perot again experienced the most change, with a 58 percent net gain. Clinton and Bush were rated virtually identically, with net gains of 5 percent and 4 percent, respectively. However, given Clinton's lead prior to the debates, these figures show that Perot obtained some measure of respectability, while Bush failed to catch Clinton in the polls. These data are displayed in table 10.

Given the fact that Clinton won the election definitively, these data (on who won the debates) could mean several things. First, the voters may have been judging performance, not preference for the candidates. The opinion poll question did ask: "Regardless of which candidate you happen to support, who do you think did the best job in the debate—George Bush, Bill Clinton, or Ross Perot?" Second, the debates may not have been an important factor in deciding the outcome of the election. Third, and in our view most likely, Perot made a favorable impression in the debates but was not a viable candidate

Table 10. "How has your opinion of George Bush/Bill Clinton/Ross Perot been affected by the debate?" (percent)

Candidate	More Favorable	Less Favorable	Not Changed Much	No Opinion
		After Debate 1		
Bush	13	24	62	1
Clinton	29	14	57	—
Perot	62	5	33	—
		After Debate 3		
Bush	29	25	46	0
Clinton	27	22	50	1
Perot	63	5	32	0

Source: Data from Gallup Polls October 12, 1994, and October 19, 1994. Gallup Opinion Polls (1994a, October 12, October 19). Roper Center, University of Connecticut, *Public Opinion Online.*

(e.g., his folksy image may have improved his image for many, but it is not a presidential image); Clinton did as well as or better than Bush in the debates and managed to preserve his lead going into the debates and through to the election. Or in other words, Perot's image was enhanced more by the debates than Clinton's, but Perot's image started out so much lower that Clinton still won the election.

There is no way to determine with certainty the extent to which the first possible explanation accounts for the discrepancy between who won the debates and who won the election. Perhaps experimental research on voting and the election will appear, which will provide a direct answer to the question of how much the 1992 debates influenced the outcome of this election. While of course the debates were only part of a long and complex campaign, we do want to argue against the possibility that the debates were unimportant to the outcome of the election.

First, the 1992 presidential debates were widely watched. As we noted in chapter 1, the first debate had 81 million viewers, debate 2 was watched by 90 million, and the final debate had 99 million viewers. For comparison purposes, the first debate of 1988 had markedly fewer viewers, 74 million ("The Aftermath," 1992, p. 3336). Voters who may have missed some or all of the debates had the opportunity to read about it in the newspaper and to see media coverage of the debates as well (and most of the commentary seemed to suggest that Clinton was holding his own in the debates, while Bush was not making significant headway). Thus vast numbers of voters were exposed to the debates, and the debates unquestionably had the opportunity to influence them. The fact that the 1992 debates came near the end of the campaign was particularly significant for potential influence on undecided and conflicted voters.

A second reason for not discounting the debates as one important force affecting the election results is the previous research, reviewed in chapter 1, on effects of debates. While this work is not univocal, it seems to demonstrate that presidential debates can influence voting patterns. For example, on the basis of their review of the literature, Becker and Kraus concluded that campaign messages "can affect voting decisions rather directly—at least when 'one of the candidates is not well known, many voters are undecided, the contest appears to be a close one, and party allegiances are weak' " (1978, p. 267). The presence of Ross Perot alone indicates that several of these factors were present in 1992, indicating a potential for important effects from the debates. Because so many people watched one or more of these debates (and heard and read reports and commentary on the debates), the potential for influence from the 1992 presidential debates was vast.

The debates provided an event (if not a spectacle) in which literally millions of voters could directly contrast the utterances of the three candidates on the issues. While we would not characterize the debates as the most important influence on the election outcome (if for no other reason than because Clinton had a sizable lead going into the debates), it seems reasonable to conclude that they were an important factor in Clinton's victory. Clinton's superior performance in his persuasive attack and defense in the presidential debates was arguably an important contribution to his victory. The situation may have favored Clinton, and Perot's discourse may have had the effect of attacking Bush much more than Clinton, but Clinton clearly took better advantage of the situation in the debates than Bush.

Evidence of the influence of the debates can be found in ABC's exit poll data (1992). Of those who reported that the debates had been an important influence on their voting decision, 45 percent supported Clinton, 30 percent Perot, and only 25 percent Bush. Thus for those who said the debates were an important factor in determining their vote, Clinton benefited from the debates almost twice as much as Bush. While this particular poll does not answer one important question (how many voters believed their decision was influenced by the debates), and while we cannot be certain that voters are aware of what information shaped their voting decision, it does provide an indication of the relative gains from the debate for the three candidates and one that is consistent with our analysis. Finally, Pfau and Eveland's analysis indicates that "the debates were responsible for less likelihood of voting for Bush" (1994, p. 165). There is both conceptual and empirical evidence for the claim that the debates hurt Bush and probably helped Clinton.

Commentary

In chapter 1 we discussed the situation before the debates to provide a context for chapters 3 and 4. Here we turn our attention to description of the discursive context of the debates into utterances that concern the state of affairs after each of the debates. It will be interesting to see whether the political commentary supports or contradicts our analysis.

After the First Debate

Commentators could hardly miss the fact that Bush pressed his attacks against Clinton in the first debate. Safire observed that judgment and character were "the President's main shot at his challenger, and he kept at it. . . . But it wasn't a knockout blow; it was neatly blocked and countered" (Safire, 1992, p. A19). Balz agreed that "Clinton effectively countered Bush's attack on his antiwar activities as a college student" (1992b, p. A1). On the other hand, Balz reported that Bush was frequently "put on the defensive by Clinton and Perot, particularly on the economy" (1992b, p. A14). Thus Bush's attacks were not seen by political observers as yielding a net gain for him. Although he was expected to be the attacker, he often found himself reacting defensively to Clinton and Perot.

Pundits also recognized that Bush tended to discuss foreign affairs rather than the economy. For example, in his closing statement, Bush "dwelt on his foreign, not domestic, record" (Apple, 1992, p. A12). When Bush did mention the economy, he promised to use Baker to solve America's domestic problems. Apple explained that Bush's use of Baker "was an effort to suggest that he [Bush] understood the urgency of American economic problems, something many voters doubt, but it also suggested that Mr. Baker, not Mr. Bush, was the man who gets things done" (Apple, 1992, p. A1). Thus commentators indicated that Bush had not focused his remarks in the first debate on the issues most important to the voters—and when he did address them, he may inadvertently have undermined the impression that he (personally) was a problem solver.

Perot, still not likely to win the presidency, was seen as having improved his image in the eyes of the electorate. Balz explained that "Perot, who salted his answers with simple phrases and results-oriented language, may have done himself the most good and likely helped erase some of the negative impressions formed by his abrupt withdrawal in July" (1992b, p. A14). Thus commentators seemed to believe that Bush had failed to make significant inroads on Clinton's lead with the voters, Clinton had held his own, and Perot had enhanced his image in the first debate.

The pollsters were active after the first debate. Evidence from a *Times*/CNN public opinion poll indicates that most people (79 percent) were not moved by Bush's attacks on Clinton's antiwar protests in the sixties. Furthermore, "An overwhelming majority of those who said the attacks made them more likely to vote against Mr. Clinton were already Bush supporters" (Toner, 1992a, p. A1). Thus Bush's attacks seemed to sway few people, and those swayed were likely to already support him, meaning no shift in his favor. This led Estrich to conclude, "As long as Bill Clinton doesn't admit it, he's already won the election" (1992, p. A27). Similarly, Safire opined, "Clinton won because he did not lose. . . . It's not over yet, but if the President cannot flatten the challenger in the next two matches, it's over" (1992, p. A19). Thus Clinton was able to retain his lead in the polls in the debates.

Polls confirmed commentators' perception that Perot had helped to restore his reputation with his performance in the first debate. Toner reported that "57 percent of the voters who watched the debate said Mr. Perot's performance made them think better of him" (1992a, p. A22). His positive ratings increased from 7 percent (when he reentered the race) to 18 percent, while his negative ratings dropped from 59 percent to 35 percent (1992a).

After the Second Debate

Toner indicated that, "despite the occasional personal jab, the debate was dominated by domestic concerns. The only question on foreign policy came more than an hour into the debate, and it was a general inquiry about how the country should participate in the 'new world order' " (1992b, p. A10). According to Dowd, "The President, cut off on character and foreign policy issues for the most part and boxed into a situation where he was forced to confront his weakest issue, the economy, seemed uncomfortable and sometimes grew testy" (1992, p. A1). Broder and Marcus commented, "front running Democratic presidential nominee Bill Clinton sailed unscathed through the second of three television debates tonight" (1992, p. A1).

Thus the second debate focused on domestic issues (and the economy in particular), which were Clinton's strong suit, not on foreign affairs, Bush's strength.

Furthermore, commentators reported that Bush's strategy of personal attack was derailed by the audience. Dowd reported that "when George Bush tried to press the attack that his advisers see as his best hope to beat Bill Clinton, the audience cut him off" (1992, p. A1). Similarly, Toner wrote, "Several questioners expressed disgust at what they said was the mud-slinging tone of the campaign and asked the candidates to discuss national issues rather than dwelling on character questions" (1992b, p. A10). Thus the voters who participated in the second debate made it clear that they wanted the candidates to focus on the economy, not on personal attack, and this attitude favored Clinton.

Public opinion polls confirmed that Clinton maintained a lead of around fifteen percentage points after the second debate. Toner reported that a *Newsweek* poll "showed Mr. Clinton retaining the lead with the support of 46%, Mr. Bush with 31%, and the independent candidate Ross Perot at 14 percent" (1992c, pp. A1–A24). On the day of the third debate, Berke explained, "The President's efforts to turn the campaign dialogue to matters of character and trust have shown no signs of moving him out of second place in polls, and tonight's debate may be his last opportunity" (1992, p. A1). Bush had thus far failed to close the gap between his numbers and Clinton's.

After the Third Debate

The *Washington Post* observed that Bush "spent little time defending his own domestic record or program. The President devoted himself instead to attacking Gov. Clinton; most of the attack was pretty well repelled" ("After the Debates," 1992, p. A18). Ronald Brown declared that Bush "was definitely more aggressive, but not necessarily more effective. The American people are fed up with these personal attacks" (Broder, 1992, p. A1). Balz and Devroy reported, "President Bush tonight mounted a sharp assault on Gov. Bill Clinton's record in Arkansas and his changing positions on issues but found himself on the defensive over the economy and Iran" (1992, p. A1). The *Washington Post* also observed that "the shots he [Perot] fired did some damage to both sides, but more to Mr. Bush" ("After the Debates," 1992, p. A18). Bush attempted to damage Clinton's candidacy in the debates, but he was unsuccessful.

Thus political commentators generally held that Clinton had successfully negotiated the debates, maintaining the lead that he enjoyed coming into the debates. He focused on domestic issues, particularly the economy, which were most important to voters. Bush, on the other hand, erred in trying to focus on personal attacks against Clinton and on foreign affairs. Perot improved his image but was not likely to win the election. This is generally consistent with our reading of the persuasive attack and defense in these debates.

Implications of the Analysis

Certain of the observations we make in this section may seem obvious or common knowledge to some readers. However, we believe they deserve mention for the record nonetheless. Furthermore, we think that some of the implications we draw from this analysis are new insights. We offer general observations first, followed by implications specific to persuasive attack, and then suggestions for persuasive defense.

General

First, our analysis of the discourse of the debates revealed that, as we suspected, most of their utterances functioned as persuasive attack and defense. The assumption underlying this analysis, then, was strongly confirmed. All three presidential candidates engaged in copious persuasive attack and defense during the course of the debates. Beyond the simple numbers, in our opinion the persuasive attack and defense often addressed key issues and concerns in the campaign. Thus persuasive attack and defense are important parts of the 1992 presidential debates.

A second general implication is that the format of the debates influenced the production of persuasive attack and defense. Specifically, when the format permitted audience participation, audience members demanded that the candidates eschew personal invective and focus on the issues. While our analysis clearly reveals that persuasive attack does not consist solely of personal invective (Clinton and Perot attacked Bush on the issues, including the economy, and Bush attacked Clinton on policy issues at times), character assassination is certainly one component of persuasive attack. This was an especially important part of persuasive attack for Bush in the debates. The audience's demand was clearly responsible for the drop in persuasive attack in the second debate: the total number of persuasive attacks dropped from 74 in debate one to 51 in debate two. The format of the third debate allowed the number of persuasive attacks to rebound to 132 in that contest (we also think that candidates were availing themselves of their last opportunity to attack opponents in the debates). In particular, we believe that attacks on character dropped the most, a decline that significantly impaired Bush's ability to engage in persuasive attack in the second debate.

Friedenberg, however, rejects the claim that the format of the second debate kept the candidates focused on the issues. This is not the precise contrary of the claim advanced here (fewer personal attacks do not necessarily translate into a focus on the issues), but we saw fewer character attacks in the second debate, and Friedenberg apparently does not interpret the text in the same way. Specifically, he observes that, "at several points in the debate, and in his closing statement, Bush attacked Clinton's character, much as he had in the first debate" (1994, p. 102).

While we found a few attacks by Bush in the second debate, our analysis reveals that these are the exception more than the rule, especially so for Bush. Specifically, we found that the number of attacks from Bush tumbled from twenty-four in the first debate to a mere nine attacks in the second—and rebounded to forty-one in the third. Furthermore, our analysis suggests that because Bush tended to attack more on character grounds than on policy or the issues, his use of persuasive attack declined considerably more in the middle debate than either Clinton's or Perot's. Thus our reading of the debates indicates that, while Bush did try to attack Clinton's character in the second debate, the audience severely constrained his use of this strategy.[2]

Hahn (1994) concludes his analysis of the 1992 debates by asserting, "We learned that changing the format has little effect on the substance of the debates" (p. 208). Our findings suggest otherwise. As just indicated, the format was largely responsible for a dramatic drop in Bush's persuasive attack between debates 1 and 2 and for an even larger upsurge in the final debate. While we agree with Hahn that the format influences perceptions held by the public, it can also significantly influence the substance of the debate.

One important factor in such debates is the questions addressed to the candidates. Eveland, McLeod, and Natanson's (1994) analysis revealed that the audience questions (in debate 2) differed from journalistic questions (in debates 1 and 3). Reporters were more likely to ask "better" questions (questions believed to be more likely to elicit candidates' stance, according to Milic, 1979). Reporters' questions were more concise and were more likely to be argumentative, accusatory, and leading than audience questions. However, neither group was more likely to address issues important to the electorate in their questions, and neither group consistently asked questions that were high in clarity.

Thus while there are systematic differences in the questions asked in the second debate (from the audience) than in the questions asked in the other debates (from reporters), these do not seem to account for the dramatic drop in persuasive attack (especially for Bush). Again, we conclude that the format, which allowed voters to pose questions (and interject their views about personal attacks), significantly depressed the amount of persuasive attack in the second debate and particularly the amount of character attack from Bush.

Third, we found a clear relationship between persuasive attack and persuasive defense. Examination of attack and defense by debate confirms this claim. As the number of persuasive attacks dropped in the second debate, so did defensive utterances: attacks dropped from 74 to 51; defenses dropped from 184 to 156. When the number of attacks increased in debate 3, persuasive defense increased as well: attacks increased from 51 to 132; defenses increased from 156 to 195. As one would expect, then, persuasive attack and defense are related communicative phenomena.

This general principle can also be illustrated by examining attacking and defensive utterances by each candidate: Bush, 74 attacks, 231 defenses; Clinton, 106 attacks, 185 defenses; Perot, 77 attacks, 119 defenses. As we indicated before, we found that the most attacks (from Clinton and Perot) were aimed at Bush, who has the largest number of defensive utterances, and the fewest attacks were leveled (by either Bush or Clinton) at Perot, who presented the least number of defenses.

Fourth, one advantage of our approach that became clear in our analysis is that it allows us to discuss both image (personality, character) and policy (or image) in the debates. To illustrate this claim, note that candidates attack on personal grounds. For example, in the first debate, Bush discusses the fact that Clinton had demonstrated against the Vietnam War: "I questioned his judgment and his character." In the third debate, Clinton charged that Bush was wrong to promise not to raise taxes in the previous election: "The mistake that was made was making the 'read my lips' promise in the first place, just to get elected . . . , knowing what the size of the deficit was, knowing there was no plan to control health care costs, and knowing that we did not have a strategy to get real economic growth back into this economy." Both of these illustrate attacks on the character of the opponent.

However, many of the attacks focused on policy grounds as well. In the second debate, for example, Bush attacked Clinton's tax-and-spend policy: "Governor Clinton's program wants to tax more and spend more—$150 billion in new taxes, spend another 220. I don't believe that's the way to do it." In the first debate, Clinton rebuked Bush because he vetoed "a bill that has an investment tax credit, middle-class tax relief, research-and-development tax credits." Thus many attacks concerned clear policy choices.

Similarly, the candidates engaged in persuasive defense of their character. In the first debate, Bush stressed his experience and in particular his foreign policy experience: "Well, I think one thing that distinguishes is experience—I think we've dramatically changed the world. I'll talk about that a little bit later, but the changes are mind-boggling for world peace. Kids go to bed at night without the same fear of nuclear war." On the other hand, Clinton described his upbringing in debate 1: "I grew up in the segregated South, thankfully raised by a grandfather with almost no formal education but with a heart of gold, who taught me early that all people were equal in the eyes of God. I saw the winds of hatred divide people and keep the people of my state poorer than they should have been, spiritually and economically." In the first debate, Perot tried to bolster his credibility by stressing his independence from the political machines: "I was not put on the ballot by any PAC money, by any foreign lobbyist money, by any special interest money. This is a movement that came from the people. This is the way the framers of the Constitution intended our government to be, a government that comes from the people." All of these statements, and others, show that the candidates offered defenses of character.

Other defenses, however, focused more on policy choices. In the second debate, Bush discussed his economic foreign policy, declaring that "I want to continue work after we get this NAFTA agreement ratified this coming year; I want to get one with Eastern Europe. I want to get one with Chile, and free and fair trade is the answer." Clinton discussed his plans for tax reform in the first debate: "My plan triggers in at gross incomes—family incomes—of $200,000 and above. Then we want to give modest middle-class tax relief to restore fairness." In the second debate, Perot reminded viewers of his stance on the deficit: "I've already taken the pledge on cutting the deficit in half." Thus the candidates defended their policy proposals in the debates.

Thus our approach, considering the debates as instances of persuasive attack and defense, permits the analyst to consider both image or personality and policy concerns. We have shown that the candidates engaged in attack on both personal and policy grounds and that they provided persuasive defense on both personal and policy grounds. A focus on persuasive attack and defense thus permits a fuller appreciation of the diversity of topics that emerge in the debates.

Persuasive Attack

Considering implications for persuasive attack, we found that candidates used general negative attacks most frequently. Other strategies, like severity, effects on the audience, and inconsistency also occurred repeatedly, but the general negative attack—possibly because it is relatively quick and easy to devise—tended to predominate. It might be objected that "negative general" attack is a general ("miscellaneous") category and should be refined further. However, we believe that many attack strategies *are* in fact quite general, because it is more difficult and time-consuming to develop an attack more specifically. Thus, carving it up into smaller categories, while possibly advantageous for some purposes, would risk losing sight of this finding.

A second implication for persuasive attack derived from this analysis is that presidential candidates overwhelmingly relied on attacking strategies that increase offensiveness rather than on strategies that increased apparent responsibility. We believe such a tendency occurs in part because advocates want the audience to believe that *they themselves* have the ability to make positive changes. Thus they are likely to portray their opponents as doing *bad things*, but they don't have to worry about *assigning responsibility* to their opponents for those offensive actions. Because the candidates want voters to assume that the president can solve problems, they may tend to assume responsibility for good or bad.

For example, Clinton does not have to spend as much time proving *Bush is responsible* for the economy as on demonstrating that *the economy is in bad shape.* He can assume that (in general) Bush is more likely to dispute the claim that the economy is in bad shape than the claim that he (as president) is responsible for the shape of our economy. Indeed, although there are many things the president cannot control, and Bush did attempt to shift blame to Congress and/or claim defeasibility at times, in our opinion he spent more effort denying that the economy was in trouble than denying responsibility for those economic problems he did admit. In short, the fact that candidates want to claim personal responsibility for (past and future) success means that arguments for responsibility tend to be less prominent.

Furthermore, Benoit and Lindsey's (1987a) study of forms of inference in political, religious, and legal discourse found that descriptive arguments are far more common than causal ones. They conclude that causal arguments (e.g., who or what is responsible for an effect) are more difficult to devise than descriptive ones. In other words, it may be easier to dispute the health of the economy than to argue about the causes of the state of the economy.

Third, the attacker has a greater opportunity to select the grounds for debate than the respondent. The candidate who is on the defensive must either choose to ignore the persuasive attacks (which could be taken as a tacit admission of their validity) or debate the ground selected by the attacker. It is possible to begin addressing the attack and then shift to other grounds, but this maneuver is more difficult (and one still at least begins on the ground selected by the attacker). It is also possible to ignore an attack, but this option risks alienating voters. Thus the more one attacks, the more control a candidate exerts over the course of the debate. The more a candidate is on the defensive, the less control he or she has over the grounds of the debate.

A fourth implication for persuasive attack is that people (voters) may find *personal* attack offensive. Pfau and Kenski (1990) argue that while people complain about negative advertising, there is a "widespread perception among political campaign professionals that the attack strategy is an important and effective option" (p. xiii). Particularly when the format permits audience participation (as in debate 2), candidates may wish to (or be forced to) avoid personal invective. Bush relied heavily on personal attacks, and when the audience took this ground away from him, he was able to launch fewer than ten persuasive attacks in that debate.

Fifth, it is reasonable for voters to assume that a politician's past record is a relatively good predictor of future success or failure. Thus the challenger (or in this case, challengers) should be prepared to attack weaknesses in the incumbent's record. Brydon (1985b), for example, found that, when Carter was the challenger, he attacked Ford's record on unemployment, inflation, and the economy. The challenger(s) should also expect the incumbent to bolster his or her past successes and be prepared to respond appropriately. In the 1992 presidential debates, Bush was forced to defend his record as president (and to a lesser extent, Clinton his record as governor). Bush attempted to bolster his past successes (as did Clinton); unfortunately for Bush, most of the successes he touted were in foreign affairs during a campaign in which most voters were much more concerned about domestic issues.

Some of the forms of persuasive attack seem generally to be more powerful than others, a sixth implication. For example, in the debates Clinton and Perot both attacked with severity and effects on audience, which seemed relatively effective. On the other hand, Bush's charges that Clinton had planned offensive acts and was inconsistent seemed less offensive and were less effective (and Perot defused the former, and Clinton made a credible attempt to defuse the latter and in fact to turn it against Bush).

Seventh, it may be helpful to try to make one's attacks specific where possible. We contrasted several of Bush's persuasive attacks with others from Clinton. Bush's attacks seemed much more general than Clinton's attacks. It also seems reasonable that the specificity of many of Clinton's attacks made them much more powerful than Bush's many vague charges.

Furthermore, it is important to develop the attacks one uses effectively. For example, Bush charged Clinton with inconsistency, as we discussed earlier. However, it seemed to us that Bush's accusation, especially after Clinton's response, tended to make Clinton look realistic, not inconsistent (seeing both good and bad in complex legislation seems plausible) and to make Bush seem as if he sees everything as either black or white. On the other hand, Bush's "read my lips" promise not to raise taxes was directly contradicted by his tax increase.

An eighth implication for persuasive attack concerns the typology of strategies for persuasive attack employed here. While it is still in its formative stages, we found it useful for analyzing and understanding the persuasive attack in the 1992 presidential debates. Further applications may well refine or extend it, but we found this typology to be a useful beginning for analyzing the strategies for persuasive attack in such texts.

Finally, we want to stress that in at least one very important respect, the 1992 presidential debates were atypical: there were three candidates. As mentioned above, one practical implication is that Clinton and Perot attacked Bush, Bush attacked Clinton, and there was relatively little attack directed at Perot. Bush was therefore at a severe disadvantage, while Perot had the best of it, but because he was not likely to win the election, it was more important that Clinton had an advantage over Bush. Again, we do not argue that Perot liked or supported Clinton any more or less than he liked or supported Bush personally; it seems clear that he was opposed to the incumbent. Nevertheless, whenever there are three (or more) candidates, it is possible that some might "gang up" on one candidate, either by design or by effect.

Persuasive Defense

The first implication for persuasive defense is that the debaters' persuasive defense relied most heavily on bolstering and corrective action. These are both plausible choices for presidential candidates to use in a debate. Bolstering attempts to place the rhetor in a favorable light, encouraging voters to vote for the rhetor. Corrective action is also a beneficial strategy. It suggests that you have solutions to problems (and that you will implement those solutions). For the challenger, corrective action also functions implicitly to attack the incumbent (for leaving problems that need to be solved). Similarly, the incumbent must be careful in using corrective action, for this strategy may imply that there are problems that he or she failed to solve. However, if much of the audience is already convinced that there are serious problems—as was clearly the case in this election—it may be better to propose solutions than to pretend that none is needed.

Second, it is important for the incumbent to be prepared to defend his or her record in office. As indicated above, it seems reasonable for voters to assume that there is no better indication of how an elected official will perform than how he or she did in the past. Incumbents should tout their successes and be prepared to defend against allegations of failures. Of course, incumbents can claim they have gained experience and insights during their first term, and they can promise corrective action. Still, one should not underestimate the importance of an incumbent's ability to defend his or her record.

It is a mistake to bolster in areas of relatively little interest to the audience. Bush could claim to have won the Gulf War, but if the audience was more interested in domestic policy—as it appeared in this case—all the bolstering would be to little or no avail. It seems reasonable that it is better to bolster in areas salient to the audience even if those areas don't seem as important to the rhetor. In this case, perhaps Bush tried to make foreign policy seem more important than, or even as important as, domestic policy—but he didn't succeed.

We are reminded of the story of the child who was searching for money he had dropped in the gutter. When a passer-by asked if this was where he had lost the money, the boy replied, "No, but the light is so much better over here." Perhaps the Gulf War was the clearest (or most important) instance of success for Bush, but foreign policy was not at or even near the top of voters' concerns. In other words,

Bush looked for his successes where they were largest but not where the potential rewards in votes were greatest. As we mentioned earlier, Limbaugh (1992) identified several areas in domestic affairs in which Bush could have tried to claim successes. It is not merely the magnitude of the accomplishment that matters but also the salience of the success to the audience.

Shifting the blame and defeasibility may reduce the apparent blame for offensive actions. However, these strategies can also reduce the appearance that the rhetor is capable of achieving promised results. This effect is clearly related to the lack of attacks that attempted to establish responsibility, discussed earlier. Bush's occasional use of these strategies may have suggested that he was not capable of solving problems (even though it is true that presidents have limitations, this impression is likely to hurt a candidate's case).

It may be a mistake to deny or minimize problems that the audience accepts as true. In these debates, much of the audience believed that our country had serious economic problems, but Bush repeatedly attempted to deny or minimize them. Of course, it may be possible for the rhetor to change the audience's mind about whether alleged problems are real or about the magnitude of the problems. However, this task required more persuasiveness than Bush was able to muster in the debates.

A final implication concerns the typology used here for analyzing persuasive defense, or image repair strategies. The theory of image restoration discourse has been applied more extensively than our typology for persuasive attack (see, e.g., Benoit, 1995; Benoit, in press; Benoit and Anderson, under review; Benoit and Brinson, 1994; Benoit, Gullifor, and Panici, 1991; Benoit and Hanczor, 1994; Benoit and Nill, under review; or Brinson and Benoit, in press). Once again, we found it superior to other approaches available in the rhetorical literature. We found that the candidates relied most heavily on bolstering and corrective action (these two categories accounted for over 80 percent of all instances of persuasive defense). Burke (1970, 1973) discussed neither of these, and Ware and Linkugel (1973) include only bolstering. Furthermore, four of the remaining strategies were discussed in only one of these typologies (shift blame [victimage] and mortification by Burke and simple denial and differentiation by Ware and Linkugel), and three by neither (defeasibility, minimization, and good intentions, the latter mentioned as a form of denial by Ware and Linkugel). Thus while building on important previous work in the area, the theory of image restoration discourse is a clear advance over other approaches to image repair discourse. It offers a more complete conceptualization of the defensive strategies available to rhetors.

We would also like to mention a few ideas for extending the analysis reported here. First, other discourse in the campaign (including the vice-presidential debate) could be analyzed critically for use of persuasive attack and defense. Murphy (1992) argues that the campaign generally is an important context for understanding presidential debates. Ellsworth (1965) suggested that candidates were more likely to respond to their opponents' attacks in the debates than in the campaign generally. Analysis of persuasive attack and defense in the rest of the campaign would permit comparisons of the extent and nature of attack and defense in the campaign generally and in the debates specifically. Convention speeches, campaign stump speeches, and advertisements are all potentially valuable sites for further research on persuasive attack and defense in political campaigns. Investigation of them would give us a more complete understanding of persuasive attack and defense in political campaigns.

Second, this analysis ought to be applied to presidential debates from earlier (and, assuming they continue, subsequent) campaigns. The 1992 presidential debates were distinctive because of the prominence of a third party candidate. We argued that Ross Perot was infrequently attacked and that his discourse had the effect of primarily attacking Bush (because Bush was an incumbent). Therefore, regardless of his showing at the polls (and it was not clear that his purpose was to get elected as much as to focus attention on issues like the federal deficit), Perot's presence definitely affected the debates and could well have contributed to Bush's defeat in the election. Analysis of persuasive attack and defense in other debates with only two contenders would thus add to our knowledge of presidential debates.

Similarly, we argued that the format of the debate can influence persuasive attack. In the second debate, the audience's clear demand that the candidates eschew personal attack affected persuasive attack (and thus persuasive defense) from all three candidates but especially Bush. Critical analysis of persuasive attack and defense in other debates, comparing format differences, could add to our understanding of the effects of format on the debates.

Third, this initial theory of persuasive attack would benefit from application in other contexts. For example, one of the findings in this study was that candidates in these debates overwhelmingly focused on increasing offensiveness of actions attributed to others rather than on attempting to increase attributions of responsibility. We suggested in chapter 3 that part of the reason might be the fact that candidates for the office of president have a reason to assume the power of the agent (because they want voters to believe that if they are elected, they can effectuate positive outcomes). While we speculated that the emphasis on offensiveness rather than responsibility might not be limited to political debates or even to political campaigns, this speculation merits scholarly attention. Thus the nature of persuasive attack ought to be examined in nonpolitical contexts.

Notes

1. To be sure, issue and image are intertwined, as we have argued throughout the book. We believe that a candidate's stance on the issues should influence that person's image. Conversely, a candidate's image may affect perceptions of that person's stand on issues. Still, we find the distinction useful in making broad characterizations of Clinton's and Bush's emphases in their persuasive attacks.

2. Friedenberg also suggests, "Even if we hypothetically concede that this debate was more dignified and issue oriented than the prior presidential debate, this change might well be a function of President Bush's awareness that his attacks on Clinton were not working" (1994, p. 102). This speculation is belied by the fact that in the third debate, without active audience participation, Bush's attacks increased from nine (in the second debate) to forty-one.

Part II

Transcripts of the 1992 Presidential
Debates: Bush, Clinton, and Perot

We began our analysis with texts of the 1992 presidential debates
from the *New York Times* ("Transcript of First," 1992; "Transcript
of Second," 1992; "Transcript of Third," 1992): we photocopied the
transcripts of the debates in this newspaper and we downloaded computer text files of them via Lexis/Nexis. We then viewed videotapes
of the debates and corrected the transcripts of the three 1992 presidential debates between Bush, Clinton, and Perot.

6

Debate One
October 11, 1992

MODERATOR: The first topic tonight is what separates each of you from the other. Mr. Perot, what do you believe tonight is the single most important separating issue of this campaign?

PEROT: I think the principal issue that separates me is that five and a half million people came together on their own and put me on the ballot. I was not put on the ballot by either of the two parties. I was not put on the ballot by any PAC money, by any foreign lobbyist money, by any special interest money. This is a movement that came from the people. This is the way the framers of the Constitution intended our government to be, a government that comes from the people.

Over time we have developed a government that comes at the people, that comes from the top down, where the people are more or less treated as objects to be programmed during the campaign with commercials and media events and fear messages and personal attacks and things of that nature. The thing that separates my candidacy and makes it unique is that this came from millions of people in fifty states all over this country who wanted a candidate that worked and belonged to nobody but them. I go into this race as their servant. And I belong to them. So this comes from the people.

MODERATOR: Governor Clinton, one-minute response.

CLINTON: The most important distinction in this campaign is that I represent real hope for change, a departure from trickle-down economics, a departure from tax-and-spend economics to invest in growth. But before I can do that, I must challenge the American people to change and they must decide. Tonight I have to say to the president, Mr. Bush, for twelve years you've had it your way; you've had your chance and it didn't work. It's time to change. I want to bring that change to the American people. But we must all decide first: do we have the courage to change for hope in a better tomorrow?

MODERATOR: President Bush, one-minute response.

BUSH: Well, I think one thing that distinguishes me is experience— I think we've dramatically changed the world. I'll talk about that a little bit later, but the changes are mind-boggling for world peace. Kids go to bed at night without the same fear of nuclear war.

And change for change sake isn't enough. We saw that message in the late seventies. We heard a lot about change and what happened, that misery index went right through the roof. But I've—my economic program, I think, is the kind of change we want.

And the way we're going to get it done is we're going to have a brand new Congress. A lot of them were thrown because of all the scandals. I'll sit down with them, Democrats and Republicans alike, and work for my agenda for American renewal, which represents real change. But I'd say if you had to separate out, I think it's experience at this level.

QUESTION: Governor Clinton, how do you respond to the president on the—you have two minutes—on the question of experience? He says that is what distinguishes him from the other two of you.

CLINTON: I believe experience counts, but it's not everything. Values, judgment, and the record that I have amassed in my state also should count for something. I've worked hard to create good jobs and to educate people. My state now ranks first in the country in job growth this year, fourth in income growth, fourth in the reduction of poverty, third in overall economic performance, according to a major newsmagazine. That's because we believe in investing in education and in jobs.

And we have to change this country. You know, my wife, Hillary, gave me a book about a year ago in which the author defined insanity as just doing the same old thing over and over again and expecting a different result. We have got to have the courage to change. Experience is important, yes. I've gotten a lot of good experience in dealing with ordinary people over the last year, month. I've touched more people's lives and seen more heartbreak and hope, more pain and more promise, than anybody else who's run for president this year. And I think the American people deserve better than they're getting.

We have gone from first to thirteenth in the world in wages in the last twelve years, since Mr. Bush and Mr. Reagan have been in. Personal income has dropped while people have worked harder. In the last four years there have been twice as many bankruptcies as new jobs created. We need a new approach. This same old experience is not relevant. We're living in a new world after the cold war, and what works in this new world is not trickle-down, not government for the benefit of the privileged few, not tax and spend, but a commitment to invest in American jobs and American education, controlling American health care costs and bringing the American people together.

That is what works, and you can have the right kind of experience and the wrong kind of experience. Mine is rooted in the real lives of real people, and it will bring real results if we have the courage to change.

MODERATOR: President Bush, one minute to respond.

BUSH: I just thought of another, another big difference here between me—I don't believe Mr. Perot feels this way, but I know Governor Clinton did. I want to accurately quote him. He thinks, I think he said that the country is coming apart at the seams. Now, I know that the only way he can win is to make everybody believe the economy is worse than it is. But this country's not coming apart at the seams, for heaven's sakes. We're the United States of America. We—in spite of the economic problems, we are the most respected economy around the world. Many would trade for it. We've been caught up in a global slowdown. We can do much much better, but we ought not try to convince the American people that America is a country that's coming apart at the seams. I would hate to be running for president and think that the only way I could win would be to convince everybody how horrible things are. Yes, there are big problems. And yes, people are hurting. But I believe that this agenda for American renewal I have is the answer to do it, and I believe we can get it done now, whereas we didn't in the past, because you're going to have a whole brand new bunch of people in the Congress that are going to have to listen to the same American people I'm listening to.

QUESTION: Mr. Perot, a minute response, sir.

PEROT: Well, they got a point. I don't have any experience in running up a $4 trillion debt. I don't have any experience in gridlock government, where nobody takes responsibility for anything and everybody blames everybody else. I don't have any experience in creating the worst public school system in the industrialized world, the most violent crime-ridden society in the industrialized world. But I do have a lot of experience in getting things done. So if we're at a point in history where we want to stop talking about it and do it, I've got a lot of experience in figuring out how to solve problems, making the solutions work, and then moving on to the next. One, I've got a lot of experience in not taking ten years to solve a ten-minute problem. So if it's time for action, I think I have experience that counts.

If there's more time for gridlock and talk and finger pointing, I'm the wrong man.

QUESTION: President Bush, the question goes to you. You have two minutes. And the question is this: are there important issues of character separating you from these other two men?

BUSH: I think the American people should be the judge of that. I think character is a very important question.

I said something the other day where I was accused of being like Joe McCarthy, because I questioned—I put it this way: I think it's wrong to demonstrate against your own country or organize demonstrations against your own country in foreign soil. I just think it's wrong.

I—that maybe they say, well, it's a youthful indiscretion. I was nineteen or twenty, flying off an aircraft carrier, and that shaped me to be commander in chief of the armed forces.

And I'm sorry, but demonstrating—it's not a question of patriotism. It's a question of character and judgment. They get on me—Bill's gotten on me about "Read my lips" some. When I make a mistake, I'll admit it.

But he has made—made, not admitted—a mistake. And I just find it impossible to understand how an American can demonstrate against his own country in a foreign land, organizing demonstrations against it, when young men are held prisoner in Hanoi or kids out of the ghetto were drafted.

Some say, well, you're a little old-fashioned. Maybe I am, but I just don't think that's right.

Now, whether it's character or judgment, whatever it is, I have a big difference here on this issue. And so we'll just have to see how it plays out, but I—I couldn't do that. And I don't think most Americans could do that.

And they all say, well, it was a long time ago. Well, let's admit it, then. Say I made a terrible mistake. How could you be commander in chief of the armed forces and have some kid say, when you have to make a tough decision, as I did in Panama or in, in Kuwait, and then have some kid jump up and say, "Well, I'm not going to go." The commander in chief was organizing demonstrations halfway around the world during another era.

So there are differences. But that's about the main area where I think we have a difference. I don't know about—we'll talk about that a little with Ross here in a bit.

MODERATOR: Mr. Perot, you have one minute.

PEROT: I think the American people will make their own decisions on character, and at a time when we have work to do and we need action, I think they need to clearly understand the backgrounds of each person. And I think the press can play a huge role in making sure that the backgrounds are clearly presented in an objective way. Then make a decision. Certainly anyone in the White House should have the character to be there. But I think it's very important to measure when and where things occurred. Did they occur when you were a young person in your formative years? Or did they occur while you were a senior official in the federal government? When you're a senior official in the federal government spending billions of dollars of taxpayers' money, and you're a mature individual and you make a mistake, then that was on our ticket. If you make it as a young man, time passes. So I would say, just, you know, look at all three of us. Decide who you think will do the job, pick that person in November, because believe me, as I've said before, the party's over and it's time for the cleanup crew. And we do have to have change and people who never take responsibility for anything when it happens on their watch and people who are in charge—

MODERATOR: Your time is up.

PEROT: Your time is up.

MODERATOR: Time is up.

PEROT: Time is up. More later.

MODERATOR: Governor Clinton, you have one minute.

CLINTON: Ross gave a good answer, but I've got to respond directly to Mr. Bush. You have questioned my patriotism. You even brought some right-wing congressmen into the White House to plot how to attack me for going to Russia in 1969–1970 when over 50,000 other Americans did. Now, I honor your service in World War II. I honor Mr. Perot's service in uniform and the service of every man and woman who ever served, including Admiral Crowe, who was your chairman of the Joint Chiefs and who is supporting me. But when Joe McCarthy went around this country attacking people's patriotism, he was wrong. He was wrong. And a senator from Connecticut stood up to him named Prescott Bush. Your father was right to stand up to Joe McCarthy. You were wrong to attack my patriotism. I was opposed to the war, but I love my country, and we need a president who will bring this country together, not divide it. We've got enough division. I want to lead a unified country.

MODERATOR: All right, we move now to the subject of taxes and spending. The question goes to Governor Clinton for a two-minute answer. It will be asked by Ann Compton.

QUESTION: Governor Clinton, can you lock in a level here tonight on where middle-income families can be guaranteed a tax cut, or at the very least, at what income level they can be guaranteed no tax increase?

CLINTON: The tax increase I have proposed triggers in at family incomes of $200,000 and above. Those are the people who in the 1980s had their incomes go up while their taxes went down. Middle-class people, defined as people with incomes of $52,000 and down, had their incomes go down while their taxes went up in the Reagan-Bush years because of six increases in the payroll taxes. So that is where my income limit would trigger.

QUESTION: So there would be no tax increases below $200,000?

CLINTON: That's right. My plan, notwithstanding my opponent's ad, my plan triggers in at gross incomes—family incomes—of $200,000 and above. Then we want to give modest middle-class tax relief to restore some fairness, especially to middle-class people with families with incomes of under $60,000. In addition to that, the money that I raise from upper-income people and from asking foreign corporations just to pay the same income tax on their income earned in America that American corporations do will be used to give incentives back to upper-income people.

I want to give people permanent incentives, an investment tax credit like President Kennedy and the Congress inaugurated in the early sixties, to get industry moving again; a research-and-development tax credit; a low-income-housing tax credit, a long-term capital gains proposal for new business and business expansions.

We've got to have no more trickle-down. We don't need across-the-board tax cuts for the wealthy for nothing. We need to say, "Here's your tax incentive if you create American jobs the old-fashioned way." I'd like to create more millionaires than were created under Mr. Bush and Mr. Reagan. But I don't want to have four years where we have no growth in the private sector, and that's what's happened in the last four years. We're down 35,000 jobs in the private sector. We need to invest and grow, and that's what I want to do.

MODERATOR: President Bush, one minute, sir.

BUSH: Well, let me—I have to correct one thing. I didn't question the man's patriotism. I questioned his judgment and his character. If—what he did in Moscow, that's fine. Let him explain it. He did. I accept that. What I don't accept is demonstrating and organizing demonstrations in a foreign country when your country's at war. I'm sorry. I cannot accept that.

In terms of—this one on taxes spells out the biggest difference between us. I do not believe we need to go back to the Mondale proposals or the Dukakis proposals of tax and spend. Governor Clinton says 200,000, but he also says he wants to raise 150 billion. The two—taxing people over 200,000 will not get you a 150 billion, and then when you add in his other spending proposals, regrettably you end up socking it to the workingman. That old adage that they use—we're going to soak the rich, we're going to soak the rich—it always ends up being the poor cab driver or the workingman that ends up paying the bill.

And so I just have a different approach. I believe the way to get the deficit down is to control the growth of mandatory spending programs and not raise taxes on the American people, you got a big difference there.

MODERATOR: Mr. Perot, one minute.

PEROT: We've got to have a growing, expanding job base to give us a growing, expanded tax base. Right now we have a flat to deteriorating job base, and where it appears to be going is minimum wage jobs. So we've got to really rebuild our job base. That's going to take money for infrastructure and investment to do that. Our foreign competitors are doing it; we're not. We cannot pay off the $4 trillion debt, balance the budget, and have—the industry is the future and the high-paying jobs in this country—without having the revenue. We're going to go through a period of shared sacrifice. There's one challenge; it's got to be fair. We've created a mess; don't have much to show for it. And we have got to fix it. And that's about all I can say in a minute.

MODERATOR: Next question goes to President Bush for a two-minute answer, and it will be asked by Sandy Vanocur.

QUESTION: Mr. President, this past week your secretary of the army, Michael Stone, said he had no plans to abide by a congressional mandate to cut U.S. forces in Europe from 150 to 100,000 by the end of September 1996.

Now why, almost fifty years after the end of World War II and with the total collapse of the Soviet Union, should American taxpayers be taxed to support armies in Europe when the Europeans have plenty of money to do it for themselves?

BUSH: Well, Sander, that's a good question. And the answer is, for forty-some years we kept the peace. If you look at the cost of not keeping the peace in Europe, it would be exorbitant. We have reduced the number of troops that are deployed and going to be deployed. I have cut defense spending.

And the reason we could do that is because of our fantastic success in winning the cold war. We never would have got there if we'd gone for the nuclear-freeze crowd; never would have got there for—if we'd listened to those that wanted to cut defense spending.

I think it is important that the United States stay in Europe and continue to guarantee the peace. We simply cannot pull back.

Now, when anybody has a spending program they want to spend money on at home, they say, well, let's cut money out of the Defense Department. I will accept, and have accepted, the recommendations of two proven leaders—General Colin Powell and Dick, Secretary Dick Cheney. They feel that the levels we're operating at and the reductions that I have proposed are proper.

And so I simply do not think we should go back to the isolation days and start blaming foreigners. We are the sole remaining super-power, and we should be that. And we have a certain disproportionate responsibility. But I would ask the American people to understand that if we make imprudent cuts, if we go too far, we risk the peace.

And I don't want to do that. I've seen what it is like to see a war, and I—to see the burdens of a war, I don't want to see us make reckless cuts. Because of our programs we have been able to significantly cut defense spending.

But let's not cut into the muscle, and let's not cut down our insurance policy, which is participation of American forces in NATO, the greatest peacekeeping organization ever made.

Today you got problems in Europe, still bubbling along even though Europe's going democracy's route. But we—we are there, and I think this insurance policy is necessary, I think it goes with world leadership, and I think the levels we've come up with are just about right.

MODERATOR: Mr. Perot, one minute, sir.

PEROT: If I'm poor and you're rich, and I can get you to defend me, that's good. But when the tables get turned, I ought to do my share. Right now we spend about $300 billion a year on defense; the Japanese spend around $30 billion in Asia, the Germans spend around $30 billion in Europe. For example, Germany'll spend a trillion dollars building infrastructure over the next ten years. It's kind of easy to do if you only have to pick up a $30 billion tab to defend your country.

The European Community is in a position to pay a lot more than they have in the past. I agree with the president; when they couldn't, we should have. Now that they can, they should. We sort of seem to have a desire to try to stay over there and control it. They don't want us to control it, very candidly. So it's, I think, very important for us to let them assume more and more of the burden and for us to bring that money back here and rebuild our infrastructure, because we can only be a superpower if we're an economic superpower, and we can only be an economic superpower if we have a growing, expanding job base.

MODERATOR: Governor Clinton. One minute, sir.

CLINTON: I agree with the general statement Mr. Bush made. I disagree that we need 150,000 troops to fulfill our role in Europe. We certainly must maintain an engagement there. There is certainly dangers there. There is certainly other trouble spots in the world which are closer to Europe than to the United States. But two former defense secretaries recently issued a report saying that 100,000 or slightly fewer troops would be enough, including President Reagan's former defense secretary, Mr. Carlucci. Many of the military experts whom I consulted on this agreed. We're going to have to spend more money in the future on military technology and on greater mobility, greater air lift, greater sea lift, and the V-22 airplane. We're going to have to do some things that are quite costly, and I simply don't believe we can afford, nor do we need, to keep 150,000 troops in Europe, given how much the Red Army, now under the control of Russia, has been cut. The Army Control Agreement concluded between Mr. Bush and Mr. Yeltsin is something I have applauded. I don't think we need 150,000 troops.

Let me make one other point. Mr. Bush talked about taxes. He didn't tell you that he vetoed a middle-class tax cut because it would be paid for by raising taxes on the wealthy and vetoed an investment tax credit paid for by raising taxes on the wealthy.

MODERATOR: All right. We go now to Mr. Perot for a two-minute question and it will be asked by John Machek.

QUESTION: Mr. Perot, you talked about fairness just a minute ago. I'm sharing the pain. As part of your plan to reduce the ballooning federal deficit, you've suggested that we raise gasoline taxes fifty cents a gallon over five years. Why punish the middle-class consumer to such a degree?

PEROT: It's ten cents a year accumulative. It finally gets to fifty cents at the end of the fifth year. I think "punish" is the wrong word. Again, see, I didn't create this problem. We're trying to solve it. Now, if you study our international competitors, some of our international competitors collect up to $3.50 a gallon in taxes, and they use that money to build infrastructure and create jobs. We collect thirty-five cents, and we don't have it to spend. I know it's not popular, and I understand the nature of your question, but the people who will be helped the most by it are the working people who will get the jobs created because of this tax.

Why do we have to do it? Because we have so mismanaged our country over the years, and it is now time to pay the fiddler, and if we don't, we will be spending our children's money. We have spent $4 trillion worth. An incredible number of young people are active in supporting my effort because they're deeply concerned that we have taken the American dream from them. I think it's fitting that we're on the campus of a university tonight. These young people, when they get out of this wonderful university, will have difficulty finding a job. We've got to clean this mess up, leave this country in good shape, and pass on the American dream to them. We've got to collect the taxes to do it. If there's a fairer way, I'm all ears. Ahh.

But, but, see—let me make it very clear. If people don't have the stomach to fix these problems, I think it's a good time to face it in November. If they do, then they will have heard the harsh reality of what we have to do. I'm not playing Lawrence Welk music tonight.

MODERATOR: All right. Governor Clinton, you have a minute, sir.

CLINTON: I think Mr. Perot has confronted this deficit issue, but I think it's important to point out that we really have two deficits in America, not one. We have a budget deficit in the federal government, but we also have an investment of jobs and income deficit. People are working harder for less money than they were making ten years ago, two-thirds of our people. A $1,600 drop in average income in just the last two years. The problem I have with the Perot prescription is that almost all economists who've looked at it say that, if you cut the deficit this much, this quick, it will increase unemployment, it will slow down the economy. That's why I think we shouldn't do it that quickly. We have a disciplined reduction in the deficit of 50 percent over the next four years, but first, get incentives to invest in this economy, put the American people back to work. We've got to invest in growth.

Nine Nobel Prize–winning economists and 500 others, including numerous Republican and Democratic business executives, have endorsed this approach because it offers the best hope to put America back to work and get our incomes rising instead of falling.

MODERATOR: President Bush, one minute, sir.

BUSH: The question was on fairness, and I, I just disagree with Mr. Perot. I don't believe it is fair to slap a fifty-cents-a-gallon tax over whatever many years on the people that have to drive for a living. People that go long distances. I don't think we need to do it.

You see, I have a fundamental difference. I agree with what he's talking about in trying to get this spending down and the discipline, although I think we ought to totally exempt Social Security. But he's talking tough medicine, and I think that's good.

I disagree with the tax-and-spend philosophy. You see, I don't think we need to tax more and spend more and then say that's going to make the problem better. And I'm afraid that's what I think I'm hearing from Governor Clinton.

I believe what you need to do is some of what Ross is talking about—control the growth of mandatory spending and get taxes down. He's mentioned some ways to do it, and I agree with those.

I've been talking about getting a capital gains cut forever, and his friends in Congress have been telling me that's a tax break for the rich. It would stimulate investment. I'm for an investment tax allowance. I am for a first-time tax break for first-time home buyers, and with this new Congress coming in, gridlock will be gone, and I'll sit down with them and say, Let's get this done. But I do not want to go the tax-and-spend route.

MODERATOR: All right, let's move on now to the subject of jobs. And the first question goes to President Bush for two minutes, and John will ask that question. John.

QUESTION: Mr. President, last month you came to St. Louis to announce a very lucrative contract for McDonnell Douglas to build F-15's for Saudi Arabia. In today's *Post Dispatch,* a retired saleswoman, a seventy-five-year-old woman named Marjorie Roberts, asked if she could ask a question of the candidates, said she wanted to register her concern about the lack of a plan to convert our defense-oriented industries into other purposes. How would you answer her?

BUSH: Well, I assume she was supportive of the decision on McDonnell Douglas. I assume she was supporting me on the decision to sell those airplanes. I think it's a good decision—took a little heat for it. But I think it was the correct, the correct decision to do, and we worked it out, and indeed, we're moving forward all around the world in a much more peaceful way. So that one we came away with which—in creating jobs for the American people, I would simply say to her look, take a look at what the president has proposed on job retraining. When you cut back on defense, defense spending, some people are going to be thrown out of work. If you throw another 50,000 kids on the street because of cutting recklessly in troop levels, you're going to put a lot more out of work. I would say to him, look at the job retraining programs that we're proposing, therein is the best answer to her. And another one is: stimulate investment in savings. I mean, we've got big economic problems, but we are not coming apart at the seams. We're ready for a recovery, with interest rates down and inflation down, the cruelest tax of all, caught up in a global slowdown right now, but that will change if you go with the programs I've talked about and if you help with job retraining and education. I am a firm believer that our America 2000 education program is the answer. A little longer run—it's going to take a while to educate, but it is a good program.

So her best hope for the short term is job retraining if she was thrown out of work at a defense plant, but tell her it's not all that gloomy. We're the United States. We got—we've faced tough problems before. Look at the misery index when the Democrats had both the White House and the—and the Congress. It was just right through the roof. Now, we can do better, and the way to do better is not to tax and spend but to retrain, get that control of the mandatory spending programs. I—I am much more optimistic about this country than some.

MODERATOR: Mr. Perot, you have one minute, sir.

PEROT: Well, your defense industries are going to have to convert to civilian industries. Many of them are. And the sooner they start, the sooner they'll finish. And there will be a significant transition. And it's very important that we not continue to let our industrial base deteriorate. We have someone who I'm sure regrets having said it, in the president's staff, said he didn't care whether we made potato chips or computer chips. Well, anybody who thinks about it cares a great deal.

Number 1, you make more making computer chips than you do potato chips. Number 2, nineteen out of twenty computer chips we have in this country now come from Japan. We've given away whole industries. So as we phase these industries over, there's a lot of intellectual talent in these industries. A lot of these people and industries can be converted to the industries of tomorrow. And that's where the high-paying jobs are. We need to have a very carefully thought through phase-over.

See, we practice nineteenth-century capitalism. The rest of the world practices twenty-first-century capitalism. We've got—I can't handle that in a minute, but I hope we can get back into it later. In the rest of the world, the countries and the businesses would be working together to make this transition in an intelligent way.

MODERATOR: Governor Clinton, you have one minute, sir.

CLINTON: We must, we must have a transition plan, to plan to convert from a defense to a domestic economy. No other nation would have cut defense as much as we already have without that. There are 200,000 people unemployed in California alone because we have cut defense without planning to retrain them and to reinvest in the technologies of the future here at home. That is what I want to do. This administration may say they have a plan, but the truth is they have not even released all the money—the paltry sum of money—that Congress appropriated.

I want to take every dollar by which we reduce defense and reinvest it in technologies for the twenty-first century—in new transportation, in communication and environmental cleanup technologies. Let's put the American people to work, and let's build the kind of high-tech high-wage high-growth economy that the American people deserve.

MODERATOR: The next question goes to Mr. Perot for a two-minute answer. It will be asked by Ann.

QUESTION: Mr. Perot, you talked a minute ago about rebuilding the job base. Is it true what Governor Clinton just said, that means that unemployment will increase, that it will slow the economy? And how would you specifically use the powers of the presidency to get more people back into good jobs immediately?

PEROT: Step 1, the American people send me up there. The day after election, I get with the congressional—we won't even wait until inauguration. And I'll ask the president to help me. And I'll ask his staff to help me. And we will start putting together teams to put together, to take all the plans that exist and do something with them.

Please understand, there are great plans lying all over Washington nobody ever executes. It's like having a blueprint for a house you never built, and don't have anywhere to sleep. Now, the challenge is to take these things and do something with them.

Step 1, you want to put America back to work? Clean up the small-business problem. Have one task force work on that.

The second, you've got your big companies that are in trouble, including the defense industries. Have another one on that.

Have a third task force on new industries of the future, to make sure we nail those for our country, and they don't wind up in Europe and Asia.

Convert from nineteenth-century to twenty-first-century capitalism. See, we have an adversarial relationship between government and business, international competitors that are cleaning our plate. Have an intelligent relationship between government and business and a supported relationship.

Then have another task force on crime, because next to jobs, the people are concerned about their safety, health care, school. One on the debt and deficit.

In fact, in that ninety-day period before the inauguration, put together the framework for the town hall, and give the American people a Christmas present. Show them by Christmas the first cut of these plans. By the time Congress comes into session, go to work. Have those plans ready to go in front of Congress. Then get off to a flying start in '93 to execute these plans.

There are people in this room and people on this stage who've been in meetings when I would sit there and say: is this one we're going to talk about or do something about? Well, obviously my orientation is: let's go do it. Now put together your plans by Christmas. Be ready to go when Congress goes. Nail these things. Small business—you've got to have capital. You've got to have credit. Many of them need mentors or coaches. And we can create more jobs there in a hurry than any other place.

MODERATOR: Governor Clinton, one minute.

CLINTON: This country desperately needs a jobs program. And my first priority would be to pass a jobs program, to introduce it on the first day I was inaugurated. I would meet with the leaders of the Congress, with all the newly elected members of the Congress and as many others with whom I could meet between the time of the election and the inauguration. And we would present a jobs program.

Then we would present a plan to control health care costs and phase in health care coverage for all Americans. Until we control health care costs, we're not going to control the deficit. It is the Number 1 culprit. But first we must have an aggressive jobs program.

I live in a state where the manufacturing job growth has far outpaced the nation's in the last few years, where we have created more private-sector jobs since Mr. Bush has been president than have been created in the entire rest of the country, where Mr. Bush's labor secretary said the job growth has been enormous.

We've done it in Arkansas. Give me a chance to create these kinds of jobs, America. We can do it. I know we can.

MODERATOR: President Bush, one minute.

BUSH: We've got the plan announced for what we can do for small business. I've already put forward things that'll get this country working fast, some of which have been echoed here tonight—investment tax allowance, capital gains reduction, more on research and development, a tax credit for first-time home buyers.

What I'm going to do is say to Jim Baker when this campaign is over: "All right, let's sit down now. You do in domestic affairs what you've done in foreign affairs. Be the kind of economic coordinator of all the domestic side of the house, and that includes all the economic side, all the training side, and bring this program together."

We're going to have a new Congress. And we're going to say to them: "You've listened to the voters the way we have, nobody wants gridlock anymore. And so let's get the program through."

And I believe it'll work, because, as Ross said, we got the plans. The plans are all over Washington. And I've put ours together in something called the Agenda for American Renewal, and it makes sense. It's sensible. It creates jobs. It gets to the base of the kind of jobs we need. And so I'll just be asking for support to get that put into effect.

MODERATOR: All right, the next question goes to Governor Clinton, for two minutes. It will be asked by Sandy.

QUESTION: Governor Clinton, when a president running for the first time gets into the office and wants to do something about the economy, he finds in Washington there's a person who has much more power over the economy than he does, the chairman of the Federal Reserve Board, accountable to no one. That being the case, would you go along with proposals made by Treasury Secretary James Brady and Congressman Lee Hamilton to make the Federal Reserve Board chairman somehow more accountable to elected officials?

CLINTON: Well, let me say that I think that we might—ought to—review the terms and the way it works. But frankly I don't think that's the problem today. We have low interest rates today. At least we have low interest rates that the Fed can control. Our long-term interest rates are still pretty high because of our deficit and because of our economic performance. And there was a terrible reaction internationally to Mr. Bush's saying he was going to give us four more years of trickle-down economics, other across-the-board tax cuts, and most of it going to the wealthy with no real guarantee of investment.

But I think the important thing, the important thing is to use the powers the president does have, on the assumption that, given the condition of this economy, we're going to keep interest rates down if we have the discipline to increase investment and reduce the debt at the same time. That is my commitment. I think the American people are hungry for action. I think Congress is hungry for someone who will work with them instead of manipulate them, someone who will not veto a bill that has an investment tax credit, middle-class tax relief, research-and-development tax credits, as Mr. Bush has done. Give me a chance to do that. I don't have to worry, I don't think, in the near term about the Federal Reserve. Their policies so far, it seems to me, are pretty sound.

MODERATOR: President Bush, you have one minute.

BUSH: I don't think the Fed ought to be put under the executive branch. There is separation there. I think that's fine. Alan Greenspan is respected. I've had some arguments with him about the speed with which we might have lowered rates, but Governor Clinton—he talks about the reaction to the markets.

There was a momentary fear that he might win and that the markets went phweee, down like that. So I don't think we can judge on— the stock market has been strong. It's been very strong since I've been president. And they recognize we got great difficulties, but they're also much more optimistic than the pessimists we have up here tonight.

In terms of vetoing tax bills, you're darn right. I am going to protect the American taxpayer against the spend-and-tax Congress. And I'm going to keep on vetoing them, because I don't think we're taxed too little. I think the government's spending too much.

So Governor Clinton can label it tax for the rich or anything he wants; I'm going to protect the working man by continuing to veto and to threaten to veto until we get this new Congress, and then we're going to move forward on our plan. Got to protect them.

MODERATOR: Mr. Perot, one minute.

PEROT: Keep the Federal Reserve independent, but let's live in a world of reality. We live in a global economy, not a national economy. These interest rates we have now don't make any sense. We have a $4 trillion debt, and only in America would you finance 70 percent of it five years or less. So 70 percent of our debt is five years or less. It's very interest sensitive. We have a 4 percent gap between what we pay for treasuries and what Germany pays for one- to five-year treasuries.

That gap is going to close, because the Arabs, the Japanese, and folks in this country are going to start buying German treasuries because they can get more money. Every time our interest rates go up 1 percent, that adds $28 billion to the deficit or to the debt, whichever place you want to put it. We are sitting on a ticking bomb, folks, because we have totally mismanaged our country, and we had better get it back under control. Just think, in your own business, if you had all of your long-term problems financed short term, you'd go broke in a hurry.

MODERATOR: We're going to move to foreign affairs. The first question goes to Mr. Perot for a two-minute answer, and Sandy will ask.

QUESTION: Mr. Perot, in the postwar cold war environment, what should be the overriding U.S. national interest? And what can the United States do—and what can it afford to do—to defend that national interest?

PEROT: Again, if you're not rich, you're not a superpower. So we have two that I'd put as Number 1. I have 1 and 1A. One is we've got to have the money to be able to pay for defense. And we've got to manufacture here. Believe it or not, folks, you can't ship it all overseas. You've got to make it here. And you can't convert from potato chips to airplanes in an emergency. See, Willow Run could be converted from cars to airplanes in World War II because it was here. We've got to make things here. You just can't ship them overseas anymore. I hope we talk more about that.

Second thing, on priorities, we've got to help Russia succeed in its revolution and all of its republics. When we think of Russia, remember, we're thinking of many countries now. We've got to help them. That's pennies on the dollar compared to renewing the cold war.

Third, we've got all kinds of agreements on paper and some that are being executed on getting rid of nuclear warheads. Russia and its republics are out of control or at best in weak control right now. It's a very unstable situation.

You've got every rich Middle Eastern country over there trying to buy nuclear weapons, as you well know. And that will lead to another five-star migraine headache down the road. We really need to nail down the intercontinental ballistic missiles, the ones that can hit us from Russia. And we've focused on the tactical. We've made real progress there. We've got some agreement on the nuclear, but we don't have those things put away yet. The sooner the better. So in terms of priorities, we've got to be financially strong.

Number 2, we've got to take care of this missile situation and try to get the nuclear war behind us and give that a very high priority. And Number 3, we need to help and support Russia and the republics in every possible way to become democratic capitalistic societies and not just sit back and let those countries continue in turmoil, because they could go back worse than things used to be. And believe me there are a lot of old boys in the K.G.B. and the military that liked it better the way it used to be.

MODERATOR: Governor Clinton, one minute.

CLINTON: In order to keep America the strongest nation in the world, we need some continuity and some change. There are three fundamental challenges. First of all, the world is still a dangerous and uncertain place. We need a new military and a new national security policy equal to the challenges of the post-cold-war era, a smaller permanent military force but one that is more mobile, well trained with high-technology equipment. We need to continue the negotiations to reduce the nuclear arsenals in the Soviet Union, the former Soviet Union, and the United States. We need to stop this proliferation of weapons of mass destruction.

Second, we have to face that, in this world, economic security is a whole lot of national security. Our dollar's at an all-time low against some foreign currencies. We're weak in the world. We must rebuild America's strength at home.

And finally, we ought to be promoting the democratic impulses around the world. Democracies are our partners. They don't go to war with each other. They're reliable friends in the future. National security, economic strength, democracy.

MODERATOR: President Bush, one minute.

BUSH: Well, we still are the envy of the world in terms of our military, there's no question about that. We're the envy of the world in terms of our economy, in spite of the difficulties we're having, there's no question about that. Our exports are dramatically up. I might say to Mr. Perot, "I can understand why you might have missed it, because there's so much fascination by trivia, but I worked out a deal with Boris Yeltsin to eliminate—get rid of entirely—the most destabilizing weapons of all, the SS-18, the big intercontinental ballistic missile." I mean, that's been done. And thank God it has, because the parents of these young people around here go to bed at night without the same fear of nuclear war. We made dramatic progress.

And so, we've got a good military. The question, to sort of get a new military, get the best in the world, we got it—and they're keeping the peace, and they're respected around the world. And we're more respected because of the way we have conducted ourselves. We didn't listen to the nuclear freeze crowd; we said "peace through strength," and it worked and the cold war is over. And America understands that.

But we're so—turned so inward we don't understand the global picture, and we are helping democracy, Ross. The Freedom Support Act is something that I got through the Congress, and it's a very good thing because it does exactly what you say, and I think you agree with that, to help Russian democracy. And we're going to keep on doing that.

MODERATOR: Next question is for Governor Clinton, and John will ask it.

QUESTION: Governor Clinton, you accused the president of coddling tyrants, including those in Beijing. As president, how would you exert U.S. power to influence affairs in China?

CLINTON: I think our relationships with China are important, and I don't think we want to isolate China, but I think it is a mistake for us to do what this administration did when all those kids went out there carrying the Statue of Liberty in Tiananmen Square. Mr. Bush sent two people in secret to toast the Chinese leaders and basically tell them not to worry about it. They rewarded him by opening negotiations with Iran to transfer nuclear technology. That was their response to that sort of action. Now that voices in the Congress and throughout the country have insisted that we do something about China, look what has happened. China has finally agreed to stop sending us products made with prison labor, not because we coddled them but because the administration was pushed into doing something about it. And recently the Chinese have announced that they are going to lower some barriers to our products, which they ought to do, since they have a $15 billion trade surplus with the United States under Mr. Bush, the second biggest surplus of all, second to Japan. So I would be firm. I would say if you want to continue most-favored-nation status for your government-owned industries as well as your private ones, observe human rights in the future. Open your society. Recognize the legitimacy of those kids that were carrying the Statue of Liberty. If we can stand up for our economic interests, we ought to be able to preserve the democratic interests of the people in China, and over the long run they will be more reliable partners.

MODERATOR: President Bush, you have one minute.

BUSH: Well, the administration is the first major country to stand up against the abuse in Tiananmen Square. We are the one that worked out the prison labor deal. We are the ones that have lowered the barrier to products with Carla Hill's negotiation.

I am the one that said let's keep the M.F.N., because you see China moving towards a free market economy. To do what the Congress and Governor Clinton is suggesting, you'd isolate and ruin Hong Kong. They are making some progress, not enough for us.

We were the first ones to put sanctions on. We still have them on some things.

But Governor Clinton's philosophy is isolate them. He says don't do it, but the policies he's expounding of putting conditions on M.F.N. and kind of humiliating them is not the way you make the kind of progress we are getting.

And I've stood up with these people, and I understand what you have to do to be strong in this situation, and it's moving not as fast as we'd like. But you isolate China and turn them inward, and then we've made a tremendous mistake.

And I'm not going to do it, and I've had to fight a lot of people that were saying "human rights," and we are the ones that put the sanctions on and stood for it.

And he can insult General Scowcroft if he wants to. They didn't go over to coddle; he went over to say we must make the very changes they're making now.

MODERATOR: One minute, Mr. Perot.

PEROT: It's huge. China's a huge country, broken into many provinces. It has some very elderly leaders that will not be around too much longer. Capitalism is growing and thriving across big portions of China. Asia will be our largest trading partner in the future. It will be a growing and a closer relationship. We have a delicate tightwire walk that we must go through at the present time to make sure that we do not cozy up to tyrants, to make sure that they don't get the impression that they can suppress their people.

But time is our friend there, because their leaders will change in not too many years, worst case, and their country is making great progress.

One last point on the missiles. I don't want the American people to be confused. We have written agreements, and we have some missiles that have been destroyed. But we have a huge number of intercontinental ballistic missiles that are still in place in Russia. The fact that you have an agreement is one thing. Till they're destroyed, some crazy person can either sell them or use them.

MODERATOR: All right, the next question goes to President Bush for a two-minute answer, and Ann will ask it.

QUESTION: Mr. President, how can you watch the killing in Bosnia and the "ethnic cleansing," or the starvation and anarchy in Somalia, and not want to use America's might, if not America's military, to try to end that kind of suffering?

BUSH: Ann, both of them are very complicated situations. And I vowed something, because I learned something from Vietnam, I am not going to commit U.S. forces until I know what the mission is, till the military tell me that it can be completed, until I know how they can come out. We are helping, American airplanes are helping today on humanitarian relief for Sarajevo. It is America that's in the lead in helping with humanitarian relief for Somalia. But when you go to put somebody else's son or daughter into war, I think you've got to be a little bit careful, and you have to have—be sure that there's a military plan that can do this. You have ancient ethnic rivalries that have cropped up as Yugoslavia has dissolved, or getting dissolved, and it isn't going to be solved by sending in the Eighty-second Airborne. And I'm not going to do that as commander in chief.

I am going to stand by and use the moral persuasion of the United States to get satisfaction in terms of prison camps—and we're making some progress there—and in terms of getting humanitarian relief in there. And right now, as you know, the United States took the lead in a no-fly operation up there in—a no-fly order up in the United Nations. We're working through the international organizations. That's one thing I learned by forging that tremendous and highly successful coalition against Saddam Hussein, the dictator. Use—work internationally to do it. I'm very concerned about, I'm concerned about ethnic cleansing. I'm concerned about attacks on Muslims, for example, over there. But I must stop short of using American force until I know how those young men and women are going to get out of there, as well as get in—know what the mission is and define it.

And I think I'm on the right track.

QUESTION: Are you designing a mission—

MODERATOR: Ms., Ann, sorry, time is up. We have to go to Mr. Perot for a one-minute response.

PEROT: I think if we learned anything in Vietnam, it's: you first commit this nation before you commit the troops to the battlefield. We cannot send our people all over the world to solve every problem that comes up. This is basically a problem that is a primary concern to the European Community. Certainly we care about the people, we care about the children, we care about the tragedy. But it is inappropriate for us, just because there's a problem somewhere around the world, to take the sons and daughters of working people, and make no mistake about it, our all-volunteer armed force is not made up of the sons and daughters of the beautiful people, it's the working folks who send their sons and daughters to war, with a few exceptions. It's very unlike World War II when FDR's sons flew missions, everybody went. It's a different world now and very important that we not just, without thinking it through, just rush to every problem in the world and have our people torn to pieces.

MODERATOR: Governor Clinton, one minute.

CLINTON: I agree that we cannot commit ground forces to become involved in the quagmire of Bosnia or in the tribal wars of Somalia. But I think that it's important to recognize that there are things that can be done short of that and that we do have interest there. There are, after all, 2 million refugees now because of the problems in what was Yugoslavia, the largest number since World War II. And there may be hundreds of thousands of people who will starve or freeze to death in this winter. The United States should try to work with its allies and stop it. I urged the president to support this air cover, and he did, and I applaud that. I applaud the no-fly zone, and I know that he's going back to the United Nations to try to get authority to enforce it. I think we should stiffen the embargo on the Belgrade government, and I think we have to consider whether or not we should lift the arms embargo now on the Bosnians, since they are in no way in a fair fight with a heavily armed opponent bent on ethnic cleansing. We can't get involved in the quagmire, but we must do what we can.

MODERATOR: Moving on now to divisions in our country. First question goes to Governor Clinton for two minutes, and Ann will ask it.

QUESTION: Governor Clinton, can you tell us what your definition of the word "family" is?

CLINTON: A family involves at least one parent, whether natural or adopted, or foster, and children. A good family is a place where love and discipline and good values are transmuted from the elders to the children. A place where people turn for refuge and where they know they're the most important people in the world. America has a lot of families that are in trouble today. There's been a lot of talk about family values in this campaign. I know a lot about that. I was born to a widowed mother who gave me family values and grandparents. I've seen the family values in my people in Arkansas. I've seen the family values of all these people in America who are out there killing themselves working harder for less, in a country that's had the worst economic years in fifty years—the first decline in industrial production ever. I think the president owes it to family values to show that he values America's families, whether they are people on welfare you're trying to move from welfare to work, the working poor, who I think deserve a tax break to lift them above poverty if they've got a child in the house and working forty hours a week, working families who deserve a fair tax system and the opportunity for constant retraining. They deserve a strong economy, and I think they deserve a family-and-medical-leave act. Seventy-two other nations have been able to do it. Mr. Bush vetoed it twice because he says we can't do something seventy-two other countries do even though it was a small business exemption. So with all the talk about family values, I know about family values. I wouldn't be here without them. The best expression of my family values is that tonight's my seventeenth wedding anniversary, and I'd like to close my question by just wishing my wife a happy anniversary and thanking my daughter for being here.

MODERATOR: President Bush, one minute.

BUSH: Well, I'd say that one meeting that made a profound impression on me was when the mayors of the big cities, including the mayor of Los Angeles, a Democrat, came to see me and they unanimously said the decline in urban America stems from the decline in the American family. So I do think we need to strengthen family. When Barbara holds an AIDS baby, she's showing a certain compassion for family; when she reads to children, the same thing. I believe that discipline and respect for the law, all of these things should be taught to children—not in our schools, but families have to do that.

I'm appalled at the highest—outrageous numbers of divorces; it happens in families, it's happened in ours, but it's gotten too much. And I just think we ought to do everything we can to respect the American family. It can be a single-parent family—those mothers need help, and one way to do it is to get these deadbeat fathers to pay their obligations to these mothers; that'll help strengthen the American family. And there's a whole bunch of other things that I can't click off in this short period of time.

MODERATOR: All right, Mr. Perot, you have one minute.

PEROT: If I had to solve all the problems that face this country and I could be granted one wish as we started down the trail to rebuild the job base, the schools, and so on and so forth, I would say a strong family unit in every home, where every child is loved, nurtured, and encouraged. A little child before they're eighteen months learns to think well of himself or herself or poorly. They develop a positive or negative self-image. At a very early age they learn how to learn.

If we have children who are not surrounded with love and affection—see, I look at my grandchildren and wonder if they'll ever learn to walk, because they're always in someone's arms. And I think, my gosh, wouldn't it be wonderful if every child had that love and support. But they don't.

We will not be a great country unless we have a strong family unit in every home. And I think you can use the White House as a bully pulpit to stress the importance of these little children, particularly in their young and formative years, to mold these little precious pieces of clay so that they, too, can live rich full lives when they're grown.

MODERATOR: New question, two-minute answer, goes to President Bush. Sandy will ask it.

QUESTION: Mr. President, there's been a lot of talk about Harry Truman in this campaign, so much so that I think tomorrow I'll wake up and see him named as the next commissioner of baseball.

BUSH: They could use one.

QUESTION: But the thing that Mr. Truman didn't have to deal with was drugs. Americans are increasingly alarmed about drug-related crimes in cities and suburbs, and your administration is not the first to have grappled with this. And are you at all of a mind that maybe it ought to go to another level? If not to what's advocated by William F. Buckley, Jr., and Milton Friedman—legalization, somewhere between there and where we are now?

BUSH: No, I don't think that's the right answer. I don't believe legalizing narcotics is the answer. I just don't believe that's the answer. I do believe that there's some fairly good news out there. The use of cocaine, for example, by teenagers is dramatically down.

But we've got to keep fighting on this war against drugs. We're doing a little better in interdiction. Many of the countries below that used to say, "Well, this is a United States problem—if you get the demand down, then we wouldn't have the problem," are working cooperatively with the D.E.A. and other, the military. We're using the military more now in terms of interdiction. Our funding for recovering is up, recovering the addicts.

Where we're not making the progress, Sander, is—we're making it in teenagers, and thank God, because I thought what Ross said was most appropriate about these families and these children. But where we're not making it is with the confirmed addicts.

I'll tell you one place that's working well, and that is the private sector, Jim Burke and his task force that he has. You may know about it. I'll tell the American people, but this man said, "I'll get you $1 million a day in pro bono advertising," something that's very hard for the government to do, and he went out and he did it. And people are beginning to educate through this program, teaching these kids you shouldn't use drugs.

So we're still in the fight. But I must tell you, I think legalization of narcotics or something of that nature in the face of the medical evidence would be totally counterproductive. And I oppose it and I'm going to stand up and continue to oppose it.

MODERATOR: Mr. Perot—Mr. Perot, one minute.

PEROT: Anytime you think you want to legalize drugs, go to a neonatal unit, if you can get in. They're between 100 and 200 percent capacity up and down the East Coast. And the reason is crack babies being born. The baby's in the hospital forty-two days; the typical cost to you and me is $125,000. Again and again and again the mother disappears in three days, and the child becomes a ward of the state because he's permanently and genetically damaged. Just look at those little children, and if anybody can even think about legalizing drugs, they've lost me.

Now let's look at priorities. You know, we went on the Libyan raid. You remember that one? Because we were worried to death that Qaddafi might be building up chemical weapons. We've got chemical warfare being conducted against our children on the streets in this country all day every day, and we don't have the will to stamp it out. And again, if I get up there, if you send me, we're going to have some blunt talks about this. And we're really going to get down to the trenches and say, is this one you want to talk about or fix, because talk won't do it, folks. There are guys that couldn't get a job third shift in a Dairy Queen driving BMWs and Mercedes selling drugs. And these old boys are not going to quit easy.

MODERATOR: Governor Clinton, one minute.

CLINTON: Like Mr. Perot, I have held crack babies in my arms, but I know more about this, I think, than anybody else up here, because I have a brother who is a recovering drug addict. I'm very proud of him, but I can tell you this: if drugs were legal, I don't think he'd be alive today. I am adamantly opposed to legalizing drugs. He is alive today because of the criminal justice system. That's a mistake.

What should we do? First, we ought to prevent more of this on the street. Thirty years ago there were three policemen for every crime; now there are three crimes for every policeman. We need 100,000 more police on the street. I have a plan for that. Secondly, we ought to have treatment on demand. Thirdly, we ought to have boot camp for first-time nonviolent offenders so they can get discipline and treatment and education and get reconnected to the community before they are severed and sent to prison, where they can learn how to be first-class criminals. There is a crime bill that lamentably was blocked from passage once again, mostly by Republicans in the United States Senate, which would have addressed some of these problems. That crime bill is going to be one of my highest priorities next January if I become president.

MODERATOR: Next question is to you, Mr. Perot; you have two minutes to answer it, and John will ask it.

QUESTION: Mr. Perot, racial division continues to tear apart our great cities, the last episode being this thing in Los Angeles. Why is this still happening in America, and what would you do to end it?

PEROT: This is a relevant question here tonight. First thing I'd do is, during political campaigns I would urge everybody to stop trying to split this country into fragments and appeal to the differences between us and then wonder why the melting pot all broke into pieces after November 3. We are all in this together. We ought to love one another, because united teams win and divided teams lose. If we can't love one another—and if you can't get fair—just recognize we're all stuck with one another because nobody's going anywhere, right? Now, that ought to get everybody back up to let's get along together and make it work.

Our diversity is a strength; we've turned it into a weakness. Now again, the White House is a bully pulpit. I think whoever is in the White House should just make it absolutely unconscionable and inexcusable, and if anybody's in the middle of a speech at a, you know, one of these conventions, I would expect the candidate to go out and lift him off the stage if he starts preaching hate. Because we don't have time for it. See, our differences are our strengths. We have got to pull together. In athletics we know it. See, divided teams lose; united teams win. We have got to unite and pull together, and there's nothing we can't do, but if we sit around blowing all this energy out the window, on a racial strife and hatred, we are stuck with a sure loser, because we have been a melting pot; we're becoming more and more of a melting pot; let's make it a strength, not a weakness.

MODERATOR: Governor Clinton, one minute.

CLINTON: I grew up in the segregated South, thankfully raised by a grandfather with almost no formal education but with a heart of gold, who taught me early that all people were equal in the eyes of God. I saw the winds of hatred divide people and keep the people of my state poorer than they would have been, spiritually and economically. And I've done everything I could in my public life to overcome racial divisions. We don't have a person to waste in this country. We are being murdered economically because we have too many dropouts, we have too many low-birth-weight babies, we have too many drug addicts as kids, we have too much violence, we are too divided by race, by income, by region. And I have devoted a major portion of this campaign to going across this country and looking for opportunities to go to white groups and African-American groups and Latino groups and Asian-American groups and say the same thing. If the American people cannot be brought together, we can't turn this country around. If we can come together, nothing, nothing, can stop us.

MODERATOR: Mr. President, one minute.

BUSH: Well, I think Governor Clinton is committed. I do think it's fair to note—he can rebut it—that Arkansas is one of the few states that doesn't have any civil rights legislation. I've tried to use the White House as the bully pulpit, speaking out against discrimination. We've passed two very forward-looking civil rights bills. It's not going to be all done by legislation, but I do think that you need to make an appeal every time you can to eliminate racial divisions and discrimination. And I'll keep on doing that and pointing to some legislative accomplishment to back it up.

I have to take ten seconds here at the end—the red light isn't on yet—to say to Ross Perot, please don't say to the D.E.A. agents on the street that we don't have the will to fight drugs. Please—I have watched these people. The same for our local law enforcement people. We're backing them up at every way we possibly can. But maybe you meant that some in the country don't have the will to fight it. But those that are out there on the front line, as you know—you've been a strong backer of law enforcement—really I just want to clear that up, have the will to fight it, and frankly, some of them are giving their lives.

MODERATOR: Time, Mr. President. All right, let's go now to another subject, the subject of health. The first question, for two minutes, is to President Bush, and John will ask it.

QUESTION: Mr. President, yesterday tens of thousands of people paraded past the White House to demonstrate their concern about the disease AIDS; a celebrated member of your commission, Magic Johnson, quit, saying that there was too much inaction. Where is this widespread feeling coming from that your administration is not doing enough about AIDS?

BUSH: It's coming from the political process. We have increased funding for AIDS, we've doubled it, on research and on every other aspect of it. My request for this year was $4.9 billion for AIDS, ten times as much per AIDS victims as per cancer victim. I think that we're showing the proper compassion and concern, so I can't tell you where it's coming from but I am very much concerned about AIDS and I believe that we've got the best researchers in the world out there at N.I.H. working the problem. We're funding them. I wish there was more money, but we're funding them far more than any time in the past, and we're going to keep on doing that.

I don't know, I was a little disappointed in Magic because he came to me and I said, "Now, if you see something we're not doing, get a hold of me, call me, let me know." He went to one meeting and then we heard that he was stepping down. So he's been replaced by Mary Fisher, who electrified the Republican convention by talking about the compassion and the concern that we feel. It was a beautiful moment, and I think she'll do a first-class job on that commission.

So I think the appeal is: yes, we care. And the other thing is part of AIDS—it's one of the few diseases where behavior matters. And I once called on somebody, "Well, change your behavior; if the behavior you're using is prone to cause AIDS, change the behavior." Next thing I know, one of these Act-Up groups is out saying, "Bush ought to change his behavior." You can't talk about it rationally; the extremes are hurting the AIDS cause. To go into a Catholic mass, in a beautiful cathedral in New York, under the cause of helping in AIDS, and start throwing condoms around in the mass—I'm sorry, I think it sets back the cause. We cannot move to the extreme. We've got to care, we've got to continue everything we can at the federal and the local level. Barbara, I think, is doing a superb job in destroying the myth about AIDS. And all of us are in this fight together, all of us care. Do not go to the extreme.

MODERATOR: One minute, Mr. Perot.

PEROT: First, I think Mary Fisher was a great choice; we're lucky to have her heading the commission. Secondly, I think one thing—if we're set to do the job, I would sit down with F.D.A., look exactly where we are. Then I would really focus on let's get these things out. If you're going to die, you don't have to go through this ten-year cycle the F.D.A. goes through on new drugs. I believe the people with AIDS are more than willing to take that risk, and we could be moving out to the human population a whole lot faster than we are on some of these new drugs. So I would think we could expedite the problem there.

Let me go back a minute to racial divisiveness. All-time low in our country was the Judge Thomas–Anita Hill hearings, and those senators ought to be hanging their heads in shame for what they did there. The second thing, how many times in your life do you get to talk to a whole country? Let me just say this to all of America. If you hate people, I don't want your vote. That's how strongly I feel about it.

MODERATOR: Governor Clinton, one minute.

CLINTON: Over 150,000 Americans have died of AIDS, well over a million and a quarter of Americans are HIV positive. We need to put one person in charge of the battle against AIDS, to cut across all the agencies that deal with it.

We need to accelerate the drug approval process. We need to fully fund the act named for that wonderful boy Ryan White to make sure we're doing everything we can on research and treatment.

And the president should lead a national effort to change behavior, to keep our children alive in the schools—responsible behavior to keep people alive. This is a matter of life and death. I've worked in my state to reduce teen pregnancy and illness among children, and I know it's tough.

The reason Magic Johnson resigned from the AIDS Commission is because the statement you heard tonight from Mr. Bush is the longest and best statement he's made about it in public.

I'm proud about—I'm proud of what we did at the Democratic convention, putting two HIV-positive people on the platform, and I'm proud of the leadership that I'm going to bring to this country in dealing with the AIDS crisis.

MODERATOR: New question for Mr. Perot. You have two minutes to answer, and Ann will ask it.

QUESTION: Mr. Perot, even if you've got what people say are the guts to take on changes in the most popular and the most sacred of the entitlements, Medicare, people say you haven't a prayer of actually getting anything passed in Washington. Since a president isn't a Lone Ranger, how in the world can you make some of those unpopular changes?

PEROT: Two ways. Number 1, if I get there it will be a very unusual and historical event, because the people, not the special interests, put me there. I will have a unique mandate. I have said again and again, and this really upsets the establishment in Washington, that we're going to inform the people in detail on the issues through an electronic town hall so that they really know what's going on. They will want to do what's good for our county. Now, all these fellows with $1,000 suits and alligator shoes, running up and down the halls of Congress, that make policy now—the lobbyists, the PAC guys, the foreign lobbyists, and what have you—they'll be over there in the Smithsonian, you know, because we're going to get rid of them, and the Congress will be listening to the people and the American people are willing to have fair, shared sacrifice.

They're not as stupid as Washington thinks they are. The American people are bright, intelligent, caring, loving people who want a great country for their children and grandchildren, and they will make those sacrifices. So I welcome that challenge, and just watch, because if the American people send me there, we'll get it done. Now, everybody will faint in Washington—they've never seen anything happen in that town. This is a town where the White House says, "Congress did it." Congress says, "The White House did it." And I'm sitting there, too. Well, who else could be around, you know. Then when they get off by themselves they say, "Nobody did it." And yet the cash register's empty, and it used to have our money—the taxpayer's money—in it, and we didn't get the results. No, we'll get it done. We'll have to—

MODERATOR: Governor, one minute.

CLINTON: Ross, that's a great speech, but it's not quite that simple. I mean, look at the facts. Both parties in Washington, the president and the Congress, have cut Medicare. The average senior citizen is spending a higher percentage of income on health care today than they were in 1965 before Medicare came in. The president's got another proposal that will require them to pay $400 a year more for the next five years, but if you don't have the guts to control costs by changing the insurance system, in taking on the bureaucracies and the regulation of health care in the private and public sector, you can't fix this problem. Costs will continue to spiral, and just remember this, folks, a lot of folks on Medicare are out there every day, making the choice between food and medicine—not poor enough for Medicare, Medicaid, not wealthy enough to buy their medicine. I've met them, people like Mary Annie and Edward Davis in Nashua, New Hampshire, all over this country—they cannot even buy medicine, so let's be careful. When we talk about cutting health care costs, let's start with the insurance companies and the people that are making a killing instead of making our people healthy.

MODERATOR: One minute, President Bush.

BUSH: Well, in the first place I'd like to clear up something, because every four years the Democrats go around and say, hey, Republicans are going to cut Social Security and Medicare. They started it again. I'm the president that stood up and said, don't mess with Social Security. And I'm not going to, and we haven't, and we are not going to go after the Social Security recipient. I have one difference with Mr. Perot on that, because I don't think we need to touch Social Security. What we do need to do, though, is control the growth of these mandatory programs, and Ross properly says, O.K., there's some pain in that. But Governor Clinton refuses to touch that. Simply refuses. So what we've go to do is control it—the growth, let it grow for inflation, let it grow for the amount of new people added, population, and then hold the line. And I believe that is the way you get the deficit down, not by the tax-and-spend program that we hear every four years, whether it's Mondale, Dukakis, whoever else it is. I just don't believe we ought to do that, so hold the line on these—on Social Security and put a cap on the growth of the mandatory program.

MODERATOR: New question. It is for Governor Clinton. Two-minute answer. Sandy will ask it.

QUESTION: Governor Clinton, Ann Compton has brought up Medicare. I remember in 1965 when Wilbur Mills of Arkansas, the chairman of Ways and Means, was pushing it through the Congress. The charge against it—was it socialized medicine. One, you never—

CLINTON: Mr. Bush made that charge.

QUESTION: Well, he served with him two years later in 1967, where I first met him. The second point, though, is that it is now skyrocketing out of control. People want it; we say it's going bonkers. Is not the Oregon plan applied to Medicaid rationing the proper way to go, even though the federal government last August ruled that it violated the Americans with Disabilities Act of 1990?

CLINTON: I thought the Oregon plan should at least have been allowed to be tried, because at least the people in Oregon were trying to do something. But let me go back to the main point, Sander. Mr. Bush is trying to run against Lyndon Johnson and Jimmy Carter and everybody in the world but me in this race. I have proposed a managed-competition plan for health care.

I will say again: you cannot control health care costs simply by cutting Medicare. Look what's happened. The federal government has cut Medicare and Medicaid in the last few years. States have cut Medicaid. We've done it in Arkansas under budget pressures. But what happens? More and more people get on the rolls as poverty increases. If you don't control the health care costs, tied to inflation and population growth, set by health care providers, not by the government. We provide for managed competition, not government models, in every state. And we control private and public health care costs. Now, just a few days ago a bipartisan commission of Republicans and Democrats—more Republicans than Democrats—said my plan will save the average family $1,200 a year more than the Bush plan will by the year 2000, $2.2 trillion in the next twelve years; $400 billion a year by the end of this decade. I've got a plan to control health care costs. But you can't just do it by cutting Medicare. You have to take on the insurance companies, the bureaucracies, and you have to have cost controls, yes. But keep in mind: we are spending 30 percent more on health care than any country in the world, any other country. And yet we have 35 million people uninsured. We have no preventive and primary care. The Oregon plan is a good start if the federal government's going to continue to abandon its responsibilities. I say if Germany can cover everybody and keep costs under inflation, if Hawaii can cover 98 percent of their people at lower health care costs than the rest of us, if Rochester, New York, with two-thirds the cost of the rest of us, America can do it, too. I'm tired of being told we can't. I say we can. We can do better and we must.

MODERATOR: President Bush, one—

BUSH: Well I don't have time in thirty seconds or whatever—minute to talk—

MODERATOR: One minute.

BUSH: About our health care reform plan. Oregon plan made some good sense. But it's easy to dismiss the concerns of the disabled. As president, I have to be sure that those waivers which we're approving all over the place are covered under the law. Maybe we can work it out.

But the Americans for Disabilities Act, speaking about sound and sensible civil rights legislation, was the most—foremost piece of legislation passed in modern times. And so we do have something more than a technical problem.

Governor Clinton clicked off the things—you've got to take on insurance companies and bureaucracies—he failed to take on somebody else: the malpractice-suit people. Those that bring these lawsuits—against these frivolous trial-lawyer lawsuits that are running the cost of medical care up by 25 to 50 billion.

And he refuses to put anything, controls, on these crazy lawsuits. If you want to help somebody, don't run the costs up by making doctors have to have five or six tests where one would do for fear of being sued. Or have somebody along the highway not stop to pick up a guy and help him because he's afraid a trial lawyer will come along and—and sue him.

We're suing each other too much and caring for each other too little.

MODERATOR: Mr. Perot, one minute.

PEROT: We've got the most expensive health care system in the world. It ranks behind fifteen other nations in—when we come to life expectancy and twenty-two other nations when we come to infant mortality. So we don't have the best.

Pretty simple, folks. If you're paying more, and you don't have the best, if all else fails, go copy the people who have the best who spend less, right? Well, we can do better than that.

Again, we've got plans lying all over the place in Washington—nobody ever implements them. Now, I'm back to Square 1: if you want to stop talking about it and do it, then I'll be glad to go up there, and we'll get it done.

But if you just want to keep the music going, just stay traditional this next time around, and this—four years from now you'll have everybody blaming everybody else for a bad health care system.

Talk is cheap, words are plentiful, deeds are precious. Let's get on with it.

MODERATOR: That was, in fact, the final question and answer. We're now going to move to closing statements. Each candidate will have up to two minutes. The order, remember, was determined by a drawing, and Mr. Perot, you were first.

Closing Statements

PEROT: Well, it's been a privilege to be able to talk to the American people tonight. I make no bones about it, I love this country; I love the principle it's founded on; I love the people here. I don't like to see the country's principles violated. I don't like to see the people in a deteriorating economy, in a deteriorating country, because our government has lost touch with the people. The people in Washington are good people. We just have a bad system. We've got to change the system. It's time to do it, because we have run up so much debt that time is no longer our friend. We've got to put our house in order.

When you go to bed tonight, look at your children. Think of their dreams, think of your dreams as a child, and ask yourself: "Isn't it time to stop talking about it? Isn't it time to stop creating images? Isn't it time to do it?" Aren't you sick of being treated like an unprogrammed robot? Every four years they send you all kinds of messages to tell you how to vote and then go back to business as usual. They told you at the tax and budget summit that if you agreed to a tax increase, we could balance the budget. They didn't tell you that that same year they increased spending $1.83 for every dollar we increased taxes. That's Washington in a nutshell right there. In the final analysis, I'm doing this for your children, when you look at them tonight.

There's another group that I feel very close to, and these are the men and women who fought on the battlefield; the children, the families of the ones who died; the people who left parts of their bodies over there.

I'd never ask you to do anything for me, but I owe you this, and I'm doing it for you. I can't tell you what it means to me at these rallies when I see you and you come up and the look in your eyes, and I know how you feel and you know how I feel.

And then I think of the older people who are retired. They grew up in the depression. They fought and won World War II. We owe you a debt we can never repay, and the greatest repayment I can ever give is to create the American dream for your children and grandchildren. I'll give it everything I have if you want me to do it.

MODERATOR: Governor Clinton, your closing statement.

CLINTON: I'd like to thank the people of St. Louis and Washington University, the Presidential Debate Commission, and all those who made this night possible, and I'd like to thank those of you who are watching. Most of all, I'd like to thank all of you who have touched me in some way over this last year, all the thousands of you whom I've seen. I'd like to thank the computer executives and the electronics executives in Silicon Valley, two-thirds of whom are Republicans who said they wanted to sign on to change to create a new America.

I'd like to thank the hundreds of executives who came to Chicago—a third of them Republicans—who said they wanted a change. I'd like to thank the people who started with Mr. Perot who've come on to help our campaign.

I'd like to thank all the folks around America that no one ever knows about: the woman who was holding the AIDS baby she adopted in Cedar Rapids, Iowa, who asked me to do something more for adoption; the woman who stopped along the road in Wisconsin and wept because her husband had lost his job after twenty-seven years; all of the people who are having a tough time and the people who are winning but who know how desperately we need to change.

This debate tonight has made crystal clear a challenge that is as old as America, the choice between hope and fear, change or more of the same, the courage to move into a new tomorrow or to listen to the crowd who says things could be worse.

Mr. Bush has said some very compelling things tonight that don't quite square with the record. He was president for three years before he proposed a health care plan that still hasn't been sent to Congress in total, three years before an economic plan, and he still hasn't sent to Congress in total, three years before an economic plan, and he still didn't say tonight that that tax bill he vetoed raised taxes only on the rich and gave the rest of you a break. But he vetoed it, anyway.

I offer a new direction. Invest in American jobs, American education, control health care costs, bring this country together again. I want the future of this country to be as bright and brilliant as its past, and it can be if we have the courage to change.

MODERATOR: President Bush, your closing statement.

BUSH: Let me tell you a little what it's like to be president. In the Oval Office, you can't predict what kind of crisis is going to come up. You have to make tough calls, you can't be on one hand with this way and one hand another. You can't take different positions on these difficult issues. And then you need a philosophical—I'd call it a philosophical underpinning. Mine for foreign affairs is democracy and freedom, and look at the dramatic changes around the world. The cold war is over, Soviet Union is no more, and we're working with a democratic country. Poland, Hungary, Czechoslovakia, the Baltics are free. Take a look at the Middle East. We had to stand up against a tyrant. The United States came together as we haven't in many, many years, and we kicked this man out of Kuwait. And in the process, as a result of that will and that decision and that toughness, we now have ancient enemies talking peace in the Middle East. Nobody would have dreamed it possible.

And I think the biggest dividend of making these tough calls is the fact that we are less afraid of nuclear war. Every parent out there has much less worry that their kids are going to be faced with nuclear holocaust. All this is good.

On the domestic side, what we must do is have change that empowers people, not change for the sake of change, tax and spend. We don't need to do that anymore. What we need to do is empower people. We need to invest and save. We need to do better in education. We need to do better in job training. We need to expand our exports, and they're going very, very well indeed, and we need to strengthen the American family.

I hope as president that I've earned your trust. I've admitted it when I make a mistake, but then I go on and help try to solve the problems. I hope I've earned your trust because a lot of being president is about trust and character. And I ask for your support for four more years to finish this job.

Thank you very, very much.

7

Debate Two
October 15, 1992

MODERATOR: Tonight's program is unlike any other presidential debate in history—we're making history now, and it's pretty exciting. An independent polling firm has selected an audience of 209 uncommitted voters from this area. The candidates will be asked questions by these voters on a topic of their choosing—anything they want to ask about. My job as moderator is to, you know, take care of the questioning, ask questions myself if I think there needs to be continuity and balance, and sometimes I might ask the candidates to respond to what another candidate may have said.

Now, the format has been agreed to by representatives of both the Republican and Democratic campaigns. And there is no subject matter that is restricted—anything goes, we can ask anything.

After the debate, the candidates will have an opportunity to make a closing statement. So, President Bush, I think you said it earlier, let's get it on.

BUSH: Let's go.

MODERATOR: And I think the first question is over here.

QUESTION: Yes, I'd like to direct my question to Mr. Perot. What will you do as president to open foreign markets to fair competition from American business and to stop unfair competition here at home from foreign countries so that we can bring jobs back to the United States?

PEROT: That's right at the top of my agenda. We've shipped millions s overseas, and we have a strange situation, because we have a process in Washington where after you've served for a while you cash in and become a foreign lobbyist, make $30,000 a month, then take a leave, work on presidential campaigns, make sure you got good contacts, and then go back out. Now, if you just want to get down to brass tacks, the first thing you ought to do is get all these folks who've got these one-way trade agreements that we've negotiated over the years and say, "Fellows, we'll take the same deal we gave you." And they'll gridlock right at that point, because, for example, we've got international competitors who simply could not unload their cars off the ships if they had to comply—you see, if it was a two-way street—just couldn't do it. We have got to stop sending jobs overseas.

To those of you in the audience who are business people, pretty simple: if you're paying twelve dollars, thirteen dollars, fourteen dollars an hour for factory workers and you can move your factory south of the border, pay a dollar an hour for labor, hire young—let's assume you've been in business for a long time and you've got a mature work force—pay a dollar an hour for your labor, have no health care—that's the most expensive single element in making a car—have no environmental controls, no pollution controls, and no retirement, and you don't care about anything but making money, there will be a giant sucking sound going south.

So we—if the people send me to Washington, the first thing I'll do is study that 2,000-page agreement and make sure it's a two-way street. One last part here—I decided I was dumb and didn't understand it, so I called the *Who's Who* of the folks who've been around it and I said, "Why won't everybody go South?" They say, "It'd be disruptive." I said, "For how long?" I finally got them up from twelve to fifteen years. And I said, "Well, how does it stop being disruptive?" And that is when their jobs come up from a dollar an hour to six dollars an hour, and ours go down to six dollars an hour, and then it's leveled again. But in the meantime, you've wrecked the country with these kinds of deals. We've got to cut it out.

MODERATOR: Thank you, Mr. Perot. I see that the president has stood up, so he must have something to say about this.

BUSH: Well, Carole, the thing that saved us in this global economic slowdown is in our exports. And what I'm trying to do is increase our exports. And if, indeed, all the jobs were going to move south because of lower wages, there are lower wages now, and they haven't done that. And so I have just negotiated with the president of Mexico, the North American Free Trade Agreement, and the prime minister of Canada, I might add, and I'm—I want to have more of these free trade agreements. Because export jobs are increasing far faster than any jobs that may have moved overseas; that's a scare tactic, because it's not that many. But anyone that's here, we want to have more jobs here, and the way to do that is to increase our exports.

Some believe in protection. I don't. I believe in free and fair trade, and that's the thing that saved us, and so I will keep on as president, trying to get a successful conclusion to the GATT round, the big Uruguay round of trade which will really open up markets for our— for our agriculture particularly—I want to continue to work after we get this NAFTA agreement ratified this coming year; I want to get one with Eastern Europe. I want to get one with Chile, and free and fair trade is the answer, not protection. And as I say we've had tough economic times, and it's exports that have saved us. Exports that have built.

MODERATOR: Governor Clinton.

CLINTON: I'd like to answer the question because I've actually been a governor for twelve years, so I've known a lot of people who've lost their jobs because of jobs moving overseas, and I know a lot of people whose plants have been strengthened by increasing exports. The trick is to expand our export base and to expand trade on terms that are fair to us. It is true that our exports to Mexico, for example, have gone up and our trade deficit's gone down. It's also true that just today a record high trade deficit was announced with Japan. So what is the answer?

Let me just mention three things very quickly.

Number 1, make sure that other countries are as open to our markets as our markets are to them. And if they're not, have measures on the books that don't take forever and a day to implement.

Number 2, change the tax code. There are more deductions in the tax code for shutting plants down and moving overseas than there are for modernizing plant and equipment here. Our competitors don't do that. Emphasize and subsidize modernizing plant and equipment here, not moving plants overseas.

Number 3, stop the federal government's program that now gives low-interest loans and job training funds to companies that will actually shut down and move to other countries, but we won't do the same thing for plants that stay here. So more trade but on fairer terms and favor investment in America.

MODERATOR: Thank you. I think we have a question over here.

QUESTION: This is for Governor Clinton. In the real world, that is, outside of Washington, D.C., compensation and achievement are based on goals defined and achieved. The deficit is my—my question is about the deficit. Would you define in specific dollar goals how much you would reduce the deficit in each of the four years of a Clinton administration and then enter into a legally binding contract with the American people that if you did not achieve those goals, that you would not seek a second term? Answer yes or no and then comment on your answer, please.

CLINTON: No, and here's why. And I'll tell you exactly why. Because the deficit now has been building up for twelve years. I'll tell you exactly what I think can be done. I think we can bring it down by 50 percent in four years and grow the economy. Now, I could get rid of it in four years in theory on the books now, but to do it, you'd have to raise taxes too much and cut benefits too much to people who need them. And it would even make the economy worse.

Mr. Perot will tell you, for example, that the expert he hired to analyze his plan said that it will bring the deficit down in five years, but it will make unemployment bad for four more years. So my view is, sir, you have to increase investment, grow the economy, and reduce the deficit by controlling health care costs, prudent reductions in defense, cuts in domestic programs, and asking the wealthiest Americans and foreign corporations to pay their fair share of taxes and investing in growing this economy.

I asked everybody to look at my economic ideas, and nine Nobel Prize winners and over 500 economists and hundreds of business people, including a lot of Republicans, said this is the way you got to go. If you don't grow the economy, you can't get it done. But I can't foresee all the things that will happen, and I don't think a president should be judged solely on the deficit. Let me also say we're having an election today. You'll have a shot at me in four years and you can vote me right out if you think I've done a lousy job. And I would welcome you to do that.

MODERATOR: Mr. President.

BUSH: Well, I, I got to—I'm a little confused here, because I don't see how you can grow the deficit down by raising people's taxes. You see, I don't think the American people are taxed too little. I think they're taxed too much. I went for one tax increase. And when I make a mistake I admit it. Say that wasn't the right thing to do.

Governor Clinton's program wants to tax more and spend more: $150 billion in new taxes, spend another 220. I don't believe that's the way to do it.

Here's some things that'll help. Give us a balanced budget amendment. He always talks about Arkansas having a balanced budget, and they do. But he has a balanced budget amendment—have to do it. I'd like the government to have that. And I think it would discipline not only the Congress, which needs it, but also the executive branch. I'd like to have what forty-three governors have—the line item veto, so if the Congress can't cut—we've got a reckless spending Congress— let the president have a shot at it by wiping out things that are pork barrel or something of that nature.

I'd like to—I proposed another one. Some sophisticates think it may be a little gimmicky. I think it's good. It's a check-off. It says to you as a taxpayer—say you're going to pay a tax of a thousand bucks or something. You can check 10 percent of that, if you want to, in one box, and that 10 percent, $100—or if you're paying 10,000, or whatever it is, a thousand dollars—check it off and make the government—make it lower the deficit by that amount. And if the Congress won't do it—if they can't get together and negotiate how to do that— then you'd have a sequester across the board. You'd exempt Social Security—I don't want to tax or touch Social Security. I'm the president that said, "Hey, don't mess with Social Security." And we haven't.

So I believe we need to control the growth of mandatory spending—back to this gentleman's question. That's the main growing thing in the economy, in the budget. The whole—the program that the president—two-thirds of the budget I, as president, never get to look at, never get to touch. We've got to control that growth to inflation and population increase. But not raise taxes on the American people now. I just don't believe that would stimulate any kind of growth at all.

MODERATOR: How about you, Mr. Perot?

PEROT: Well, we're $4 trillion in debt. We're going into debt an additional $1 billion—a little more than a billion dollars every working day of the year.

Now, the thing I love about it—I'm just a businessman. I was down in Texas taking care of business, tending to my family. This situation got so bad that I decided I'd better get into it. The American people asked me to get into it.

But I just find it fascinating that while we sit here tonight, we will go into debt an additional $50 billion—$50 million dollars in an hour and a half.

Now, it's not the Republicans' fault, of course. And it's not the Democrats' fault. And what I'm looking for is: who did it? Now, they're the two folks involved, so maybe if you put them together, they did it.

Now, the facts are: we have to fix it. We are leaving—I'm here tonight for these young people up there in the balcony from this college. When I was a young man, when I got out of the navy, I had multiple job offers. Young people with high grades can't get a job.

People—the eighteen- to twenty-four-year-old high school graduates ten years ago were making more than they are now. In other words, we were down to, 18 percent of them were making—ah, of the eighteen- to twenty-four-year-olds—were making less than $12,000. Now that's up to 40 percent. And what's happened in the meantime, the dollar's gone through the floor.

Now, whose fault is that? Not the Democrats, not the Republicans. Somewhere out there there's an extraterrestrial that's doing this to us, I guess. And everybody says they take responsibility. Somebody somewhere has to take responsibility for this.

Put it to you bluntly, American people. If you want me to be your president, we're going to face our problems, we'll deal with the problems, we'll solve our problems. We'll pay down our debt. We'll pass on the American dream to our children, and I will not leave our children a situation that they have today.

When I was a boy it took two generations to double the standard of living. Today, it will take twelve generations. Our children will not see the American dream because of this debt that somebody somewhere dropped on us.

MODERATOR: You're all wonderful speakers, and I know you have lots more to add, but I've talked to this audience, and they have lots of questions on other topics. Can we move to another topic, please? We have one up here, I think.

QUESTION: Yes, I'd like to address all the candidates with this question. The amount of time the candidates have spent on this campaign trashing their opponents' character and their programs is depressingly large. Why can't your discussions and proposals reflect the genuine complexity and the difficulty of the issues to try to build a consensus around the best aspects of all proposals?

MODERATOR: Who wants to take that one? Mr. Perot, you have an answer for everything, don't you? Go right ahead, sir.

PEROT: No, no, I don't have an answer for everything.

QUESTION: Why?

PEROT: As you all know, I've been buying thirty-minute segments to talk about issues. And tomorrow night, on NBC, from 10:30 to 11:00 Eastern we're going to talk about how you pay the debt down, so we're going to come right down to that one. See, we'll be on again Saturday night, eight to nine o'clock on ABC, so—

[All talking together.]

PEROT: Finally, I couldn't agree with you more. Couldn't agree with you more. And I have said again and again and again, let's get off mud wrestling; let's get off personalities, and let's talk about jobs, health care, crime, the things that concern the American people. I'm spending my money, not PAC money, not foreign money, my money, to take this message to the people.

MODERATOR: Thank you, Mr. Perot. So that seems directed; he

would say it's you gentlemen who have been doing that. Mr. Clinton, Governor Clinton, how do you—or President Bush, how would you like to respond?

BUSH: Well, in the first place, I believe that character is a part of being president. I think you have to look at it. I think that has to be a part of—of a candidate for president or being president.

In terms of programs, I've submitted, what, four different budgets to the United States Congress? In great detail. They're so heavy they'd give you, you know, a broken back. And everything in there says what I am for. Now I've come out with a new agenda for America's renewal, a plan that I believe really will help stimulate the growth of this economy. My record on world affairs is pretty well known, because I've been president for four years. So I feel I've been talking issues.

You know, nobody likes—likes "Who shot John?" but I think the first negative campaign run in this election was by Governor Clinton. And I'm not going to sit there and be a punching bag. I'm going to stand up and say, "Hey, listen, here's my side of it." But character is an important part of the equation.

The other night, Governor Clinton raised—I don't know if you saw the debate the other night? Suffered through that? Well, he raised the question of my father; it was a good line, well rehearsed and well delivered. But he raised the question of my father and said, "Well, your father, Prescott Bush, was against McCarthy. You should be ashamed of yourself. McCarthyism." I remember something my dad told me. I was eighteen years old, going to Penn Station to go into the navy, and he said, "Write your mother"—which I faithfully did—he said, "Serve your country"—my father was an honor, duty, and country man—and he said, "Tell the truth." And I've tried to do that in public life, all through it. And that says something about character.

My argument with Governor Clinton—you can call it mud wrestling, but I think it's fair to put in focus—is I am deeply troubled by someone who demonstrates and organizes demonstrations in a foreign land when his country's at war. Probably a lot of kids here disagree with me, but that's what I feel. That's what I feel passionately about. I'm thinking of Ross Perot's running mate sitting in the jail; how would he feel about it? But maybe that's generational, I don't know.

But the big argument I have with the governor on this is this taking different positions on different issues, trying to be one thing to one person here that's opposing the NAFTA agreement and then for it—what we call waffling. And I do think that you can't turn the White House into the Waffle House, you've got to say what you're for and you've got to—

MODERATOR: Mr. President, I'm getting time cues, and with all due respect, I'm sorry.

BUSH: Excuse me, I don't want to—I don't want to, no, go ahead, Carole.

MODERATOR: Governor Clinton.

BUSH: I get wound up because I feel strongly—

MODERATOR: Yes, you do.

CLINTON: Let me say, first of all, to you that I believe so strongly in the question you ask that I suggested this format tonight. I started doing these formats a year ago in New Hampshire. And I found that we had huge crowds, because all I did was let people ask questions and I tried to give very specific answers. I also had a program starting last year. I've been disturbed by the tone and the tenor of this campaign. Thank goodness the networks have a fact check so I don't have to just go blue in the face anymore. Mr. Bush said once again tonight I was going to have a $150 billion tax increase. When Mr. Quayle said that, all the networks said, "That's not true. He's got over $100 billion of tax cuts and incentives." So I'm not going to take up your time tonight.

But let me just say this. We'll have a debate in four days, and we can talk about this character thing again. But the *Washington Post* ran a long editorial today saying they couldn't believe Mr. Bush was making character an issue, and they said he was the greatest quote political chameleon for changing his positions of all times. Now, I don't want to get into it—

BUSH: Please don't judge me by the *Washington Post*.

CLINTON: Let's don't—let's don't—you don't have to believe that. I—here's my point. I'm not interested in his character. I want to change the character of the presidency. And I'm interested in what we can trust him to do and what you can trust me to do and what you can trust Mr. Perot to do for the next four years. So I think you're right, and I hope the rest of the night belongs to you.

MODERATOR: May I—I talked to this audience before you gentlemen came, and I asked them about how they felt about the tenor of the campaign. Would you like to let them know what you thought about that when I said are you pleased with how the campaign's been going?

Who wants to say why you don't like the way the campaign is going? We have a gentleman back here.

QUESTION: If I may, and forgive the notes here, but I'm shy on camera. The focus of my work as domestic mediator is meeting the needs of the children that I work with by way of their parents and not the wants of their parents. And I ask the three of you, how can we, as symbolically the children of the future president, expect the two of you, the three of you, to meet our needs: the needs in housing and,

and, and in crime, and you name it, as opposed to the wants of your political spin doctorism, and your political parties?

MODERATOR: So your question is—

QUESTION: Can we focus on the issues and not the personalities and the mud? I think there is, there is a need, if we can take a poll here, with the folks from Gallup, perhaps. I think there is a real need here to focus at this point on the needs.

MODERATOR: How do you respond? How do you gentlemen respond to—

PEROT: I agree with him.

MODERATOR: President Bush?

BUSH: Let's do it. Let's do it. Let's talk about programs for children.

QUESTION: One other thing?

BUSH: Yes?

QUESTION: Could we cross our hearts? It sounds silly here, but could we make a commitment? You know, we're not under oath at this point, but could you make a commitment to the citizens of the United States to meet our needs, and we have many, and not yours. Again, I have to repeat that, it's a real need, I think, that we all have.

BUSH: It depends on how you define it. I mean, I—I think, in general, let's talk about these—let's talk about these issues, let's talk about the programs, but in the presidency a lot goes into it. Caring is—goes into it; that's not particularly specific. Strength goes into it, that's not specific; standing up against aggression, that's not specific in terms of a program. This is what a president has to do. So I, in principle, I'll take your point and think we ought to discuss child care, or whatever else it is.

QUESTION: And you two?

CLINTON: Ross had his hand up.

MODERATOR: Yes, Ross.

PEROT: No hedges, no ifs, ands, and buts. I'll take the pledge. Because I know the American people want to talk about issues and not tabloid journalism. So I'll take the pledge and we'll stay on the issues.

Now, just for the record, I don't have any spin doctors. I don't have any speechwriters. Probably shows. I make those charts you see on television; even that shows.

But you don't have to wonder if it's me talking. What you see is what you get. And if you don't like it, you got two other choices, right?

CLINTON: Now, wait a minute. I want to say just one thing, now, Ross, in fairness. The ideas I express are mine. I've worked on these things for twelve years, and I'm the only person up here who hasn't been part of Washington in any way for the last twenty years. So I don't want the implication to be that somehow everything we say is just cooked up and put in our head by somebody else. I worked twelve years very hard as a governor on the real problems of real people. I'm just as sick as you are by having to wake up and figure out how to defend myself every day.

PEROT: I got—

CLINTON: I never thought I'd ever be involved in anything like this.

PEROT: May I finish?

MODERATOR: Yes, you may finish.

PEROT: Very briefly?

MODERATOR: Yes. Very briefly.

PEROT: I don't have any foreign money in my campaign. I don't have any foreign lobbyist on leave in my campaign. I don't have any PAC money in my campaign. I got five and a half million hardworking people who put me on the ballot. And I belong to them.

MODERATOR: O.K.

PEROT: And they want or are interested in what you're interested in. I take the pledge—I've already taken the pledge on cutting the deficit in half. I never got to say that. It's a great young group. Lead or leave. College students. Young people who don't want us to spend their money. I took the pledge we'd cut it out.

MODERATOR: Thank you. We have a question here.

QUESTION: Yes, I would like to get a response from all three gentlemen, and the question is: what are your plans to improve the physical infrastructure of this nation, which includes the water system, the sewer system, our transportation systems, etc. Thank you.

MODERATOR: The cities, who's going to fix the cities and how?

BUSH: Be glad to take a shot at it.

MODERATOR: Please.

BUSH: I'm not sure that—and I can understand if you haven't seen this, because there's been a lot of hue and cry—we passed, this year, the most farthest-looking transportation bill in the history of this country, since Eisenhower started the interstate highways, $150 billion for improving the infrastructure. That happened when I was president, and so I'm very proud of the way that came about, and I think it's a very, very good beginning. Like Mr. Perot, I am concerned about the deficits, and $150 billion is a lot of money, but it's awful hard to say we're going to go out and spend more money when we're trying to get the deficit down. But I would cite that as a major accomplishment.

We hear all the negatives. When you're president you expect this, everybody's running against the incumbent, they can do better, everyone knows that. But here's something that we can take great pride in, because it really does get to what you're talking about. Our home initiative, our home ownership initiative—hope it'll pass the Congress—is a good start for having people own their own homes instead of living in these deadly tenements. Our enterprise zones that we hear a lot of lip service about in Congress would bring jobs into the inner city. There's a good program, and I need the help of everybody across this country to get it passed in a substantial way by the Congress.

When we went out to South Central in Los Angeles—some of you may remember the riots there—I went out there, I went to a boys' club and every one of them—the boys' club leaders, the ministers, all of them were saying, "Pass enterprise zones." We go back to Washington and very difficult to get it through the Congress. But there's going to be a new Congress. No one likes gridlock, there's going to be a new Congress, because the old one—I don't want to get this man mad at me, but there was a post office scandal and a bank scandal. You're going to have a lot of new members of Congress, and then you can sit down and say, "Help me do what we should for the cities, help me pass these programs."

MODERATOR: Mr. President, aren't you threatening to veto the bill, the Urban Aid Bill, that included enterprise zones?

BUSH: Sure, but the problem is, you get so many things included in a great big bill that you have to look at the overall good. That's the problem with our system; if you had a line item veto you could knock out the pork, you could knock out the tax increases, and you could do what the people want, and that is create enterprise zones.

MODERATOR: Governor Clinton, you're chomping at the bit.

CLINTON: That bill pays for these urban enterprise zones by asking the wealthiest Americans to pay a little more, and that's why he wants to veto it. Just like you vetoed an earlier bill this year; this is not mud-slinging, this is fact-slinging. A bill early this year—this is facts—that would have given investment tax credits and other incentives to reinvest in our cities, in our country, but it asked the wealthiest Americans to pay a little more.

Mr. Perot wants to do the same thing. I agree with him. I mean, we agree with that. Let me tell you specifically what my plan does. My plan would dedicate $20 billion a year in each of the next four years for investments and new transportation, communications, environmental cleanups, and new technologies for the twenty-first century, and we would target it especially in areas that have been either depressed or which have lost a lot of defense-related jobs. There are 200,000 people in California, for example, who've lost their defense-related jobs. They ought to be engaged in making high-speed rail; they ought to be engaged in breaking ground in other technologies, doing waste recycling, clean water technology, and things of that kind. We can create millions of jobs in these new technologies more than we're going to lose in defense if we target it, but we're investing a much smaller percentage of our income in the things you just asked about than all of our major competitors, and our wealth growth is going down as a result of this, it's making the country poorer, which is why I answered the gentleman the way I did before. We have to both bring down the deficit and get our economy going through these kinds of investments in order to get the kind of wealth and jobs and incomes we need in America.

MODERATOR: Mr. Perot, what about your plans for the cities? You want to tackle the economy and the deficit first—

PEROT: First, you've got to have money to pay for these things. So, you've got to create jobs. There are all kinds of ways to create jobs in the inner city.

Now, I'm not a politician, but I think I could go to Washington in a week and get everybody holding hands and get this bill signed. Because I talked to the Democratic leaders and they want it; I talked to Republican leaders and they want it. But since they are bred from childhood to fight with one another rather than get results—you know, I would be glad to drop out and spend a little time and see if we couldn't build some bridges. Now, results is what counts. The president can't order Congress around. Congress can't order the president around. That's not bad for a guy that's never been there, right? But you have to work together.

Now, I have talked to the chairmen of the committees that want this. They're Democrats. The president wants it, but we can't get it, because we sit here in gridlock because it's a campaign year.

We didn't fund a lot of other things this year, like the savings-and-loan mess. That's another story we're getting to pay a big price for right after the election.

The facts are, though—the facts are, the American people are hurting. These people are hurting in the inner cities. We're shipping the low-paying jobs—quote low-paying jobs—overseas. What are low-paying jobs? Textiles, shoes, things like that we say are yesterday's industries. They're tomorrow's industries in the inner cities.

Let me say in my case, if I'm out of work, I'll cut grass tomorrow to take care of my family. I'll be happy to make shoes, I'll be happy to make clothing, I'll make sausage. You just give me a job. Put those jobs in the inner cities instead of doing diplomatic deals and shipping them to China, where prison labor does the work.

MODERATOR: Mr. Perot, everybody thought you won the first debate, because you were plain-speaking and you made it sound oh, so simple: we'll just do it. What makes you think that you're going to be able to get the Democrats and Republicans together any better than these guys?

PEROT: If you asked me if I could fly a fighter plane or launch—or be an astronaut, I can't. I spent my life creating jobs—it's something I know how to do. And very simply, in the inner city they're starved. See, small business is the way to jump-start the inner city, not—

MODERATOR: Are you answering my question?

PEROT: You want jobs in the inner city? Do you want jobs in the inner city, is that your question?

MODERATOR: No, I want you to tell me how you're going to be able to get the Republicans and Democrats in Congress—

PEROT: Oh, I'm sorry.

MODERATOR: —to work together better than these two gentlemen.

PEROT: Well, I've listened to both sides, and if they would talk to one another instead of throwing rocks, I think we could get a lot done. And among other things, I would say, O.K., over here in this Senate committee, to the chairman who is anxious to get this bill passed—the president is anxious—I'd say, rather than just yelling at one another, why don't we find out where we're apart, try to get together, get the bill passed, and give the people the benefits and not play party politics right now?

And I think the press would follow that so closely that probably they would get it done. That's the way I would do it. I doubt if they'll give me the chance, but I will drop everything and go work on it.

QUESTION: O.K. I have a question here. My question was originally for Governor Clinton, but I think I would welcome a response from all three candidates. As you are aware, crime is rampant in our cities. And in the Richmond area, and I'm sure it's happening elsewhere, twelve-year-olds are carrying guns to school. And I'm sure when our Founding Fathers wrote the Constitution they did not mean for the right to bear arms to apply to twelve-year-olds. So I'm asking: where do you stand on gun control and what do you plan to do about it?

MODERATOR: Governor Clinton.

CLINTON: I support the right to keep and bear arms. I live in a state where over half the adults have hunting or fishing licenses or both. But I believe we have to have some way of checking handguns before they're sold—to check the criminal history, the mental health history, and the age of people who are buying them. Therefore I support the Brady bill, which would impose a national waiting period unless and until a state did what only Virginia has done now, which is to automate its records. Once you automate your records, then you don't have to have a waiting period. But at least you can check. I also think we should have, frankly, restrictions on assault weapons, whose only purpose is to kill. We need to give the police a fighting chance in our urban areas where the gangs are building up.

The third thing I would say doesn't bear directly on gun control, but it's very important. We need more police on the street. There is a crime bill which would put more police on the street which was killed for this session by a filibuster in the Senate, mostly by Republican senators. And I think it's a shame it didn't pass. I think it should be made the law, but it had the Brady bill in it—the waiting period.

I also believe that we should offer college scholarships to people who will agree to work them off as police officers and I think, as we reduce our military forces, we should let people earn military retirement by coming out and working as police officers. There—thirty years ago there were three police officers on the street for every crime. Today there are three crimes for every police officer. In the communities which have had real success putting police officers near schools where kids carry weapons, to get the weapons out of the schools, or on the same blocks, you've seen crime go down. In Houston, there's been a 15 percent drop in the crime rate in the last year because of the work the mayor did there in increasing the police force. So I know it can work. I've seen it happen.

MODERATOR: Thank you. President Bush.

BUSH: I think you put your finger on a major problem. I talk about strengthening the American family, and it's very hard to strengthen the family if people are scared to walk down to the corner store and you know, send their kid down to get a loaf of bread, it's very hard. I have been fighting for very strong anticrime legislation. Habeas corpus reform so you don't have these endless appeals, so when somebody gets sentenced, hey, this is for real. I've been fighting for changes in the exclusionary rule, so if an honest cop stops somebody and makes a technical mistake, the criminal doesn't—doesn't go away. I'll probably get into a fight in this room with some, but I happen to think that we need stronger death penalties for those that kill police officers. Virginia's in the lead in this, as Governor Clinton properly said, on this identification system for firearms. I am not for national registration of firearms.

Some of the states that have the toughest antigun laws have the highest levels of crime. I am for the Right, as the governor says; I'm a sportsman, and I don't think you ought to eliminate all kinds of weapons. But my—I was not for the bill that he was talking about, because it was not tough enough on the criminal. I'm very pleased that the fraternal order of police in Little Rock, Arkansas, endorsed me, because I think they see I'm trying to strengthen the anticrime legislation. We've got more money going out for local police than—than any previous administration.

So we've got to get it under control, and there is one last thing—point I'd make. Drugs. We have got to win our national strategy against drugs, the fight against drugs. And we're making some progress, doing a little better on interdiction. We're not doing as well amongst the—amongst the—the people that get to be habitual drug users.

The good news is, and I think it's true in Richmond, teenage use is down of cocaine substantially, 60 percent in the last couple of years. So we're making progress, but until we get that one done, we're not going to solve the neighborhood crime problem.

MODERATOR: Mr. Perot, there are young black males in America dying at unprecedented rates.

PEROT: I'd just like to comment on this.

MODERATOR: Yes, I'm getting to—

PEROT: Oh, you're going to elaborate, O.K. Excuse me.

MODERATOR: —the fact that homicide is the leading cause of death among young black males fifteen to twenty-four years old. What are you going to do to get the guns off the street?

PEROT: On any program, and this includes crime, you'll find we have all kinds of great plans lying around that never get enacted into law and implemented. I don't care what it is—competitiveness, health care, crime, you name it—the Brady bill, I agree that it's a tentative step in the right direction, but it won't fix it. So why pass a law that won't fix it? Now, what it really boils down to is: can you live? We have become so preoccupied with the rights of the criminal that we've forgotten the rights of the innocent. And in our country we have evolved to a point where we've put millions of innocent people in jail, because you go to the poor neighborhoods, and they put bars on their windows and bars on their doors and put themselves in jail to protect the things that they're acquired legitimately. That's where we are.

We have got to become more concerned about people who play by the rules and get the balance we require. This is going to take first building a consensus in grassroots America; right from the bottom up, the American people have got to say they want it. And at that point, we can pick from a variety of plans and develop new plans, and the way you get things done is bury yourselves in a room with one another, put together the best program, take it to the American people, use the electronic town hall—the kind of thing you're doing here tonight—build a consensus, and then do it and then go on to the next one. But don't just sit here slow dancing for four years doing nothing.

MODERATOR: Thank you, thank you, Mr. Perot. We have a question up here?

QUESTION: Please state your position on term limits, and if you are in favor of them, how will you get them enacted?

BUSH: Any order? I'll be glad to respond. I strongly support term limits for members of the United States Congress. I believe it would return the government closer to the people, in a way that Ross Perot is talking about. The president's terms are limited to two—a total of eight years; what's wrong with limiting the terms of members of Congress to twelve? Congress has gotten kind of institutionalized; for thirty-eight years one party has controlled the House of Representatives, and the result, a sorry little post office that can't—you know, can't do anything right and a bank that has more overdrafts than all the Chase Bank and Citibank put together. We've got to do something about it, and I think you get a certain arrogance—bureaucratic arrogance—if people stay there too long. And so I favor—strongly favor—term limits.

And how to get them passed? Send us some people that'll pass the idea. And I think you will. I think the American people want it now. Every place I go I talk about it, and I think they want it done. Actually, you'd have to have some amendments to the Constitution because of the way the Constitution reads.

MODERATOR: Thank you. Governor Clinton?

CLINTON: I know they're popular, but I'm against them. I'll tell you why. I believe, Number 1, it would pose a real problem for a lot of smaller states in the Congress, would have enough trouble now making sure their interests are heard. Number 2, I think it would increase the influence of unpaid unelected staff members in the Congress who have too much influence already. I want to cut the size of the congressional staffs, but I think you're going to have too much influence there with people who were never elected who have lots of expertise. Number 3, if the people really have a mind to change, they can. You're going to have 120 to 150 new members of Congress.

Now, let me tell you what I favor instead; I favor strict controls on how much you can spend running for Congress. Strict limits on political action committees. Requirements that people running for Congress appear in open public debates like we're doing now. If you did that, you could take away the incumbent's advantage, because challengers like me would have a chance to run against incumbents like him for House races and Senate races, and then the voters could make up their own minds without being subject to an unfair fight. So that's how I feel about it. I think if we have the right kind of campaign reform, we'd get the changes you want.

MODERATOR: Mr. Perot, would you like to address term limitations?

PEROT: Yes. Let me do it, first, on a personal level. If the American people send me up to do this job, I intend to be there one term. I do not intend to spend one minute of one day thinking about reelection.

And as a matter of principle, and my situation is unique and I understand it, I would take absolutely no compensation. I'd go as their servant.

Now, I have set as strong an example as I can, and at that point when we sit down over at Capitol Hill, tomorrow night, I'm going to be talking about government reform. It's a long subject; you wouldn't let me finish tonight. You want to hear it, you can get it tomorrow night.

[All talking together]

But the point is, you'll hear it tomorrow night. But we have got to reform government. If you put term limits in, and don't reform government, you won't get the benefit you thought. It takes both. So we need to do the reform and the term limits, and after we reform it, it won't be a lifetime career opportunity. Good people will go serve and then go back to their homes. And not become foreign lobbyists and cash in at $30,000 bucks a month and then take time off to run some president's campaign. This, they're all nice people, they're just in a bad system. I don't think there are any villains but, boy, is the system rotten.

MODERATOR: Thank you very much. We have a question over here.

QUESTION: I'd like to ask Governor Clinton: do you attribute the rising cost of health care to the medical profession itself? Or do you think the problem lies elsewhere, and what specific proposals do you have to tackle this problem?

CLINTON: I've had more people talk to me about their health care problems, I guess, than anything else. All across America, you know, people that lost their jobs, lost their businesses, had to give up their jobs because of sick children.

So let me try to answer you in this way. Let's start with a premise. We spend 30 percent more of our income than any nation on earth on health care. And yet we insure fewer people. We have 35 million people without any insurance at all. I see them all the time. A hundred thousand Americans a month have lost their health insurance just in the last four years. So if you analyze where we're out of line with other countries, you come up with the following conclusions. Number 1, we spend at least $60 billion a year on insurance, administrative costs, bureaucracy, and government regulation that wouldn't be spent in any other nation. So we have to have, in my judgment, a drastic simplification of the basic health insurance policies of this country. Be very comprehensive for everybody.

Employers would cover their employees. Government would cover the unemployed. Number 2, I think you have to take on specifically the insurance companies and require them to make some significant change in the way they rate people into big community pools. I think you have to tell the pharmaceutical companies they can't keep raising drug prices at three times the rate of inflation. I think you have to take on medical fraud. I think you have to help doctors stop practicing defensive medicine. I've recommended that our doctors be given a set of national practice guidelines and that if they follow those guidelines, that raises the presumption that they didn't do anything wrong. I think you have to have a system of primary and preventive clinics in our inner cities and our rural areas so people can have access to health care.

The key is to control the cost and maintain the quality. To do that you need a system of managed competition where all of us are covered in big groups and we can choose our doctors and our hospitals across a wide range, but there is an incentive to control costs, and I think there has to be—I think Mr. Perot and I agree on this, there has to be a national commission of health care providers and health care consumers that set ceilings to keep health costs in line with inflation plus population growth.

Now, let me say, some people say we can't do this, but Hawaii does it. They cover 98 percent of their people and their insurance premiums are much cheaper than the rest of America. And so does Rochester, New York. They now have a plan to cover everybody and their premiums are two-thirds of the rest of the country. This is very important. It's a big human problem and a devastating economic problem for America. And I'm going to send a plan to do this within the first hundred days of my presidency. It's terribly important.

MODERATOR: Thank you. Sorry to cut you short, but President Bush, health care reform.

BUSH: Can I—I just have to say something. I don't want a stampede—Ross was very articulate—across the country. I don't want anybody to stampede to cut the president's salary off altogether. Barbara's sitting over here and I—I—but what I have proposed, 10 percent cut, downsize the government and we can get that done. She asked the question, I think, is whether the health care profession was to blame.

No. One thing to blame is these malpractice lawsuits. They are breaking the system. It costs $20 to $25 billion a year, and I want to see those outrageous claims capped. Doctors don't dare to deliver babies sometimes because they're afraid that somebody's going to sue them. People don't dare—medical practitioners—to help somebody along the highway that are hurt, because they're afraid that some lawyer's going to come along and get a big lawsuit. So you can't blame the practitioners for the health problem.

And my program is this. Keep the government as far out of it as possible. Make insurance available to the poorest of the poor through vouchers, next range in the income bracket through—through tax credits. And get on about the business of pooling insurance. A great big company can buy—Ross got a good-size company, been very successful. He can buy insurance cheaper than mom and pop store on the corner. But if those mom and pop stores all get together and pool, they too can bring the cost of insurance down. So I want to keep the quality of health care—that means keep government out of it. I want to do—I don't like this idea of these boards. It all sounds to me like you're going to have some government setting price. I want competition, and I want to pool the insurance and take care of it that way.

And have—here's another point. I think medical care should go with the person. If you leave a business, I think your insurance should go with you to some other business. You shouldn't be worrying if you get a new job as to whether that's going to—and part of our plan is to make it what they call portable. A big word, but that means, if you're working for the Jones company, you go to the Smith company, your insurance goes with you. And I think it's a good program. I'm really excited about getting it done, too.

MODERATOR: Mr. Perot.

PEROT: We have the most expensive health care system in the world; 12 percent of our gross national product goes to health care. Our industrial competitors who are beating us in competition spend less and have better health care. Japan spends a little over 6 percent of its gross national product; Germany spends 8 percent. It's fascinating. You bought a front-row box seat, and you're not happy with your health care, and you're saying we've got bad health care but very expensive health care. Folks, here's why. Go home and look in the mirror. You own this country, but you have no voice in it the way it's organized now. And if you want to have a high-risk experience comparable to bungee jumping, go into Congress sometime when they're working on this kind of legislation, when the lobbyists are running up and down the halls. Wear your safety-toe shoes when you go.

And as a private citizen, believe me, you are looked on as a major nuisance. The facts are, you now have a government that comes at you, and you're supposed to have a government that comes from you. Now, there are all kinds of good ideas, brilliant ideas, terrific ideas on health care. None of them ever get implemented, because—let me give you an example. A senator runs every six years; he's got to raise 20,000 bucks a week to have enough money to run. Who's he going to listen to, us? Or the folks running up and down the aisles with money—the lobbyists, the PAC money? He listens to them. Who do they represent? The health care industry. Not us.

Now, you've got to have a government that comes from you again;

you've got to reassert your ownership in this country, and you've got to completely reform our government. And at that point they'll just be like apples falling out of a tree—the programs will be good because the elected officials will be listening to—I said the other night I was all ears? And I would listen to any good idea? I think we ought to do plastic surgery on a lot of these guys so that they are all ears, too, and listen to you. Then you get what you want, and shouldn't you? You pay for it, why shouldn't you get what you want as opposed to what some lobbyist who cuts a deal, writes the little piece in the law, and it goes through. That's the way the game's played now. Until you change it, you're going to be unhappy.

MODERATOR: Thank you. Governor Clinton, you wanted one brief point—

CLINTON: One brief point. We have elections so people can make decisions about this. The point I want to make to you is a bipartisan commission reviewed my plan and the Bush plan and concluded—there were as many Republicans as Democratic health care experts on it—they concluded that my plan would cover everybody, and his would leave two—27 million behind by the year 2000.

And that my plan in the next twelve years would save $2.2 trillion in public and private money to reinvest in this economy. And the average family would save $1,200 a year under the plan that I offered without any erosion in the quality of health care.

So I ask you to look at that. And you have to vote for somebody with a plan. That's what you have elections for. If people say, well, he got elected to do this, and then the Congress says, O.K., I'm going to do it—that's what the election was about.

MODERATOR: Brief, Governor Clinton, thank you. We have a question right here.

QUESTION: Yes. How has the national debt personally affected each of your lives? And if it hasn't, how can you honestly find a cure for the economic problems of the common people if you have no experience in what's ailing them?

PEROT: May I, may I answer that?

MODERATOR: Well, Mr. Perot, yes, of course.

PEROT: Who do you want to start with? Go right ahead.

QUESTION: Each of you—

PEROT: It caused me to disrupt my private life and my business to get involved in this activity. That's how much I care about it. And believe me, if you knew my family and if you knew the private life I have, you would agree in a minute that that's a whole lot more fun than getting involved in politics.

But I became—I have lived the American dream. I came from a very modest background; nobody's been luckier than I've been. All the way across the spectrum and the greatest riches of all are my wife and children. Just as it's true of any family.

But I want all the children—I want these young people up here to be able to start with nothing but an idea like I did and build a business. But they've got to have a strong basic economy. And if you're in debt, you're—it's like having a ball and chain around you.

I'm doing—I just figure, as lucky as I've been, I owe it to them. And I owe it to the future generations. And on a very personal basis, I owe it to my children and grandchildren.

MODERATOR: Thank you, Mr. Perot. Mr. President.

BUSH: Well, I think the national debt affects everybody. Obviously it has a lot to do with interest rates. It has—

MODERATOR: She's saying you personally.

QUESTION: On a personal basis, how has it affected you—has it affected you personally?

BUSH: Well, I'm sure it has. I love my grandchildren and I want to think that—

QUESTION: How?

BUSH: I want to think that they're going to be able to afford an education. I think that that's an important part of being a parent. I—if the question—if you're—maybe I get it wrong. Are you suggesting that if somebody has means that the national debt doesn't affect them?

QUESTION: Well, what I'm saying—

BUSH: I'm not sure I get it. Help me with the question, and I'll try to answer it.

QUESTION: Well, I've had friends that have been laid off from jobs. I know people who cannot afford to pay the mortgage on their homes, their car payment. I have personal problems with the national debt. But how has it affected you? And if you have no experience in it, how can you help us if you don't know what we're feeling?

MODERATOR: I think she means more the recession, the economic problems today the country faces, rather than the deficit.

BUSH: Well, listen, you ought to—you ought to be in the White House for a day and hear what I hear and see what I see and read the mail I read and touch the people that I touch from time to time. I was in the Lomax A.M.E. Church. It's a black church just outside of Washington, D.C. And I read in the—in the bulletin about teenage pregnancies, about the difficulty that families are having to meet ends—to make ends meet. I talk to parents. I mean, you've got to care. Everybody cares if people aren't doing well. But I don't think—I don't think it's fair to say, You haven't had cancer, therefore you don't know what it's like. I don't think it's fair to say, you know, whatever it is, that if you haven't been hit by it personally—but everybody's affected by the debt because of the tremendous interest that goes into paying on that debt, everything's more expensive. Everything comes out of your pocket and my pocket.

So it's, it's sad, but I think in terms of the recession, of course you feel it when you're president of the United States. And that's why I'm trying to do something about it by stimulating the exports, investing more, better education system. Thank you. I'm glad to clarify it.

MODERATOR: Governor Clinton.

CLINTON: Tell me how it's affected you again. You know people who've lost their jobs and lost their homes.

QUESTION: Well, yeah, uh-huh.

CLINTON: Well, I've been governor of a small state for twelve years. I'll tell you how it's affected me. Every year, Congress and the president sign laws that makes us—make us do more things and give us less money to do it with. I see people in my state, middle-class people, their taxes have gone up in Washington and their services have gone down while the wealthy have gotten tax cuts. I have seen what's happened in this last four years when in my state, when people lose their jobs, there's a good chance I'll know them by their names. When a factory closes, I know the people who ran it. When the businesses go bankrupt, I know them. And I've been out here for thirteen months meeting in meetings just like this ever since October with people like you all over America, people that have lost their jobs, lost their livelihood, lost their health insurance.

What I want you to understand is: the national debt is not the only cause of that. It is because America has not invested in its people. It is because we have not grown. It is because we've had twelve years of trickle-down economics.

We've gone from first to twelfth in the world in wages. We've had four years where we've produced no private-sector jobs. Most people are working harder for less money than they were making ten years ago. It is because we are in the grip of a failed economic theory. And this decision you're about to make better be about what kind of economic theory you want. Not just people saying I want to go fix it but what are we going to do. What I think we have to do is invest in American jobs, American education, control American health care costs, and bring the American people together again.

MODERATOR: Thank you, Governor Clinton. We are a little more than halfway through this program, and I'm glad that we're getting the diversity of questions that we are, and I don't want to forget these folks in the wings over here. So let's go over here. Do you have a question?

QUESTION: Yes, I do. My name is Vin Smith. I work in the financial field counseling retirees, and I'm personally concerned about three major areas. One is the Social Security Administration where the trust fund is projected to be insolvent by the year 2036, and we funded the trust fund with IOUs in the form of treasury bonds. The pension guarantee fund, which backs up our private retirement plans for retirees, is projected to be bankrupt by the year 2026, not to mention the cutbacks by private companies, and Medicare is projected to be bankrupt, maybe as soon as 1997. And I would like from each of you a specific response as to what you intend to do for retirees relative to these issues. Not generalities but specifics, because I think they're very disturbing issues.

MODERATOR: President Bush, may we start with you?

BUSH: Well, the Social Security—you're an expert, and I can, I'm sure, learn from you the details of the pension guarantee fund and the Social Security fund. The Social Security system was fixed about five years, and I think it's projected out to be sound beyond that. So at least we have time to work with it.

But on all of these things, a sound economy is the only way to get it going. Growth in the economy is going to add to these—add to the overall prosperity and wealth. I can't give you a specific answer on pension guarantee funds; all I know is that we have firm government credit to guarantee the pensions, and that is very important. But it's—it's the full faith and credit of the United States in space—in spite of our difficulties is still pretty good. It's still the most respected credit. So I would simply say, as these dates get close, you're going to have to reorganize and refix as we did with the Social Security fund. And I think that's the only answer, but the most—more immediate answer is to do what this lady was suggesting we do, and that is to get this deficit down and get on without adding to the woes and then restructure. One thing I've called for has been stymied, and I'll keep on working for it, is a whole financial reform legislation. It is absolutely essential in terms of bringing our banking system and credit system into the new age instead of having it living back in the Dark Ages. And it's a big fight, and I don't want to give my friend Ross another shot at me here, but I am fighting with the Congress to get this through. And you can't just go up and say, "I'm going to fix it." You've got some pretty strong-willed guys up there that argue with you. But that's what the election's about. I agree with the governor. That's what the election is about. And sound fiscal policy is the best answer I think to the—all the three problems you mentioned.

MODERATOR: Thank you. Mr. Perot.

PEROT: Yes, on the broad issue here. When you're trying to solve a problem, you get the best plans. You have a raging debate about those plans. Then out of that debate with leadership comes consensus.

Then if the plans are huge and complex, like health care, I would urge you to implement pilot programs. Like the old carpenter who says: measure twice and cut once. Let's make sure this thing's as good as we all think it is at the end of the meeting. Then finally our government passes laws and freezes the plan in concrete. Anybody that's ever built a successful business will tell you, you optimize, optimize, optimize after you put something into effect. The reason Medicare and Medicaid are a mess is we froze them. Everybody knows how to fix them. There are people all over the federal government, if they could just touch it with a screwdriver, could fix it.

Now back over here. See, we've got a $4 trillion debt and only in America would you have 2.8 trillion of it, or 70 percent of it, financed five years or less. Now, that's another thing for you to think about when you go home tonight. You don't finance long-term debt with short-term money. Why did our government do it? To get the interest rates down. A 1 percent increase in the interest rates, and that $2.8 trillion is $28 billion a year. Now, when you look at what Germany pays for money and what we don't pay for money, you realize it's quite a spread, right. And you realize this is a temporary thing, and there's going to be another sucking sound that runs our deficit through the roof. You know, and everybody's ducking it, so I'm going to say it, that we are not letting that surplus stay in the bank. We are not investing that surplus like a pension fund. We are spending that surplus to make the deficit look smaller to you than it really is.

Now, that'd put you in jail in corporate America if you kept books that way, but in government it's just kind of the way things are. That's because it comes at you, not from you. Now then, that money needs to be—they don't even pay interest on it, they just write a note for the interest.

MODERATOR: Mr. Perot, can you wrap it up?

PEROT: So now then, that's important. See, do you want to fix the problem or sound bite it? I understand the importance of time but— see here's how we get to this mess we're in. This is just 1 of 1,000—

MODERATOR: But we've got to be fair.

PEROT: Now then, to nail it, there's one way out. A growing expanding job base, a growing expanding job base to generate the funds and the tax revenues to pay off the mess and rebuild America. We got a double hit. If we're $4 trillion down, we should have everything perfect, but we don't. We've got to pay it off and build money to renew it—spend money to renew it, and that's going to take a growing expanding job base. That is Priority 1 in this country. Put everybody that's breathing to work. And I'd love to be out of workers and have to import them like some of our international competitors.

MODERATOR: Mr. Perot, I'm sorry I'm going to—

PEROT: Sorry.

MODERATOR: And I don't want to sound bite you, but we are trying to be fair to everyone.

PEROT: O.K. No, absolutely. I apologize.

MODERATOR: All right. Governor Clinton.

CLINTON: I think I remember the question. And let me say first of all—I want to answer your specific question, but first of all, we all agree that there should be a growing economy. What you have to decide is who's got the best economic plan. And we all have ideas out there, and Mr. Bush has a record. So I don't want you to read my lips, and I sure don't want you to read his. I just—I do hope you will read our plans. Now, specifically—

BUSH: That's the first rule.

CLINTON: Specifically, one: on Medicare, it is not true that everyone knows how to fix it; there are different ideas. The Bush plan, the Perot plan, the Clinton—we have different ideas. I am convinced, having studied health care for a year, hard, and talking to hundreds and hundreds of people all across America, that you cannot control the costs of Medicare until you control the costs of private health care and public health care, with managed competition, a ceiling on costs, and radical reorganization of the insurance markets. You've got to do that. We've got to get those costs down.

Number two, with regard to Social Security. That program—a lot of you may not know this. It provides a $70 billion surplus a year. Social Security is in surplus $70 billion.

Six increases in the payroll tax—that means people with incomes of $51,000 a year or less pay a disproportionately high share of the federal tax burden, which is why I want some middle-class tax relief. What do we have to do? By the time the century turns, we have got to have our deficit under control. We have to work out of it so that surplus is building up so when the baby boomers like me retire, we're O.K. Number 3, on the pension funds, I don't know as much about it, but I will say this. What I would do is to bring in the pension experts of the country, take a look at it, and strengthen the pension requirements further, because it's not just enough to have a guarantee. We had a guarantee on the S&L's, right? We had a guarantee, and what happened? You picked up a $500 billion bill because of the dumb way the federal government deregulated. So I think we are going to have to change and strengthen the pension requirements on private retirement plans.

MODERATOR: Thank you. I think we have a question here on international affairs, hopefully.

QUESTION: We've come to a position where we're in the new world order. And I'd like to know what the candidates feel our position is in this new world order and what our responsibilities are as a super-power.

MODERATOR: Mr. President.

BUSH: Well, we have come to that position since I became president. Forty-three, forty-four countries have gone democratic—no longer totalitarian, no longer living under dictatorship or Communist rule. This is exciting. This is—"new world order" to me means freedom and democracy. I think we will have a continuing responsibility as the only remaining superpower to stay involved. If we pull back in some isolation and say we don't have to do our share or more than our share anymore, I believe you can just ask for conflagration that we'll get involved in the future. NATO, for example, has kept the peace for many many years, and I want to see us keep fully staffed in NATO so we'll continue to guarantee the peace in Europe.

But the exciting thing is the fear of nuclear war is down, and you hear all the bad stuff that's happened on my watch. I hope people will recognize that this is something pretty good for mankind. I hope they'll think it's good that democracy and freedom is on the move. And we're going to stay engaged, as long as I'm president, working to improve things. You know, it's so easy now to say, Hey, cut out foreign aid, we got a problem at home. I think the United States has to still have the Statue of Liberty as a symbol of caring for others. We're—right this very minute we're sending supplies in to help these little starving kids in Somalia. We're trying to get—we're—it's the United States that's taken the lead in, in humanitarian aid into Bosnia. We're doing this all around the world. Yes, we got problems at home, and I think I got a good plan to help fix those problems at home. But because of our leadership, because we didn't listen to the freeze, the nuclear freeze group, you remember? Freeze it back in about 19—the late seventies. Freeze. Don't touch it. We're going to lock it in now, or else we'll have war.

President Reagan said, "No, peace through strength." It worked. The Soviet Union is no more, and now we're working to help them become totally democratic through the freedom support act that I led on. A great Democratic ambassador, Bob Strauss, over there. Jim Baker. All of us got this thing passed through cooperation, Ross, it worked with cooperation, and you're for that, I'm sure. Helping Russia become democratic. So the new world order, to me, means freedom and democracy, keep engaged. Do not pull back into isolation, and we are the United States, and we have a responsibility to lead and to guarantee the security. If it hadn't been for us, Saddam Hussein would be sitting on top of three-fifths of the oil supply of the world, and he'd have nuclear weapons. And the—only the United States could do that. Excuse me, Carole.

MODERATOR: Thank you. Mr. Perot?

PEROT: Well, it's cost effective to help Russia succeed in its revolution. Pennies on the dollar compared to going back to cold war. Russia's still very unstable; they could go back to Square 1 and worse. Still, all the nuclear weapons are not dismantled. I'm particularly concerned about the intercontinental weapons, the ones that can hit us. We've got agreements but they're still there. With all this instability and breaking in the republics, and all the Middle Eastern countries going over there shopping for weapons, we've got our work cut out for us, so we need to stay right on top of that and constructively help them move toward democracy and capitalism. We have to have money to do that. We have to have our people at work.

See, for forty-five years we were preoccupied with the Red Army. I suggest now that our Number 1 preoccupation is red ink in our country, and we've got to put our people back to work, so that we can afford to do these things we want to do in Russia. We cannot be the policemen for the world any longer. We spent $300 billion a year defending the world. Germany and Japan spend around $30 billion apiece. It's neat. If I can get you to defend me, and I can spend all my money building industry, that's a home run for me. Coming out of World War II it made sense. Now, the other superpowers need to do their part. I close on this point. You can't be a superpower unless you're an economic superpower. If we're not an economic superpower, we are a "used to be," then we will no longer be a force good throughout the world. And if nothing else gets you excited about rebuilding our industrial base, maybe that will because it's Job 1, is to put our people back to work.

MODERATOR: Governor Clinton, the president mentioned Saddam Hussein. Your vice president and you have had some words about the President and Saddam Hussein. Would you care to comment?

CLINTON: I'd rather answer a question first, then I'll be glad to. 'Cause the question you ask is important. The end of the cold war brings an incredible opportunity for change. Winds of freedom blowing around the world. Russia demilitarizing. And it also requires us to maintain some continuity, some bipartisan American commitment to certain principles. And I would just say—there are three things that I would like to say.

Number 1, we do have to maintain the world's strongest defense. We may differ about what the elements of that are. I think the defense needs to be with fewer people and permanent armed services but with greater mobility on the land, in the air, and on the sea, with a real dedication to continuing the development of high-technology weaponry and well-trained people. I think we're going to have to work to stop the proliferation of weapons of mass destruction. Got to keep going until all those nuclear weapons in Russia are gone and the other republics.

Number 2, if you don't rebuild the economic strength of this country at home, we won't be a superpower. We can't have any more instances like what happened when Mr. Bush went to Japan and the Japanese prime minister said he felt sympathy for our country. We have to be the strongest economic power in the world. That's what got me into this race. So we could rebuild the American economy.

And Number 3, we need to be a force for freedom and democracy, and we need to use our unique position to support freedom whether it's in Haiti, or in China, or in any other place; wherever the seeds of freedom are sprouting. We can't impose it, but we need to nourish it. And that's the kind of thing that I would do as president. Follow those three commitments into the future.

MODERATOR: O.K., we have a question up there.

QUESTION: Yes, you've talked a lot tonight about creating jobs, but we have an awful lot of high school graduates who don't know how to read a ruler, who cannot fill out an application for a job. How can we create high-paying jobs with the education system we have, and what would you do to change it?

MODERATOR: Who would like to begin? The education president?

PEROT: Go ahead, yeah, go ahead.

BUSH: I'd be delighted to. Because you can't do it the old way. You can't do it with the school bureaucracy controlling everything. And that's why we have a new program that I hope people have heard about. It's being worked now in 1,700 communities—bypassed Congress on this one, Ross—1,700 communities across the country. It's called America 2000. And it literally says to the communities: reinvent the schools, not just the bricks and mortar but the curriculum and everything else. Think anew. We have a concept called the New American School Corporation where we're doing exactly that.

And so I don't—I believe that we've got to get the power in the hands of the teacher, not the teachers' union. I—what's happening up there.

And so our America 2000 program also says this. It says, "Let's give parents the choice of a public, private, or public school"—public, private, or religious school. And it works. It works in Milwaukee. Democratic woman up there taken the lead in this—the mayor up there—on the program. And the schools that are not chosen are improved; competition does that.

So we've got to innovate through school choice; we've got to innovate through this America 2000 program. But she is absolutely right—the programs that we've been trying where you control everything and mandate it from Washington don't work.

The governors—and I believe Governor Clinton was in on this, but maybe—I don't want to invoke him here. But they come to me and they say, "Please get the Congress to stop passing so many mandates telling us how to control things. We know better how to do it in California" or Texas or wherever it is.

So this is what our program is all about, and I believe you're right on to something. If we don't change the education, we're not going to be able to compete. Federal funding for education is up substantially, Pell Grants are up, but it isn't going to get the job done if we don't change K through 12.

MODERATOR: Governor Clinton?

CLINTON: First of all, let me say that I've spent more of my time and life on this in the last twelve years than any other issue. Seventy percent of my state's money goes to the public schools, and I was really honored when *Time* magazine said that our schools had shown more improvement than any other state in the country except one other— they named two states showing real strides forward in the eighties. So I care a lot about this, and I've spent countless hours in schools. But let me start with what you said. I agree with some of what Mr. Bush said, but it's nowhere near enough. We live in a world where what you earn depends on what you can learn, where the average eighteen-year-old will change jobs eight times in a lifetime and where none of us can promise any of you that what you now do for a living is absolutely safe from now on.

Nobody running can promise that, there's too much change in the world. So what should we do? Let me reel some things off real quick, because you said you wanted specifics.

Number 1, under my program we would provide matching funds to states to teach everybody with a job to read in the next five years and give everybody with a job a chance to get a high school diploma; in big places, on the job.

Number 2, we would provide two-year apprenticeship programs to high school graduates who don't go to college, in community colleges or on the job.

Number 3, we'd open the doors to college education to high school graduates without regard to income; they could borrow the money and pay it back as a percentage of their income over the couple of years of service to our nation here at home.

Number 4, we would fully fund the Head Start program to get little kids off to a good start.

And 5, I would have an aggressive program of school reform, more choices. I favor public schools or these new charter schools; we can talk about that if you want. I don't think we should spend tax money on private schools but I favor public school choice, and I favor radical decentralization and giving more power to better-trained principals and teachers with parent councils to control their schools.

Those things would revolutionize American education and take us to the top economically.

MODERATOR: Thank you, Governor Clinton. What the question is, what is it going to cost? What is it going to cost?

CLINTON: In six years the—I budget all this in my budget—in six years, the college program would cost $8 billion, over and above what—the president's student loan program costs 4. You pay $3 billion for busted loans because we don't have an automatic recovery system and a billion dollars in bank fees. So the net cost would be 8 billion six years from now in a trillion-plus budget, not very much.

The other stuff, all the other stuff I mentioned, costs much less than that. The Head Start program: full funding would cost about 5 billion more. And it's all covered in my budget from the plans that I've laid out from raising taxes on families with incomes above $200,000 and asking foreign corporations to pay the same tax that American corporations do on the same income. From $140 billion budget cuts including what I think are very prudent cuts in the defense budget. It's all covered in the plan.

MODERATOR: Thank you. Mr. Perot, you on education, please.

PEROT: Yes. I've got scars to show from being around education reform. And the first words you need to say in every city and state, and just draw a line in the sand, is: public schools exist for the benefit of the children. You're going to see a lot of people fall over. Because anytime you're spending $199 billion a year, somebody's getting it. And the children get lost in the process. So that's Step 1.

Keep in mind in 1960, when our schools were the envy of the world, we were spending $16 billion on them. Now we spend more than any other nation in the world, $199 billion a year, and ranked at the bottom of the industrialized world in terms of education achievement. One more time, you bought a front-row box seat and got a third-rate performance, because the government is not serving you.

By and large it should be local. The more local the better. An interesting phenomenon. Small towns have good schools; big cities have terrible schools. The best people in a small town will serve on the school board. You get into big cities, it's political patronage, stepping-stones. You get the job, you gave your relatives the janitors' jobs at $57,000 a year, more than the teachers make, and with luck they clean the cafeteria once a week. Now, you're paying for that. Those schools belong to you. And we put up with that. Now, as long as you put up with that, that's what you're going to get. And these folks are just dividing up 199 billion bucks the children get lost. If I could wish for one thing for great public school's it'd be a strong family unit in every home. Nothing will ever replace that.

You say, well, gee, what are you going to do about that. Well, the White House is a bully pulpit, and I think we ought to be pounding on the table every day. There's nothing—the most efficient unit of government the world will ever know is a strong, loving family unit.

Next thing, you need small schools, not big schools. In a little school everybody's somebody. Individualism is very important. These big factories, everybody told me they were cost effective. I did a study on it. They're cost ineffective. Five thousand students, why is a high school that big? One reason. Sooner or later you'll get eleven more boys that can run like the devil that weigh 250 pounds, and they might win district. Now that has nothing to do with learning.

Secondly, across Texas typically half the school day, was nonacademic pursuits. In one place it was 35 percent. In Texas you can have unlimited absences to go to livestock shows. I found a boy—excuse me, but this gives the flavor—a boy in Houston kept a chicken in the bathtub in downtown Houston. He missed sixty-five days going to livestock shows. Finally had to come back to school. The chicken lost his feathers. That's the only way we got him back. Now, that's your tax money being wasted.

Now, neighborhood schools, it is terrible to bus tiny little children across town. And it is particularly terrible to take poor tiny little children and wait until the first grade and bus them across town to Mars, where the children know their numbers, know their letters, have had every advantage. The end of the first day that little child wants out. I close on this.

You've got to have world-class teachers, world-class books. If you ever got close to how textbooks were selected, you wouldn't want to go back the second day. I don't have time to tell the stories.

MODERATOR: No, you don't.

PEROT: Finally, finally, if we don't fix this, you're right, we can't have the industries of tomorrow unless we have the best educated workforce. And here you've got for the disadvantaged children, you've got to have early childhood development; cheapest money you'll ever spend. First contact should be with the mother when she's pregnant. That little child needs to be loved and hugged and nurtured and made to feel special. Like your children were. They learn to think well or poorly of themselves in the first eighteen months—

MODERATOR: Thank you. Thank you, Mr. Perot.

PEROT: —In the first two years they learn how to learn or don't know how to learn how to learn, and if they don't, they wind up in prison. And it costs more to keep them in prison—

MODERATOR: Thank you, Mr. Perot.

PEROT: —than it does to send them to Harvard. I rest my case.

MODERATOR: Thank you. President Bush, you wanted to—

BUSH: I just have a word of clarification because of something Governor Clinton said. My school choice program, G.I. Bill for kids, does not take public money and give it to private schools. It does what the G.I. Bill itself did, when I came out of World War II. It takes public money and gives it to families or individuals to choose the school they want. And where it's been done—those schools like in Rochester—those schools that weren't chosen find that they then compete and do better.

So I think it's worth a shot. We've got a pilot program. It ought to be tried. School choice: public, private, or religious. Not to the schools, but—you know, 46 percent of the teachers in Chicago, public school teachers, send their kids to private school. Now, I think we ought to try to help families and see if it will do what I think make all schools better.

CLINTON: I just want to mention, if I could, just—

MODERATOR: Very briefly.

CLINTON: Very briefly. Involving the parents in the preschool education of their kids, even if they're poor and uneducated, can make a huge difference. We have a big program in my state that teaches mothers or fathers to teach their kids to get ready for school. It's the most successful thing we've ever done.

Just a fact clarification, real quickly. We do not spend a higher percentage of our income on public education than every other country. There are nine countries that spend more than we do on public education. We spend more on education because we spend so much more on colleges. But if you look at public education alone, and you take it into account, the fact that we have more racial diversity and more poverty, it makes a big difference. There are great public schools where there's public school choice, accountability and brilliant principles. I'll just mention one. The Beasley Academic Center in Chicago. I commend it to anybody; it's as good as any private school in the country.

MODERATOR: We have very little time left, and it occurs to me that we have talked all this time, and there has not been one question about some of the racial tensions and ethnic tensions in America. Is there anyone in this audience that would like to pose a question to the candidates on this?

QUESTION: What I'd like to know—and this is to any of the three of you—is aside from the recent accomplishments of your party, aside from those accomplishments in racial representation, and without citing any of your current appointments or successful elections, when do you estimate your party will both nominate and elect an Afro-American and female ticket to the presidency of the United States?

MODERATOR: Governor Clinton, why don't you answer that first.

CLINTON: Well, I don't have any idea, but I hope it will happen sometime in my lifetime.

BUSH: I do, too.

CLINTON: I believe that this country is electing more and more African-Americans and Latinos and Asian-Americans who are representing districts that are themselves not necessarily of a majority of their race. The American people are beginning to bolt across racial lines, and I hope it will happen more and more.

More and more women are being elected. Look at all these women Senate candidates we have here. And you know, according to my mother and my wife and my daughter, this world would be a lot better place if women were running it most of the time. I do think there are special experiences and judgments and backgrounds and understandings that women bring to this process, by the way. This lady said here, how have you been affected by the economy. I mean, women know what it's like to be paid an unequal amount for equal work. They know what it's like not to have flexible working hours. They know what it's like not to have family leave or child care. So I think it would be a good thing for America if it happened, and I think it will happen in my lifetime.

MODERATOR: O.K., I'm sorry. We have just a little time left. Let's try to get responses from each of them. President Bush or Mr. Perot.

BUSH: If Barbara Bush were running this year, she'd be elected. But she—it's too late. You don't want us to mention appointees, but when you see the quality of people in our administration, see how Colin Powell performed—I say administration; he's in the—

[Unintelligible]

BUSH: You weren't impressed with the fact that he—

QUESTION: Excuse me, I'm extremely impressed with that.

BUSH: Yeah, but wouldn't that suggest to the American people, then, here's a quality person, if he decided that he could automatically get the nomination of either party or—

[Unintelligible]

BUSH: Huh?

QUESTION: I'm totally impressed with that. I just want to know: when's your guess, when?

BUSH: You mean time?

QUESTION: Yeah.

BUSH: I don't know. Starting after four years. No, I think you'll—I think you'll see more—

MODERATOR: Mr. Perot.

BUSH: I think you'll see more minority candidates and women candidates coming forward.

MODERATOR: Thank you.

BUSH: This is supposed to be the women's—the Year of the Woman in the Senate; let's see how they do. I hope a lot of them lose.

MODERATOR: Mr. Perot, I don't want to cut you off any more, but we only have a minute left.

PEROT: I have a fearless forecast. Unless he just won't do it, Colin Powell will be on somebody's ticket four years from now, right? Right?

[Unintelligible]

PEROT: You, you, you wanted—that's it: four years.

QUESTION: How about a woman?

PEROT: Now, if he won't be, General Waller would be a—you say, why do you keep picking, picking military people? These, these are people that I just happen to know and have a high regard for. I'm sure there are hundred of others.

BUSH: How about Dr. Lou Sullivan?

PEROT: Absolutely.

BUSH: Yeah, a good man.

QUESTION: What about a woman?

PEROT: Oh, oh.

BUSH: My candidate's back there.

PEROT: O.K. I can think of many.

QUESTION: Many?

PEROT: Absolutely.

QUESTION: Who?

PEROT: How about Sandra Day O'Connor, as an example. Dr. Bernadine Healy.

QUESTION: Good.

PEROT: National Institute of Health. I'll yield the floor. Name some more.

MODERATOR: Thank you. I, I, I want to apologize to our audience, because there were 209 people here, and there were 209 questions. We only got to a fraction of them, and I'm sorry to those of you that didn't get to ask your questions, but we must move to the conclusion of the program.

It is time now for the two-minute closing statements, and by prior agreement, President Bush will go first.

BUSH: May I ask for an exception because I think we owe Carole Simpson a—anybody can stand in between these three characters here and get the job done, we owe her a round of applause. Just don't take it out of my time. I feel strongly about it, but I don't want it to come out of my time.

MODERATOR: Give this man more time.

Closing Statements

BUSH: No, but let me just say to the American people in, in two and a half weeks we're going to choose who should sit in this Oval Office. Who to lead the economic recovery, who to be the leader of the free world, who to get the deficit down.

Three ways to do that: one is to raise taxes; one is to reduce spending, controlling that mandatory spending; another one is to invest and save and to stimulate growth.

I do not want to raise taxes. I differ with the two here on that. I'm just not going to do that. I do believe that we need to control mandatory spending. I think we need to invest and save more. I believe that we need to educate better and retrain better. I believe that we need to export more, so I'll keep working for export agreements where we can sell more abroad. And I believe that we must strengthen the family. We've got to strengthen the family.

Now, let me pose this question to America: if in the next five minutes, a television announcer came on and said, There is a major international crisis—there is a major threat to the world or in this country—a major threat. My question is: who, if you were appointed to name one of the three of us, who would you choose? Who has the perseverance, the character, the integrity, the maturity to get the job done? I hope I'm that person. Thank you very, very much.

MODERATOR: Thank you, Mr. President. And now a closing statement from Mr. Perot.

PEROT: If the American people want to do it and not talk about it, then, they ought—you know, I'm one person they ought to consider. If they just want to keep slow dancing and talk about it and not do it, I'm not your man. I am results-oriented, I am action-oriented. I've built my businesses. Getting things done in three months what my competitors took eighteen months to do. Everybody says you can't do that with Congress; sure, you can do that with Congress. Congress is—they're all good people. They're all patriots. But you've got to link arms and work with them. Sure, you'll have arguments; sure, you'll have fights. We have them all day, every day. But we get the job done.

I have to come back in my close to one thing, because I am passionate about education. I was talking about early childhood education for disadvantaged little children. And let me tell you one specific pilot program, where children who don't have a chance go to this program when they're three, and now we're going back to when the mother's pregnant. They'll start right after they're born. But going—starting when they're three and going to this school until they're nine, and then going into the public schools, in the fourth grade? Ninety percent are on the honor roll. Now, that will change America.

Those children will all go to college. They will live the American dream.

And I beg the American people, anytime they think about reforming education, to take this piece of society that doesn't have a chance and take these little pieces of clay that can be shaped and molded and give them the same love and nurture and affection and support you give your children, and teach them that they are unique and that they're precious and there's only one person in the world like them, and you will see this nation bloom. And we will have so many people who are qualified for the top job that it will be terrific, and finally, if you can't pay the bills, you're dead in the water. And we have got to put our nation back to work. If you don't want to really do that I'm not your man. I'd go crazy sitting up there slow dancing that one; in other words, unless we're going to do it, then pick somebody who likes to talk about it. Now, just remember, when you think about me, I didn't create this mess, I've been paying taxes just like you. And Lord knows, I've paid my share. Over a billion dollars in taxes. For a guy that started out with everything he owns in—

MODERATOR: I'm sorry. Mr. Perot, I'm sorry once again.

PEROT: It's in your hands. I wish you well. I'll see you tomorrow night. On NBC 10:30–11:00 Eastern.

MODERATOR: And finally, last but not least, Governor Clinton.

CLINTON: Thank you, Carole. Thank you, ladies and gentlemen. Since I suggested this format, and I hope it's been good for all of you, I've really tried to be faithful to your request that we answer the questions specifically and pointedly. I thought I owed that to you, and I respect you for being here and for the impact you've had on making this a more positive experience.

These problems are not easy and not going to be solved overnight. But I want you to think about just two or three things. First of all, the people of my state have let me be the governor for twelve years because I made commitments to two things. More jobs and better schools. Our schools are now better; our children get off to a better start from preschool programs and smaller classes in the early grades, and we have one of the most aggressive adult education programs in the country. We talked about that. This year my state ranks first in the country in job growth, fourth in manufacturing job growth, fourth in income growth, fourth in the decline of poverty. I'm proud of that. It happened because I could work with people, Republicans and Democrats. That's why we've had twenty-four retired generals and admirals, hundreds of business people, many of them Republican, support this campaign.

You have to decide whether you want to change or not. We do not need four more years of an economic theory that doesn't work. We've had twelve years of trickle-down economics. It's time to put the American people first, to invest and grow this economy. I'm the only person here who's ever balanced the government budget, and I've presented twelve of them and cut spending repeatedly, but you cannot just get there by balancing the budget. We've got to grow the economy by putting people first. Real people like you. I've got into this race because I did not want my child to grow up to be part of the first generation of Americans to do worse than their parents. We're better than that. We can do better than that. I want to make America as great as it can be, and I ask for your help in doing it. Thank you very much.

8

Debate Three
October 19, 1992

MODERATOR: Gentlemen, again, welcome, and again, good evening. It seems, from what some of those voters said at your Richmond debate and from polling and other data, that each of you fairly or not faces serious voter concerns about the underlying credibility and believability of what each of you says you would do as president in the next four years. Governor Clinton, in accordance with the draw, those concerns about you are first. You are promising to create jobs, reduce the deficit, reform the health care system, rebuild the infrastructure, guarantee college education for everyone who is qualified, among many other things, all with financial pain only for the very rich. Some people are having trouble, apparently, believing that is possible. Should they have that concern?

CLINTON: No. There are many people who believe that the only way we can get this country turned around is to tax the middle class more and punish them more. But the truth is that middle-class Americans are basically the only group of Americans who have been taxed more in the 1980s and during the last twelve years even though their incomes have gone down. The wealthiest Americans have been taxed much less even though their incomes have gone up. Middle-class people will have their fair share of changing to do and many challenges to face, including the challenge of becoming constantly reeducated. But my plan is a departure from trickle-down economics, just cutting taxes on the wealthiest Americans and getting out of the way.

It's also a departure from tax-and-spend economics, because you can't tax and divide an economy that isn't growing.

I propose an American version of what works in other countries. I think we can do it better, invest and grow. I believe we can increase investment and reduce the deficit at the same time if we not only ask the wealthiest Americans and foreign corporations to pay their fair share, we also provide over $100 billion in tax relief in terms of incentives for new plants, new small businesses, new technologies, new housing, and for middle-class families.

And we have $140 billion of spending cuts, invest and grow. Raise some more money, spend the money on tax incentives to have growth in the private sector, take the money from the defense cuts and reinvest it in new transportation and communications and environmental cleanup systems.

This will work. On this, as on so many other issues, I have a fundamental difference from the present administration. I don't believe trickle-down economics will work; unemployment is up; most people are working harder for less money than they were making ten years ago. I think we can do better if we have the courage to change.

MODERATOR: Mr. President, a response. Specifically—

BUSH: There's one minute—now, just the ground rules here.

MODERATOR: Well, yes, roughly one minute. We can loosen that up a little bit, but go ahead.

BUSH: He doesn't like trickle-down government, but I think he's talking about the Reagan-Bush years, where we created 15 million jobs. The rich are paying a bigger percent of the total tax burden. And what I don't like is trickle-down government. And therein I think Governor Clinton keeps talking about trickle down, trickle down, and he's still talking about spending more and taxing more. Government, he says, invest in government, grow government. Government doesn't create jobs. If they do, they're make-work jobs.

It's the private sector that creates jobs. And yes, we've got too many taxes on the American people, and we're spending too much. And that's why I want to get the deficit down by controlling the growth of mandatory spending. It won't be painless. I think Mr. Perot put his finger on something there. It won't be painless, but we've got to get the job done. But not by raising taxes. Mr. and Mrs. America, when you hear him say "We're going to tax only the rich," watch your wallet. Because his figures don't add up, and he's going to sock it right to the middle-class taxpayer and lower if he's going to pay for all the spending programs he proposes. So we have a big difference on this trickle-down theory. I do not want any more trickle-down government. It's gotten too big. I want to do something about that.

MODERATOR: Mr. Perot, what do you think of the governor's approach, what he just laid out?

PEROT: The basic problem with it, it doesn't balance the budget. If you forecast it out, we'll still have a significant deficit under each of their plans as I understand them. Our challenge is to stop the financial bleeding. If you take a patient into the hospital that's bleeding arterially, Step 1 is to stop the bleeding. And we are bleeding arterially. There's only one way out of this, and that is to stop the deterioration of our job base, to have a growing, expanding job base to give us the tax base. See, balancing the budget is not nearly as difficult as paying off the $4 trillion debt and leaving our children the American Dream intact. We have spent their money, we've got to pay it back. This is going to take fair, shared sacrifice. My plan balances the budget within six years. We didn't do it faster than that because we didn't want to disrupt the economy. We gave it off to a slow start and a fast finish to give the economy time to recover.

But we faced it, and we did it. And we believe it's fair share and sacrifice. The one thing I have done is lay it squarely on the table in front of the American people. You've had a number of occasions to see in detail what the plan is, and at least you'll understand it. I think that's fundamental in our country, that you know what you're getting into.

MODERATOR: Governor, the word "pain"—one of the other leadership things that's put on you is that you don't speak of pain. That you speak of, of all things—nobody's going to really have to suffer under your plan. You heard what Mr. Perot has said; he said, It's got—to do the things that you want to do, you can't do it by just taking the money from the rich. That's what the president says as well. How do you respond to that, if the numbers don't add up?

CLINTON: I disagree [unintelligible]. For one thing, let me just follow up here. I disagree with Mr. Perot that the answer is to raise—put a fifty cents gas tax on the middle class and raise more taxes on the middle class and the working poor than on the wealthy. His own analysis says that unemployment will be slightly higher in 1995 under his plan than it is today. And as far as what Mr. Bush says, he is the person who raised taxes on the middle class after saying he wouldn't, and just this year Mr. Bush vetoed the tax increase on the wealthy that gave middle-class tax relief. He vetoed middle-class tax relief this year. And furthermore, under this administration, spending has increased more than it has in the last twenty years, and he asked Congress to spend more money than it actually spent.

Now, it's hard to outspend Congress, but he tried to for the last three years. So my view is that the middle class is the one—they've been suffering, Jim. Now, should people pay more for Medicare if they can? Yes. Should they pay more for Social Security if they get more out of it than they've paid in and they're upper-income people? Yes. But look what's happened to the middle class. Middle-class Americans are working harder for less money than they were making ten years ago, and they're paying higher taxes. The tax burden on them has not gone down. It has gone up. I don't think the answer is to slow the economy down more, drive unemployment up more, and undermine the health of the private sector.

The answer is to invest and grow this economy. That's what works in other countries, and that's what'll work here.

MODERATOR: As a practical matter, Mr. President, do you agree with the governor when he says that the middle class—the taxes on the middle class—do your numbers agree that the middle—the taxes on the middle class have gone up during the last—

BUSH: I think everybody's paying too much taxes. He refers to one tax increase. Let me remind you it was a Democratic tax increase, and I didn't want to do it, and I went along with it. And I said I make a mistake—if I make a mistake, I admit it. That's quite different than some. But I think that's the American way. I think everyone's paying too much. But I think this idea that you can go out and—he, then he hits me for vetoing a tax bill. Yes, I did. And the American taxpayer ought to be glad they have a president to stand up to a spending Congress. We remember what it was like when we had a spending president and a spending Congress and interest rates—who, who remembers that? They were at 21.5 percent under Jimmy Carter. And inflation was 15.

We don't want to go back to that. And so yes, everybody's taxed too much, and I want to get the taxes down. But not by signing a tax bill that's going to raise taxes on people.

MODERATOR: Mr. President, when you said just then that you admit your mistakes, and you looked at Governor Clinton, and said, what mistake is it that you want him to admit to?

BUSH: Well, the record in Arkansas. I mean, look at it. And that's what we're asking America to have. Now, look, he says, Arkansas is a poor state. They are. But in almost every category they're lagging. I'll give you an example. He talks about all the jobs he's created in one or two years. Over the last ten years since he's been governor, they're 30 percent behind—30 percent—they're 30 percent of the national average, on pay for teachers, on all these categories Arkansas is right near the very bottom. I'll—you haven't heard me mention this before, but we're getting close now, and I think it's about time I start putting things in perspective, and I'm going to do that. It's not dirty campaigning, because he's been talking about my record for a half a—half a year here—eleven months here.

And so we've got to do that. I got to get it in perspective. What's his mistake? Admit it! That Arkansas is doing very, very badly against any standard—environment, support for police officers, whatever it is.

MODERATOR: Governor, is that true?

CLINTON: Mr. Bush's Bureau of Labor Statistics says that Arkansas ranks first in the country in the growth of new jobs this year—first.

BUSH: This year.

CLINTON: Fourth in manufacturing jobs, fourth in the reduction of poverty, fourth in income increase. Over the last ten years, we've created manufacturing jobs much more rapidly than the national average. Over the last five years, our income has grown more rapidly than the national average. We are second in tax burden—the second lowest tax burden in the country. We have the lowest per capita state and local spending in the country. We're low spending, low tax burden; we dramatically increased investment, and our jobs are growing. I wish America had that kind of record, and I think most people looking at us tonight would like it if we had more jobs and a lower spending burden on the government.

MODERATOR: Mr. Perot, if you were sitting at home now and just heard this exchange about Arkansas, who would you believe?

PEROT: I grew up five blocks from Arkansas. Let's—let's put it in perspective. It's a beautiful state, it's a fairly rural state, it has a population less than Chicago or Los Angeles, about the size of Dallas and Fort Worth combined. So I think probably we're making a mistake night after night after night to cast the nation's future on a unit that small.

MODERATOR: Why is that a mistake?

PEROT: It's irrelevant. You know, Jim, I—

MODERATOR: What he did as Governor of Arkansas is irrelevant?

PEROT: Oh, no, no, but you can't—I could say, you know, that I ran a small grocery store on the corner, therefore I extrapolate that into the fact that I could run Wal-Mart; that's not true.

MODERATOR: Mr. Perot—Governor—

PEROT: I can't project an Arkansas company—

MODERATOR: Governor—

CLINTON: Mr. Perot, with all respect, I think it is highly relevant, and I think that a $4 billion budget, with state and federal funds, is not all that small. And I think the fact that I took a state that was one of the poorest states in the country and had been for 153 years and tried my best to modernize its economy and to make the kind of changes that have generated support from people like the presidents of Apple Computer and Hewlett Packard, and some of the biggest companies in this country, twenty-four retired generals and admirals and hundreds of business executives, are highly relevant, and you know, I'm frankly amazed that, since you grew up five blocks from there you would think that what goes on in that state is irrelevant. I think it's been pretty impressive. And the people who have jobs, the people who have jobs and educations and opportunities that didn't have them ten years ago, don't think it's irrelevant at all. They think it's highly relevant and they wish the rest of the—

MODERATOR: You think it is relevant.

BUSH: I don't have a dog in this fight, but I'd like to get in on it. Governor Clinton has to operate under a balanced budget amendment. He has to do it. That is the law. I'd like to see a balanced budget amendment for America to protect the American taxpayers. And then that would discipline, not only the executive branch but the spending Congress, the Congress that's been in control of one party, his party, for thirty-eight years. And we almost had it done and that institution, the House of Representatives, everyone's yelling "clean house!"—one of the reasons is, we almost had it done, and the Speaker, a very able, decent fellow, I might add, but he twisted the arms of some of the sponsors of that legislation and had them change their vote. What's relevant here is that tool, that discipline that he has to live by in Arkansas, and I'd like it for the American people. I want the line item veto, I want to check off, so if the Congress can't do it, let people check off their income tax, 10 percent of it to compel the government to cut spending. And if they can't do it, if the Congress can't do it, let them then have to do it across the board, a—what we call a sequester. That's the discipline we need. And I'm working for that, to protect the American taxpayer against the big spenders.

MODERATOR: Mr. President, let's move to some of the leadership concerns that have been voiced about you, and they relate to something you said in your closing statement in Richmond the other night about the president being the manager of crises and that relates to an earlier criticism that you began to focus on the economy, on health care, on racial divisions in this country only after they became crises. Is that a fair criticism?

BUSH: Jim, I don't think that's a fair shot. I hear it, I hear it echoed by political opponents, but I don't think it's fair. I think we've been fighting from Day 1 to do something about the inner cities. I'm for enterprise zones. I have had it in every single proposal I've sent to the Congress.

And now we hear a lot of talk: oh, well, they all want enterprise zones. And yet the House and the Senate can't send it down without loading it up with a lot of, you know, these Christmas tree ornaments they put on the legislation.

I don't think in racial, ah, racial harmony that I'm a laggard on that. I've been speaking out since Day 1. We've gotten the Americans for Disabilities Act, which I think is one of the foremost pieces of civil rights legislation.

And yes, it took me to veto two civil rights quota bills, because I don't believe in quotas. And I don't think the American people believe in quotas. And I beat back the Congress on that, and then we passed a decent civil rights bill that offers guarantees against discrimination in employment. And that is good.

I've spoken out over and over again against anti-Semitism and racism. And I think my record as a member of Congress speaks for itself on that.

What was the other part of it?

MODERATOR: Well, it's just that—you've spoken to it. I mean, but the idea, not so much in specific—

BUSH: Yes—

MODERATOR: —but that it has to be a crisis before you—it gets your attention.

BUSH: I don't think that's true at all. I don't think that's true. But you know, let others fire away on it.

MODERATOR: Do you think that's true, Mr. Perot?

PEROT: I'd like to just talk about issues and so—

MODERATOR: You don't think this is an issue?

PEROT: No, well, no. But the point is that's a subjective thing. See, the subjective thing is when does President Bush react. And I, I feel it would be very difficult for me to answer that in any short period of time.

MODERATOR: Well, then, let's phrase—I'll phrase it differently, then.

PEROT: Let's—

MODERATOR: He said the other night in his closing words in Richmond that one of the key things that he believes the American people should decide between, among, the three of you is who they want in charge if this country gets to a crisis. Now, that's what he said, and, and the rap on the president is that it's only crisis time that he focuses on some of these things. So my question to you—we're going to talk about you in a minute. My question about you—

PEROT: I thought you'd forgotten I was here.

MODERATOR: No, no, no, no, no, no. But my question to you is—if you have nothing to say about it, fine. I'll go to Governor Clinton. But, ah—

PEROT: No. I will, I will let the American people decide that. I would rather not critique the two candidates.

MODERATOR: All right. Governor, what do you think?

CLINTON: The only thing I would say about that is I think that on the economy Mr. Bush said for a long time there was no recession and then said it would be better to do nothing than to have a compromise effort with the Congress. He really didn't have a new economic program until over 1,300 days into his presidency, and not all of his health care initiative has been presented to the Congress, even now.

I think it's important to elect a president who is committed to getting this economy going again and who realizes we have to abandon trickle-down economics and put the American people first again and who will send programs to the Congress in the first hundred days to deal with the critical issues that America is crying out for leadership on—jobs, incomes, the health care crisis, the need to control the economy. Those things deserve to be dealt with from Day 1. I will deal with them from Day 1. They will be my first priority, not my election year concern.

MODERATOR: Mr. President.

BUSH: Well, I think you're overlooking that we have had major accomplishments in the first term. But if you're talking about protecting the taxpayer against his friends in the United States Congress, go back to what it was like when you had a Democratic president and a Democratic Congress. You don't have to go back to Herbert Hoover. Go back to Jimmy Carter. And interest rates were 21 percent. Inflation was 15 percent. The misery index—unemployment and inflation added together; it was invented by the Democrats—went right through the roof. We've cut it in half. And all you hear about is how bad things are. You know, remember the question: are you better off? Well, is a home buyer better off if he can refinance the home because interest rates are down? Is the senior citizen better off because inflation is not wiping out their family's savings? I think they are. Is the guy out of work better off? Of course he's not. But he's not going to be better off if we grow the government, if we invest, as Government Clinton—Governor Clinton—says, invest in more government. You've got to free up the private sector. You've got to let small business have more incentives.

For three months—three quarters—I've been fighting, three quarters been fighting to get the Congress to pass some incentives for small business: capital gains, investment tax allowance, credit for first-time home buyers. And it's blocked by the Congress, and then if a little of it comes my way, they load it up with Christmas trees and tax increases. And I have to stand up and favor the taxpayer.

MODERATOR: I have to let—we have to talk about Ross Perot now, or he'll get me, I'm sure. Mr. Perot, on this issue that I have raised at the very beginning that we've been talking about which is leadership, as president of the United States, it concerns, my reading of it at least, my concerns about you as expressed by folks in the polls and other places. It goes like this; you've got a problem with General Motors. You took your $750 million and you left. You had a problem in the spring and summer about some personal hits that you took as a potential candidate for president of the United States and you, you walked out. Does that say anything relevant to how you would function as president of the United States?

PEROT: I think the General Motors thing is very relevant. I did everything I could to get General Motors to face its problems in the mideighties while it was still financially strong; they just wouldn't do it. And everybody now knows the terrible price they're paying by waiting until it's obvious to the brain dead that they have problems. Now, hundreds—thousands—of good, decent people, whole cities up here in this state, are adversely impacted because they would not move in a timely way. Our government is at that point now. The thing that I am in this race for is to tap the American people on the shoulder and to say to every single one of you, fix it while we're still relatively strong. If you have a heart problem, you don't wait until a heart attack to address it.

So the General Motors experience is relevant. At the point when I could not get them to address those problems, I had created so much stress in the board who wanted just to keep the Lawrence Welk music going that they asked to buy my remaining shares. I sold them my remaining shares. They went their way, I went my way, because it was obvious we had a complete disagreement about what should be done with the company.

But let's take my life in perspective. Again and again on complex, difficult tasks I have stayed the course. When I was asked by our government to do the POW project, within the year the Vietnamese had sent people into Canada to make arrangements to have me and my family killed—and I had five small children—and my family and I decided we would stay the course. And we lived with that problem for three years.

Then I got into the Texans' War on Drug program and big-time drug dealers got all upset. Then when I had two people imprisoned in Iran, I could have left them there, I could have rationalized it. We went over, we got them out, we brought them back home. And since then, for years I have lived with the burden of the Middle East, where it's an "eye for an eye and a tooth for a tooth" country in terms of their unhappiness with the fact that I was successful in that effort.

Again and again and again in the middle of the night and two or three o'clock in the morning my government has called me to take extraordinary steps for Americans in distress. And again and again and again I have responded. And I didn't wilt and I didn't quit.

Now, what happened in July we've covered again and again and again. But I think in terms of the American people's concern about my commitment, I'm here tonight, folks. I've never quit supporting you as you put me on the ballot in the other twenty-six states. And when you asked me to come back in, I came back in. And talk about not quitting? I'm spending my money on this campaign. Your two parties are spending your money, taxpayer money. I—I've put my wallet on the table for you and your children, over $60 million at least, will go into this campaign to leave the American dream to you and your children, to get this country straightened out, because if anybody owes it to you, I do. I've lived the American dream. I'd like for your children to be able to live it, too.

MODERATOR: Governor, does—do you have a response to the staying-the-course question about Mr. Perot?

CLINTON: I don't have any criticism of Mr. Perot. I think the—what I'd like to talk about a minute is, since you're asking the question, was the—the General Motors issue. I don't think there's any question that the automobile executives made some errors in the 1980s. But I also think we should look at how much productivity has increased lately, how much labor has done to increase productivity and how much management has done. And we're still losing a lot of auto jobs, in my judgment, because we don't have a national economic strategy that will build the industrial base of this country. Now, just today I met with the presidents and the vice presidents of the Willow Run union here—near here. They both said they were Vietnam veterans supporting me because I had an economic program to put them back to work.

We need an investment, incentive to modernize plant and equipment. We've got to control the health care costs for those people, otherwise we can't keep the manufacturing jobs here, and we need a tough trade policy that is fair, that insists on open markets in return for open markets. We ought to have a strategy that will build the economic and industrial base. So I think Mr. Perot was right in questioning the management practices, but they didn't have much of a partner in government here as compared with the policies the Germans and the Japanese followed, and I believe we can do better. That's one of the things I want to change. We—I know that we can grow manufacturing jobs. We did it in my state and we can do it nationally.

MODERATOR: Mr. President, do you have a response?

BUSH: To this?

MODERATOR: Yes.

BUSH: Well, I wondered when Governor Clinton was talking to the auto workers whether he talked about his and Senator Gore's favoring CAFE standards. Those fuel efficiency standards of forty miles per gallon. That would break the auto industry and throw a lot of people out of work.

As regarding Mr. Perot, I take back something I said about him. I once said in a frivolous moment when he got out of the race, if you can't stand the heat, buy an air conditioning company. And I take it back. Because I think he ex—he said he made a mistake. And the thing I find is, if I make a mistake, I admit it. I've never heard Governor Clinton make a mistake. But the one mistake he's made is: fuel efficiency standards at forty to forty-five miles per gallon will throw many auto workers out of work, and you can't have it both ways. There's a pattern here of appealing to the auto workers and then trying to appeal to the spotted owl crowd. Or the extremes in the environmental movement. You can't do it as president. You can't have a pattern of one side of the issue one day and another the next. So my argument is not with Ross Perot. It is more with Governor Clinton.

MODERATOR: Governor, what about that charge? That you want it both ways on this issue.

CLINTON: Let's just talk about the CAFE standards.

MODERATOR: All right.

CLINTON: That's the fuel efficiency standards that are now 27.5 miles per gallon per automobile free, fleet. I never said—and I defy you to find where I said—I gave an extensive environmental speech in April, and I said that we ought to have a goal of raising the fuel efficiency standards to forty miles a gallon. I think that should be a goal. I've never said we should write it into law if there is evidence that that goal cannot be achieved. The National Science Foundation did a study which said it would be difficult for us to reach fuel efficiency standards in excess of thirty-seven miles per gallon for the year 2000. I think we should try to raise the fuel efficiency. And let me say this. I think we ought to have incentives to do it. I think we ought to push to do it. That doesn't mean we have to write it into the law.

Look, I am a job creator, not a job destroyer. It is the Bush administration that has had no new jobs in the private sector in the last four years. In my state we're leading the country in private-sector job growth, but it is good for America to improve fuel efficiency. We also ought to concert—convert—more fuel vehicles to compressed natural gas. That's another way to improve the environment.

MODERATOR: Mr. Perot, based on your experience at General Motors, where do you come down in this? This has been thrown about, back and forth, during this campaign, from the very beginning about jobs and CAFE standards.

PEROT: Well, everybody's nibbling around the edges; let's go to the center of the bull's-eye, the core problem—and believe me, everybody on the factory floor all over this country knows it. You implement that NAFTA, the Mexican trade agreement, where they pay people one dollar an hour, have no health care, no retirement, no pollution controls, et cetera, et cetera, et cetera, and you're going to hear a giant sucking sound of jobs being pulled out of this country right at a time when we need the tax base to pay the debt and pay down the interest on the debt and get our house back in order. We've got to proceed very carefully on that. See, there's a lot I don't understand. I do understand business, I do understand creating jobs, I do understand how to make things work. And I got a long history of doing that.

Now, if you want to go to the core problem that faces everybody in manufacturing in this country, it's that agreement that's about to be put into practice. Here's—it's very simple, everybody says it'll create jobs. Yes, it'll create bubble jobs—you know, watch this, listen very carefully to this—one-time surge while we build factories and ship machine tools and equipment down there. Then year after year, for decades, they will have jobs. And I finally thought I didn't understand it—called all the experts, and they said, "Oh, it'll be disruptive for twelve to fifteen years." We haven't got twelve days, folks. We cannot lose those jobs. They were eventually saying Mexican jobs will eventually come to $7.50 an hour, ours will eventually go down to $7.50 an hour. Makes you feel real good to hear that, right?

Let's think it through here, let's be careful. I'm for free trade philosophically, but I have studied these trade agreements till the world has gone flat, and we don't have good trade agreements across the world.

I hope we'll have a chance to get into that tonight, because I can get right to the center bull's-eye and tell you why we're losing whole industries in this country. Excuse me.

MODERATOR: Just for the record, though, Mr. Perot, I take it, then, for your answer you do not have a position on whether or not enforcing the CAFE standards will cost jobs in the auto industry.

PEROT: Oh, no, it will cost jobs. But, that's not—let me say this, I'd rather—if you gave me two bad choices, I'd rather have some jobs left here than just see everything head south, see.

MODERATOR: So that means no—in other words, you agree with President Bush, is that right?

PEROT: No, I'm—I'm saying our principal need now is to stabilize the tax base, which is the job base, and create a growing dynamic base. Now please, folks, if you don't hear anything else I say, remember where the tax—millions of people at work are our tax base. One quick thought; if you confiscate the Forbes 400 wealth, take it off, you cannot balance the budget this year. It kind of gets your head straight about where the taxes, year in and year out, have got to come from: millions and millions of people at work.

MODERATOR: Yes, sir.

BUSH: Well, I'm caught—caught in the middle on NAFTA. Ross says, with great conviction, he opposes the North American Free Trade Agreement. I am for the North American Free Trade Agreement. My problem with Governor Clinton, once again, is that one time he's going to make up his mind he will see some merit in it, but then he sees a lot of things wrong with it. And then the other day he says he's for it, however, then we've got to pass other legislation. When you're president of the United States, you cannot have this pattern of saying, well, I'm for it, but I'm on the other side of it. And it's true on this and it's true on CAFE.

Look, if Ross were right, and we get a free trade agreement with Mexico, why wouldn't they have gone down there now? You have a differential in wages right now. I just have an honest philosophical difference. I think free trade is going to expand our job opportunity. I think it is exports that have saved us when we're in a global slowdown, a connected global slowdown, a recession in some countries. And it's free trade, fair trade that needs to be our—our—our hallmark. And we need more free trade agreements, not fewer.

MODERATOR: Governor, a quick answer on trade, then I want to go on to something else.

CLINTON: I'd like to respond to that. You know, Mr. Bush was very grateful when I was among the Democrats who said he ought to have the authority to negotiate an agreement with Mexico. Neither I nor anybody else, as far as I know, agreed to give him our proxy to say that whatever he did was fine for the workers of this country and for the interests of this country. I am the one who's in the middle on this. Mr. Perot says it's a bad deal. Mr. Bush says it's a hunky-dory deal. I say on balance it does more good than harm if—if we can get some protection for the environment so that the Mexicans have to follow their own environmental standards, their own labor law standards, and if we have a genuine commitment to reeducate and retrain the American workers who lose their jobs and reinvest in this economy.

I have a realistic approach to trade. I want more trade. And I know there are some good things in that agreement. But it can sure be made better. Let me just point out: just today in the *Los Angeles Times* Clyde Prestowitz, who was one of President Reagan's leading trade advisers and a lifelong conservative Republican, endorsed my candidacy because he knows that I'll have a free and fair trade policy, a hardheaded realistic policy, and not get caught up in rubber-stamping everything the Bush Administration did. If I wanted to do that, why would I run for president, Jim? Anybody else can run the middle class down and run the economy in a ditch. I want to change it. We've got—

BUSH: I think he made my case. On the one hand, it's a good deal, but on the other hand, I'd make it better.

MODERATOR: All right. We've got—

BUSH: You can't do that as president. You can't do it on the war, where he says, well, I was with the minor—minority, but I guess I would have voted with the majority. This is my point tonight. We're talking about two weeks from now you've got to decide who's going to be president. And there is this pattern that has plagued him in the primaries and now about trying to have it both ways on all these issues. You can't do that. And if you make a mistake, say you made a mistake and go on about your business, trying to serve the American people.

Right now we heard it. Ross is against it. I am for it. He says, "On the one hand, I'm for it—on the other I may be against it."

CLINTON: That's what's wrong with Mr. Bush. His whole deal is you've got to be for it or against it. You can't make it better. I believe we can be better. I think the American people are sick and tired of either-or solutions, people being pushed in the corner, polarized to extremes. I think they want somebody with common sense who can do what's best for the American people. And I'd be happy to discuss these other issues. But I can't believe he is accusing me of getting on both sides. He said trickle-down economics is voodoo economics. Now he's its biggest practitioner.

He promised, you know—

BUSH: I've always said trickle-down government is bad.

CLINTON: I could run this string out a long time, but remember this, Jim: those 209 Americans last Thursday night in Richmond told us they wanted us to stop talking about each other and start talking about Americans and their problems and their promise, and I think we ought to get back to that. I'll be glad to answer any question you have, but this election ought to be about the American people.

MODERATOR: Mr. Perot?

PEROT: Is there an equal-time rule here tonight?

BUSH: Yes.

PEROT: Or do you just keep lunging in at will? I thought we were going to have equal time, but maybe I just have to interrupt the other two, is that the way it works?

MODERATOR: Mr. Perot, you're doing fine. Go ahead. Whatever you want to say, say it.

PEROT: Now that we've talked all around the problem about free trade, let's go, again, to the center of the bull's-eye.

MODERATOR: I thought you wanted to respond to what we're talking about.

PEROT: I do. I do. I just want to make sure—foreign lobbyists, this whole thing, our country has sold out to foreign lobbyists. We don't have free trade. Both parties have foreign lobbyists on leaves and key roles in the campaigns. And if there's anything more unwise than that, I don't know what it is.

Every debate I bring this up, nobody ever addresses it. I would like for them to look you in the eye and tell you why they have people representing foreign countries working on their campaigns. And you know, you've seen the list. I've seen the list. We won't go into the names, but no wonder they—if I had those people around me all day every day telling me what's fair and free, I might believe it. But if I look at the facts as a businessman, it's so tilted, the first thing you ought to do is just say, "Guys, if you like these deals so well, we'll give you the deal you gave us."

Now, Japanese couldn't unload the cars in this country if we—if they had the same restrictions we had, and on, and on, and on, and on, and on. I suggest to you that the core problem: one country spent $400 million lobbying in 1988, our country. And it goes on and on, and you look at a *Who's Who* in these campaigns, around the two candidates, they're foreign lobbyists taking leaves. What do you think they're going to do when the campaign's over? Go back to work at 30,000 bucks a month representing some other country. I don't believe that's in the American people's interest.

I don't have a one of them, and I haven't taken a penny of foreign money, and I never will.

MODERATOR: Mr. President, how do you respond to that? Mr. Perot's made that charge several times. The fact that you have people working in your campaign who are paid foreign lobbyists.

BUSH: Most of the people that are lobbying are lobbying the Congress. And I don't think there's anything wrong with an honest person who happens to represent an interest of another country from making his case. That's the American way. And what you're assuming is that that makes the recipient of the lobbying corrupt, or the lobbyist himself corrupt. I don't agree with that. But if I found somebody that was—had a conflict of interest that would try to illegally do something as a foreign registered lobby, the laws cover this. I don't know why—I've never understood quite why Mr. Perot was so upset about it because one of the guys he used to have working for him, I believe, had—had foreign accounts. Could be wrong, but I think so.

PEROT: And as soon as I found it out, he went out the door. Truth, yes!

BUSH: I don't—I think you got to look at the integrity and the honor of the people who are being lobbied and those that are lobbyists. The laws protect the American taxpayer in this regard if the laws are violated so much, but to suggest if somebody represents a foreign country on anything, that makes him corrupt or against the taxpayer, I don't agree with that.

PEROT: One quick relevant specific. We're getting ready to dismantle an airlines industry in our country, and none of you know it. And I doubt, in all candor, if the president knows it. But this deal that we're doing with BAC and USAir and KLM and Northwest—now guess who's on the president's campaign big-time? A guy from Northwest. This deal is terribly destructive to the U.S. airline industry; one of the largest industries in the world is the travel and tourist business.

We won't be making airplanes in this country ten years from now if we let deals like this go through. I can—if the press has any interest tonight, I'll detail it to you. I won't take ten minutes tonight. All these things take a few minutes, but that's happening as we sit here today. We hammerlock the American companies, American Airlines, Delta, the last few great we have, because we're trying to do this deal with these two European companies. And never forget, they've got Airbus over there, and it's a government-owned, privately owned consortium across Europe. They're dying to get the commercial airline business. Japan is trying to get the commercial airline business. I don't think there are any villains inside government on this issue, but there sure are a lot of people who don't understand business. And maybe you need somebody up there who understands when you're getting your pocket picked.

MODERATOR: All right. We have to—Governor, I'm sorry but that concludes my time with—

CLINTON: Boy, I had a great response to that.

MODERATOR: All right, go ahead quick—quickly.

CLINTON: Just very briefly.

MODERATOR: Yeah.

CLINTON: I think Ross is right and that we do need some more restrictions on lobbyists. We ought to make them disclose the people they've given money to when they're testifying before congressional committees. We ought to close the lawyers loophole. They ought to have to disclose when they're really lobbying. And we ought to limit the—we ought to have a much longer period of time, about five years, between the time when people can leave the executive branch offices and then go out and start lobbying for foreign interest. I agree with that. We've wrecked the airline industry already because—well, there's all these leveraged buyouts and all these terrible things that have happened to the airline industry. We're going to have a hard time rebuilding it, but the real thing we've got to have is a competitive economic strategy. Look what's happening to McDonnell Douglas, even Boeing is losing market share, because we let the Europeans spend $25 to $40 billion on Airbus without an appropriate competitive response. What I want America to do is to trade more but to compete and win by investing in competitive ways, and we're in real trouble on that.

MODERATOR: I'm going to be in real trouble if I don't bring out—it's now time—

BUSH: I promise it's less than ten seconds.

MODERATOR: O.K.

BUSH: I heard Governor Clinton congratulate us on one thing—first time he said something pleasant about this administration. Productivity in this country is up. It is way up. Productivity is up, and that's a good thing. There are many other good ones, but I was glad he acknowledged that. Thank you.

MODERATOR: Now we're going to move to the second half—

PEROT: Now give me one second. I volunteered now and all—I mean, now, look, I'm just kind of a, you know, cur dog here. I was put on the ballot by the people, not the special interests. So have to stand up for myself. Now, Jim, let me net it out. On the second debate, I offered, since both sides want the enterprise zones we can't get together—I said, I'll take a few days off, go to Washington, and hold hands with you and we'll get it done. I'll take a few days off, hold hands with you and get this airline thing straightened out, because that's important to this country.

That's kind of pathetic. I have to do it, and nobody's called me yet to come up, I might mention. But if they do—

MODERATOR: I want to—

PEROT: If they do, it's easy to fix. If you all want the enterprise zones. Why don't we pass the dang thing and do it, right?

MODERATOR: All right, now we're going to bring in the three other journalists to ask questions. They are Susan Rook of CNN, Gene Gibbons of Reuters, and Helen Thomas of United Press International. You thought you'd never get in here, did you?

MODERATOR: Good evening, gentlemen. Good evening. O.K., we're going to continue on the subject of leadership, and the first question goes to Governor Clinton for a two-minute answer. It will be asked by Helen Thomas. Helen?

QUESTION: Governor Clinton, your credibility has come into question because of your different responses on the Vietnam draft. If you had it to do over again, would you put on the nation's uniform, and if elected, could you in good conscience send someone to war?

CLINTON: If I had it to do over again, I might answer the questions a little better. You know, I've been in public life a long time, and no one had ever questioned my role, and so I was asked a lot of questions about things that happened a long time ago. I don't think I answered them as well as I could have.

Going back twenty-three years, I don't know, Helen. I was opposed to the war. I couldn't help that. I felt very strongly about it, and I didn't want to go at the time. It's easy to say in retrospect I would have done something differently. President Lincoln opposed the war, and there were people who said maybe he shouldn't be president. But I think he made us a pretty good president in wartime. We got a lot of other presidents who didn't wear their country's uniform and had to order our young soldiers into battle, including President Wilson and President Roosevelt. So the answer is, I could do that. I wouldn't relish doing it, but I wouldn't shrink from it. I think that the president has to be prepared to use the power of the nation when our vital interests are threatened. When our treaty commitments are at stake. When we know that something has to be done that is in the national interest and that is a part of being president. Could I do it? Yes, I could.

MODERATOR: All right, a reminder now—we're back on the St. Louis rules, which means that the governor had his answer and then each of you will have one minute to, to respond. Mr. President.

BUSH: Well, I've expressed my heartfelt feel—difference with Governor Clinton on organizing demonstrations while in a foreign land against your country when young ghetto kids have been drafted and are dying. My argument with him on the question was about the draft—is that there is this same pattern. It—in New Hampshire, Senator Kerrey said you ought to level, you ought to tell the truth about it. On April 17 he said he'd bring out all the records on the draft. They have not been forthcoming. He got a deferment or he didn't. He got a notice or he didn't. And I, I think it's this pattern that troubles me more than the draft. A lot of decent, honorable people felt as he did on the draft. But it is this pattern. And again, you might be able to make amendments all the time, Governor, but you've got to, as president, you can't be on all these different sides. And you can't have this pattern of saying, well, I'm, I did this or I didn't. Then the facts come out. And you change it. That's my big difference with him on the draft. It wasn't failing to serve.

MODERATOR: Your minute is up, sir.

BUSH: Yes, sir.

MODERATOR: Mr. Perot, one minute.

PEROT: I've spent my whole adult life very close to the military. Feel very strongly about the people who go into battle for our country. Appreciate their idealism, their sacrifices. Appreciate the sacrifices their families make. That's been displayed again and again in a very tangible way. I look on this as history. I don't look on it personally as relevant. And I consider it really a waste of time tonight when you consider the issues that face our country right now.

MODERATOR: All right. The next question goes to President Bush. And Gene Gibbons will ask it. Gene.

QUESTION: Mr. President, you keep saying that you made a mistake in agreeing to a tax increase to get the 1990 budget deal with Congress. But if you hadn't gotten that deal, you would have either had to get repeal of the Gramm-Rudman Deficit Control Act or cut defense spending drastically at a time when the country was building up for the Gulf War and decimate domestic discretionary spending, including such things as air traffic control. If you had it to do all over again, sir, which of those alternatives would you choose?

BUSH: I wouldn't have taken any of the alternatives. I believe that—I believe I made a mistake. I did it for the very reasons you say. There was one good thing that came out of that budget agreement, that is, we put a cap on discretionary spending—one-third of the president's budget is at the president's discretion, or really the Congress, since they appropriate every dime and tell a president how to spend every dime. We put a cap on the growth of all that spending and that's good, and that's helped. But I was wrong, because I thought the tax compromise—going along with one Democratic tax increase—would help the economy. I see no evidence that it has done it.

So what would I have done, what should I have done? I should have held out for a better deal that would have protected the taxpayer and not ended up doing what we had to do—or what I thought at the time would help. So I made a mistake. I—you know, the difference, I think, is that I knew at the time I was going to take a lot of political flak, I knew we'd have somebody out there yelling, "Read my lips." And I did it because I thought it was right, and I made a mistake.

That's quite different than taking a position where you know it's best for you. That wasn't best for me, and I knew it in the very beginning. I thought it would be better for the country than it was. So there we are.

QUESTION: Mr. Perot, one minute. Mr. Perot?

PEROT: 101 in leadership is to—is be accountable for what you do. Let's go back to a tax and budget summit briefly. Nobody ever told the American people that we increase spending $1.83 for every dollar tax is raised. That's absolutely unconscionable. Both parties carry a huge blame for that on their shoulders.

This was not a way to pay down the deficit, this was a trick on the American people. That's not leadership.

Let's go back in terms of accepting responsibility for your actions. If you create Saddam Hussein over a ten-year period, using billions of dollars of U.S. taxpayer money, step up to the plate and say, "It was a mistake." If you create Noriega, using taxpayer money, step up to the plate and say, "It was a mistake." If you can't get your act together to pick him up one day when the Panamanian major has kidnapped him, and the special forces team is 400 yards away and it's a stroll across the park to get him, and if you can't get your act together, at least pick up the Panamanian major who they then killed, step up to the plate, and admit it was a mistake. That's leadership, folks.

Now, leaders will always make mistakes. We have created—and I'm not aiming at any one person here, I'm aiming at our government—nobody takes responsibility for anything. We got to change that.

MODERATOR: I'm taking responsibility for saying your time's up.

PEROT: I'm watching the light.

MODERATOR: All right. Governor Clinton, one minute, sir.

CLINTON: The mistake that was made was making the "read my lips" promise in the first place, just to get elected, knowing what the size of the deficit was—knowing what the size of the deficit was, knowing there was no plan to control health care costs, and knowing that we did not have a strategy to get real economic growth back into this economy. The choices were not good then. I think at the time the mistake that was made was signing off on the deal late on Saturday night, in the middle of the night. That's just what the president did when he vetoed the Family Leave Act. I think what he should have done is gone before the American people on the front and said, "Listen, I made a commitment and it was wrong. I made a mistake because I couldn't have foreseen these circumstances, and this is the best deal we can work out at the time."

He said it was in the public interest at the time, and most everybody who was involved in it, I guess, thought it was. The real mistake was the "read my lips" promise in the first place. You just can't promise something like that just to get elected if you know there's a good chance that circumstances may overtake you.

MODERATOR: All right, Mr. Perot, the question is for you. You have a two-minute answer, and it will be asked by Susan Rook.

QUESTION: Mr. Perot, you've talked about going to Washington to do what the people who run this country want you to do, but it is the president's duty to lead and often lead alone. How can you lead if you are forever seeking consensus before you act?

PEROT: You're talking about two different subjects. In order to lead you first have to use the White House as a bully pulpit and lead. Then you have to develop consensus or you can't get anything done, and that's where we are now. We can't get anything done. How do you get anything done when you've got all of these political action committees, all of these thousands of registered lobbyists—40,000 registered lobbyists, 23,000 special interest groups, and the list goes on and on and on. And the average citizen out here, just working hard every day. You've got to go to the people. I just love the fact that everybody, particularly in the media, goes bonkers over the town hall. I guess it's because you will lose your right to tell them what to think.

The point is, they'll get to decide what to think! What you've been—I love the fact that people will listen to a guy with a bad accent and a poor presentation manner talking about flip charts for thirty minutes because they want the details. See, all the folks up there at the top said, "People—the attention span of the American people is no more than five minutes, they won't watch it." They're thirsty for it. You ought to have a new program in this country—if you get grass-roots America excited about it and if they tap Congress on the shoulder and say, "Do it, Charlie," it'll happen, and that's a whole lot different from these fellows running up and down the halls whispering in their ears now and promising campaign funds the next election if they do it.

Now, I think that's going back to where we started. That's having a government from the people. I think that's the essence of leadership, rather than cutting deals in dark rooms in Washington.

MODERATOR: Governor Clinton, one minute.

CLINTON: Well, I believe in the town hall meetings. They started with my campaign in New Hampshire. And I think Ross Perot has done a good job in having them, and I, I, as you know, pushed for the debate to include the 209 American citizens who were part of it in Richmond a few days ago. I've done a lot of them, and I'll continue to do them as president.

But I'd also like to point out that I haven't been part of what we're criticizing in Washington tonight. Of the three of us, I have balanced a government budget twelve times. I have offered and passed campaign finance reform. Offered—pushed for and passed in public referendum lobbyist restrictions. Done the kinds of things you have to do to get legislators together, not only to establish consensus but to challenge in the change. And in twelve years as governor I guess I've taken on every interest group there was in my state at one time or another, to fight for change. It can be done. That's why I tried to be so specific in this campaign to have a mandate if elected so the Congress will know what the American people have voted for.

MODERATOR: President Bush, one minute.

BUSH: I would like the record to show to the panelists that Ross Perot took the first shot at the press. My favorite bumper sticker, though, is: "Annoy the media. Re-elect President Bush." And I just had to work that in. Sorry, Helen. I'm going to pay for this later on.

Look, you have to build a consensus, but in some things—Ross mentioned Saddam Hussein. Yes, we tried. And yes, we failed to bring him into the family of nations. He had the fourth largest army. But then when he moved against Kuwait, I said, "This will not stand." And it's hard to build a consensus. We went to the U.N., we made historic resolutions up there. The whole world was united. Our Congress was dragging its feet. Governor Clinton said, "Well, I might have been with the minority. Let's see how sanctions work. But I guess I would have voted with the majority." A president can't do that. Sometimes he has to act, and in this case I'm glad we did, because if we had let the sanctions work, and had tried to build a consensus on that, Saddam Hussein today would be in Saudi Arabia controlling the world's oil supply, and he would be there maybe with a nuclear weapon. We busted the fourth largest army, and we did it through leadership.

MODERATOR: All right, we're going to go on to another subject now, and the subject is priorities, and the first question goes to you, President Bush, and Susan will ask it.

QUESTION: President Bush, gentlemen, I acknowledge that all of you have women and ethnic minorities working for you and working with you, but when we look at the circle of the key people closest to you—your inner circle of advisers—we see white men only. Why and when will that change?

BUSH: You don't see Margaret Tutwiler sitting in there with me today?

QUESTION: The key people, President Bush.

BUSH: Huh?

QUESTION: The key people. The people—

BUSH: I happen to think she's a key person.

QUESTION: —beyond the glass ceiling.

BUSH: I think our Cabinet members are key people. I think the woman that works with me, Rose Zamaria, is about as tough as a boot out there and can make some discipline and protects the taxpayer. Look at our Cabinet—you talk about somebody strong, look at Carla Hills. Look at Lynn Martin, who's fighting against this glass ceiling and doing a first class job on it. Look at our surgeon general,

Dr. Novella. You can look all around, and you'll see first class, strong women. Jim Baker's a man. Yeah, I agree—I plead guilty to that. But look around who's—look who's around with him there. I mean, this is a little defensive on your part, Susan, to be honest with you. We've got a very good record appointing women to high positions and positions of trust, and I'm not defensive at all about it. What we got to do is keep working—as the Labor Department is doing a first class job on—to break down discrimination, to break down the glass ceiling, and I am not apologetic at all about our record with women. We've got, I think—you know you think about women in government, I think about women in business. Why not try to help them with my small business program to build some incentives into the system?

I, I, I think we're making progress here. You've got a lot of women running for office. As I said the other night, I hope a lot of them lose, because they're liberal Democrats, and we don't need more of them in the Senate or more of them in the House. But nevertheless, they're out there, and we've got some very good Republican women running. So we're making dramatic progress.

MODERATOR: Mr. Perot, one minute.

PEROT: Well, I've come from the computer business, and everybody knows women are more talented than the men. So we have a long history of having a lot of talented women. One of our first officers was a woman, the chief financial officer. She was the director, and it was so far back it was considered so odd, and even though we were a tiny little company at the time, it made all the national magazines. But in terms of being influenced by women and being a minority, there they are right out there, my wife and my four beautiful daughters, and I just have one son, so he and I are surrounded by women giving—telling us what to do, all the time.

And for the rest of my minute, I want to make a very brief comment here, in terms of Saddam Hussein. We told him that we wouldn't get involved with his border dispute and we've never revealed those papers that were given to Ambassador Glaspie on July the 25th. I suggest, in the sense of taking responsibility for your actions, we lay those papers on the table. They're not secrets to the nuclear bomb.

Secondly, we got upset when he took the whole thing. But to the ordinary American out there who doesn't know where the oil fields are in Kuwait, they're near the border. We told him he could take the northern part of Kuwait, and when he took the whole thing, we went nuts. And if we didn't tell him that, why won't we even let the Senate Foreign Relations Committee and the Senate Intelligence Committee see the written instructions for Ambassador Glaspie?

BUSH: I have to reply on that—that—that gets to the national honor.

We did not say to Saddam Hussein, Ross, you can take the northern part of Kuwait.

PEROT: Well, where are the papers?

BUSH: That is absolutely absurd.

PEROT: Where are the papers?

BUSH: Glaspie has testified, and Glaspie's papers have been presented to the United States Senate. Now, please.

PEROT: If you have time, if you have time, go to Nexis and Lexis, pull all the old news articles, look at what Ambassador Glaspie said all through the fall and what have you, and then look at what she and Kelly and others in State said at the end, when they were trying to clean it up. And talk to any head of any of those key committees in the Senate—they will not let them see the written instructions given to Ambassador Glaspie. And I suggest that in a free society owned by the people, the American people ought to know what we told Ambassador Glaspie to tell Saddam Hussein, because we spent a lot of money and risked lives and lost lives in that effort and did not accomplish most of our objectives. We got Kuwait back to the Emir, but he's still got his nuclear, his chemical, his bacteriological, and he's still over there, right? I'd like to see those written instructions. Sir.

MODERATOR: Mr. President, when you—just to make sure that everybody knows what's going on here. When you responded directly to Mr. Perot—

BUSH: Yes.

MODERATOR: —you violated the rule—your rule. Now, I'm more than willing—

BUSH: For which I apologize. When I make a mistake, I—

MODERATOR: No, it's O.K. No, no, no. I just want to make sure that everybody—I just want to make sure everybody understands it. If you all want to change the rules, we can do it.

BUSH: No, I don't. I apologize for it. But that one got right to the national honor, and I'm sorry—

MODERATOR: O.K. But, but, Governor Clinton, you have a minute.

CLINTON: Susan, I don't agree that there are no women and minorities in important positions in my campaign. There are many. But I think even more relevant is my record at home. For most of my time as governor a woman was my chief of staff. An African-American was my chief cabinet officer; an African-American was my chief economic development officer.

It was interesting today—there was a story either today or yesterday in the *Washington Post* about my economic programs, and my chief budget officer and my chief economic officer were both African-Americans, even though the *Post* didn't mention that, which I think is a sign of progress. The National Women's Political Caucus gave me an award, one of their good guy awards for my involvement of women in high levels of government. And I've appointed more minorities to positions of high level in government than all the governors in the history of my state combined before me.

So that's what I'll do as president. I don't think we've got a person to waste, and I think I owe the American people a White House staff, a Cabinet, and appointments that look like America but that meet high standards of excellence, and that's what I'll do.

MODERATOR: All right, next question goes to you, Mr. Perot. It's a two-minute—it's a two-minute question, and Helen will ask it. Helen.

QUESTION: Mr. Perot, what proof do you have that Saddam Hussein was told that he could have the oil? Do you have any actual proof? Or are you asking for the papers?

PEROT: I—

QUESTION: And also, I really came in with another question, is, what is this penchant you have to investigate everyone? Are those accusations correct? Investigating your staff, investigating the leaders of the grassroots movement, investigating associates of your family?

PEROT: No. They're not correct. And if you look at my life for the first—until I got involved in this effort, I was one person. And then after the Republican dirty tricks group got through with me, I'm another person. Which I consider an absolutely sick operation. And all of you in the press know exactly what I'm talking about. They investigated every single one of my children. They investigated my wife. They interviewed all of my children's friends from childhood on. They went to extraordinary, sick lengths.

And I just found it amusing that they would take two or three cases where I was involved in lawsuits and would engage an investigator. The lawyers would engage an investigator, which is common. And the only difference between me and any other businessman that has the range of businesses I have is I haven't had that many lawsuits. So that's just another one of those little fruit-loopy things they make up to try to—instead of facing issues, to try to redefine a person's—that's running against them. This goes on night and day. I will do everything I can, if I get up there, to make dirty tricks a thing of the past. One of the two groups has raised it to an art form. It's a sick art form.

Now let's go back to Saddam Hussein. We gave Ambassador Glaspie written instructions. That's a fact. We've never let the Congress and the Foreign Relations—Senate Intelligence Committee see them. That's a fact. Ambassador Glaspie did a lot of talking right after July the 25th. And that's a fact that's in all the newspapers, and you pull all of it at once and read it—and I did—and it's pretty clear what she and Kelly and the other key guys around that thing thought they were doing. Then, at the end of the war, when they had to go testify about it, their stories are a total disconnect from what they said in August, September, and October. So I say, this is very simple. Saddam Hussein released a tape, as you know, claiming it was a transcript of their meeting, whereas she said, "We will not become involved in your border dispute." In effect, you can take the northern part of the country. We later said, "No, that's not true." I said, "Well, this is simple. What were her written instructions?" We guard those like the secrets to the atomic bomb, literally. Now, I say, whose country is this? This is ours. Who will get hurt if we lay those papers on the table? The worst thing is, it's again, it's a mistake. Nobody did any of this with evil intent. I just object to the fact that we cover up and hide things, whether it's Iran-Contra, Iraq-gate or you name it, it's a steady stream.

MODERATOR: Governor Clinton, you have one minute.

CLINTON: Let's take Mr. Bush, for the moment, at his word. He's right, we don't have any evidence, at least, that our government did tell Saddam Hussein he could have that part of Kuwait. And let's give him the credit he deserves for organizing Operation Desert Storm and Desert Shield. It was a remarkable event.

But let's look at where I think the real mistake was made. In 1988, when the war between Iraq and Iran ended, we knew Saddam Hussein was a tyrant. We had dealt with him because he was against Iran, the enemy of my enemy may be, is, my friend. All right, the war is over. We know he's dropping mustard gas on his own people. We know he's threatened to incinerate half of Israel. Several government departments, several, had information that he was converting our aid to military purposes and trying to develop weapons of mass destruction. But in late '89 the president signed a secret policy saying we were going to continue to try to improve relations with him, and we sent him some sort of communication on the eve of his invasion of Kuwait that we still wanted better relations. So I think what was wrong, I give credit where credit is due, but the responsibility was in coddling Saddam Hussein when there was no reason to do it and when people in high levels in our government knew he was trying to do things that were outrageous.

MODERATOR: Mr. President, you have a moment. A minute, I'm sorry.

BUSH: Well, it's awful easy when you're dealing with 90/90 hindsight. We did try to bring Saddam Hussein into the family of nations. He did have the fourth largest army. All our Arab allies out there thought we ought to do just exactly that. And when he crossed the line, I stood up and looked into the camera, and I said, "This aggression will not stand." And we formed a historic coalition, and we brought him down. And we destroyed the fourth army, fourth largest army. And the battlefield was searched, and there wasn't one single iota of evidence that any U.S. weapons were on that battlefield, and the nuclear capability has been searched by the United Nations, and there hasn't been one single scintilla of evidence that there's any U.S. technology involved in it.

And what you're seeing, on all this Iraq-gate, is a bunch of people who were wrong on the war trying to cover their necks here and—and try to do a little revisionism. And I cannot let that stand, because it isn't true. Yes, we had grain credits for Iraq, and there isn't any evidence that those grain credits were diverted into weaponry. None. None whatsoever. And so I—I just have to say, it's fine.

MODERATOR: We have to go on.

BUSH: You can't say there, Governor Clinton, and say, well, I think I'd have been—I've supported the minority, let sanctions work or wish it'd go away, but I would have voted with the majority. Come on, that's not leadership.

MODERATOR: All right. The next question goes to Governor Clinton, and Gene Gibbons will ask it. Gene.

QUESTION: Governor, an important aspect of leadership is of course anticipating problems. During the 1988 campaign there was little or no mention of the savings-and-loan crisis that has cost the American people billions and billions of dollars. Now there are rumblings that a commercial bank crisis is on the horizon. Is there such a problem, sir? If so, how bad is it, and what will it cost to clean it up?

CLINTON: Gene, there is a problem in the sense that there are some problem banks, and on December 19 new regulations will go into effect which will, in effect, give the government the responsibility to close some banks that are not technically insolvent but that are plainly in trouble. On the other hand, I don't think that we have any reason to believe that the dimensions of this crisis are anywhere near as great as the savings-and-loan crisis. The mistake that both parties made in Washington with the S&L business was deregulating them without proper capital requirements, proper oversight and regulation, proper training of the executives. Many people predicted what happened, and it was a disaster.

The banking system in this country is fundamentally sound, with some weak banks. I think that our goal ought to be first of all not to politicize it, not to frighten people, secondly, to say that we have to enforce the law in two ways. We don't want to overreact as—as the federal regulators have, in my judgment, on good banks so that they've created credit crunches that has, that have, made our recession worse in the last couple of years. But we do want to act prudently with the banks that are in trouble. We also want to say that, insofar as is humanly possible, the banking industry itself should pay for the cost of any bank failures; the taxpayers should not. And that will be my policy, and I believe we have a good, balanced approach. We can get the good banks loaning money again, end the credit crunch, have proper regulation on the ones that are in trouble. And not overreact. It is a serious problem, but I don't see it as the kind of terrible, terrible problem that the S&L problem was.

MODERATOR: President Bush, one minute.

BUSH: Well, I don't—I don't believe it would be appropriate for a president to suggest that the banking system is not sound. It is sound. There are some problem banks out there. But what we need is financial reform. We need some real financial reform—banking reform legislation. And I have proposed that, and when I am reelected I believe the first—one of the first things ought to be to press a new Congress, not beholden to the old ways, to pass financial reform legislation that modernizes the banking system, doesn't put a lot of inhibitions on it, and protects the depositors through keeping the FDIC sound, but I—I think that—that—I just was watching some of the proceedings of the American Bankers Association, and I think the general feeling is most of the banks are sound. Certainly there's no comparison here between what happened to the S&Ls and where the banks stand right now, in my view.

MODERATOR: Mr. Perot, one minute.

PEROT: Well, nobody's gotten into the real issue yet on the savings and loan. Again, nobody's got a business background, I guess. The whole problem came up in 1984. The president of the United States was told officially it was a $20 billion problem. These crooks—now, Willie Sutton would have gone to own a savings and loan rather than rob banks because you—he robbed banks because that's where the money is, only the saving and loan is where the money was. Yeah. In 1984, they were told. I believe the vice president was in charge of deregulation. Nobody touched that tar baby till the day after elections in 1988, because they were flooding both parties with crooked PAC money, and it was in many cases stolen PAC money.

Now, you and I never got a ride on a lot of these yachts and fancy things it bought, but you and I are paying for it. And they buried it till right after the election. Now, if you believe the *Washington Post* and you believe this extensive study that's been done—and I'm reading it—right after election day this year, they're going to hit us with 100 banks—it'll be a $100 billion problem. Now, if that's true, just tell me now. Yeah, I'm grown up, I can deal with it, I'll pay my share. But just tell me now. Don't bury it until after the election twice. I say that to both political parties. The people deserve that, since we have to pick up the tab. You got the PAC money; we'll pay the tab. Just tell us.

MODERATOR: All right, Mr. Perot, the next question—we're going into a new round here, on a category just called differences, and the question goes to you, Mr. Perot, and Gene will ask it. Gene?

QUESTION: Mr. Perot, aside from the deficit, what government policy or policies do you really want to do something about? What really sticks in your craw about conditions in this country, beside the deficit, that you would want to fix as president?

PEROT: The debt and the deficit. Well, if you watched my television show the other night, you saw it, and if you watch it Thursday, Friday, Saturday of this week you'll get more. So a shameless plug there, Mr. President. But in a nutshell, we've got to reform our government, or we won't get anything done. We have a government that doesn't work. All these specific examples I'm giving tonight, if you had a business like that, they'd be leading you away and boarding up the doors.

We have a government that doesn't work. It's supposed to come from the people; it comes at the people. The people need to take their government back. You've got to reform Congress. They've got be servants of the people again. You've got to reform the White House. We've got to turn this thing around, and it's a long list of specific items. And I've covered it again and again in print and on television, but very specifically, the key thing is to turn the government back to the people and take it away from special interests and have people go to Washington to serve.

Who can give themselves a 23 percent pay raise anywhere in the world except Congress? Who would have 1,200 airplanes worth $2 billion a year just to fly around in? I don't have a free reserved parking place at National Airport; why should my servants? I don't have an indoor gymnasium and an indoor tennis court, an indoor every other thing they can think of. I don't have a place where I can go make free TV to send to my constituents to try to blame Washington—to elect me the next time. And I'm paying for all that for those guys. I'm going to be running an ad pretty soon that shows—they promised us they were going to hold the line on spending, a tax and budget summit, and I'm going to show how much they have increased this little stuff they do for themselves, and it is Silly Putty, folks, and the American people have had enough of it.

Step 1, if I get up there, we're going to clean that up. You say, how can I get Congress to do that? I have millions of people at my shoulder—shoulder to shoulder with me, and we will see it done warp speed. Because it's wrong. It's just—we've turned the country upside down.

MODERATOR: Governor Clinton, you have one minute. Governor.

CLINTON: I would just point out on the—the point Mr. Perot made. I agree that we need to cut spending in Congress. I've called for a 25 percent reduction in congressional staffs and expenditures. But the White House staff increased its expenditures by considerably more than Congress has in the last four years under the Bush administration. And Congress has actually spent a billion dollars less than President Bush asked them to spend. Now, when you outspend Congress, you're really swinging.

That, however, is not my only passion. The real problem in this country is that most people are working hard and falling farther behind. My passion is to pass a jobs program and get incomes up with an investment incentive program to grow jobs in the private sector, to waste less public money and invest more, to control health care costs and provide for affordable health care for all Americans. And to make sure we've got the best trained workforce in the world. That is my passion. We've got to get this country growing again and this economy strong again or we can't bring down the deficit. Economic growth is the key to the future of this country.

MODERATOR: President Bush, one minute.

BUSH: On government reform?

MODERATOR: Sir?

BUSH: Government reform?

MODERATOR: To—yes, exactly, well to respond to what the—the subject that Mr. Perot mentioned.

BUSH: Well—how about this for a government reform policy? Reduce the White House staff by a third after or at the same time the Congress does the same thing for their staff; term limits for members of the United States Congress; give the government back to the people. Let's do it that way. The president has term limits. Let's—let's limit some of these guys sitting out here tonight. Term limits and then how about a balanced budget amendment to the Constitution? Forty-three—more than that have—states have it, I believe. Let's try that.

And you want to do something about all this extra spending that concerns Mr. Perot and me? O.K., how about a line item veto. Forty-three governors have that. And give it to the president, and if the Congress isn't big enough to do it, let the president have a shot at this excess spending. A line item veto, that means you can take a line and cut out some of the pork out of a meaningful bill. Governor Clinton keeps hitting me on vetoing legislation. Well, that's the only protection the taxpayer has against some of these reckless pork programs up there. And I'd rather be able to just line it right out of there and get on about passing some good stuff but leave out the garbage.

MODERATOR: All right, we have—

BUSH: Line item veto. There is a good reform program for you.

MODERATOR: All right. A—next question goes to Governor Clinton. You have—you have two minutes, Governor, and Susan will ask it.

QUESTION: Governor Clinton, you said that you will raise taxes on the rich, people with incomes of $200,000 a year or higher. A lot of people are saying that you will have to go lower than that. Much lower. Will you make a pledge tonight below which, an income level that you will not go below? I'm looking for numbers, sir, not just a concept.

CLINTON: My plan—you can read my plan. My plan says that we want to raise marginal income tax on family incomes above $200,000 from 31 to 36 percent; that we want to ask foreign corporations simply to pay the same percentage of taxes on their income that American corporations pay in America. That we want to use that money to provide over $100 billion in tax cuts for investment in new plant and equipment, for small business, for new technologies, and for middle-class tax relief.

Now, I'll tell you this: I will not raise taxes on the middle class to pay for these programs. If the money does not come in there to pay for these programs, we will cut other government spending, or we will slow down the phase-in of the programs. I am not going to raise taxes on the middle class to pay for these programs. Now, furthermore, I am not going to tell you, "Read my lips." On anything. Because I cannot foresee what emergencies might develop in this country. And the president said never, never, never would, never would he raise taxes in New Jersey, and within a day Marlin Fitzwater, his spokesman, said, "Now, that's not a promise." So I think even he has learned that you can't say, "Read my lips," because you can't know what emergencies might come up.

But I can tell you this. I'm not going to raise taxes on middle-class Americans to pay for the programs I recommended. Read my plan. And you can—you know how you can trust me about that? Because you know, in that first debate, Mr. Bush made some news. He had just said Jim Baker was going to be secretary of state, but in the first debate he said, "No, now he's going to be responsible for domestic economic policy." Well, I'll tell you. I'll make some news in the third debate. The person responsible for domestic economic policy in my administration will be Bill Clinton. I'm going to make those decisions. And I won't raise taxes on the middle class to pay for my programs.

MODERATOR: President Bush, you have one minute.

BUSH: That's what worries me. That he's going to be responsible.

He's going to do—he would do—and he would do for the United States what he's done to Arkansas. He would do for the United States what he's done to Arkansas. We do not want to be the lowest of the low. We are not a nation in decline. We are a rising nation. Now, my problem is I heard what he said. He said I want to raise—take it from the rich. Raise $150 billion from the rich to get it—to get $150 billion in new taxes, you got to go down to the guy that's making $36,600. And if you want to pay for the rest of his plan, all the other spending programs, you're going to sock it to the workingman. So when you hear, "Tax the rich," Mr. and Mrs. America, watch your wallet. Lock your wallet; he's coming right after you. Just like Jimmy Carter did and just like you're going to get—you're going to end up with interest rates at 21 percent, and you're going to have inflation going through the roof. Yes, we're having tough times, but we do not need to go back to the failed policies of the past when you had a Democratic president and a spendthrift Democratic Congress.

MODERATOR: Mr. Perot.

CLINTON: You permitted Mr. Bush to break the rules. He said to defend the honor of the country. What about the honor of my state? We rank first in the country in job growth. We got the lowest spending state and local in the country and the second lowest tax burden, and the difference between Arkansas and the United States is that we're going in the right direction and this country is going in the wrong direction, and I have to defend the honor of my state.

MODERATOR: We've got a wash, according to my calculation we have a wash, and we go to Mr. Perot for one minute. In other words, it's a violation of the rule, that's what I meant, Mr. Perot.

PEROT: So I'm the only one that's untarnished at this point.

MODERATOR: Right, you're clean. You're clean.

CLINTON: Go ahead, Ross. Go ahead.

PEROT: I'm sure I'll do it before it's over. The key thing is, see, we all come up with images. Images don't fix anything. I think—you know, I'm starting to understand it, you stay around this long enough, you think about it—if you talk about it in Washington, you think you did it. If you've been on television about it, you think you did it. What we need is people to stop talking and start doing. Our real problem here is they have—both have plans that will not work. The *Wall Street Journal* said your numbers don't add up. And you take it out on charts, you look at all the studies that different groups have done, you go out four, five, six years, we're still drifting along with a huge deficit.

So let's come back to harsh reality. And what I—you know, everybody says, "Gee, Perot, you're tough." I'm saying, "Well, this is not as tough as World War II, and it's not as tough as the Revolution."

And it's fair-shared sacrifice to do the right thing for our country and for our children. And it will be fun, if we all work together to do it.

MODERATOR: All right, this is the last question and it goes to President Bush for a two-minute answer, and it will be asked by Helen.

QUESTION: Mr. President, why have you dropped so dramatically in the leadership polls from the high eighties to the forties? And you have said that you will do anything you have to do to get reelected. What can you do in two weeks to win reelection?

BUSH: Well, I think the answer to why the drop, I think, has been the economy in the doldrums. Why I'll win is I think I have the best plan of the three of us up here to do something about it. Mine does not grow the government, it does not invest—have government invest. It says we need to do better in terms of stimulating private business.

We got a big philosophical difference here tonight between one who thinks the government can do all these things through tax and spend, and one who thinks it ought to go the other way. And so I believe the answer is, I'm going to win it, because I'm getting into focus my agenda for America's renewal, and also I think that Governor Clinton's had pretty much of a free ride on looking at—specifically at the Arkansas record. He keeps criticizing us, criticizing me, I'm the incumbent. Fine. But he's an incumbent, and we've got to look at all the facts. They're almost at the bottom on every single category. We can't do that to the American people.

And then, Helen, I really believe we—people are going to ask this question about trust, because I do think there's a pattern by Governor Clinton of saying one thing to please one group and then trying to please another group. And I think that pattern is a dangerous thing to suggest would work for the Oval Office. It doesn't work that way when you're president. Truman is right: the buck stops there. And you have to make decisions even when it's against your own interests. And I've done that. It was against my political interests to say, "Go ahead," and go along with the tax increase, but I did what I thought was right at the time.

So I think people are going to be looking for trust and experience. And then I mentioned it the other night. I think if there's a crisis, people are going to say, "Well, George Bush has taken us through some tough crises, and we trust him to do that." And so I'll make the appeal on a wide array of issues. Also I got a philosophical difference—I've got to watch the clock here—I don't think we're a declining nation. The whole world has had economic problems; we're doing better than a lot of the countries in the world. And we're going to lead the way out of this economic recession across the world and economic slowdown here at home.

MODERATOR: Mr. Perot—

BUSH: So I think I'll win.

MODERATOR: Mr. Perot, you have—sorry, excuse me, sir. Mr. Perot, you have one minute.

PEROT: I'm the last one, right?

MODERATOR: No, Governor Clinton has a minute after you. Then we have the closing statements.

PEROT: I have one minute after you.

MODERATOR: Correct.

PEROT: I'm totally focused on the fact that we may have bank failures and nobody answered it. I'm totally focused on the fact that we are still evading the issue of the Glaspie papers. I'm totally focused on the fact that we still could have enterprise zones according to both parties, but we don't. So I'm still focused on gridlock, I guess.

And I am also focused on the fact that isn't it a paradox that we have the highest productivity in our workforce in the industrialized world and at the same time have the largest trade deficit and at the same time rank behind nine other nations in what we pay our most productive people in the world and that we're losing whole industries overseas.

Now, can't somebody agree with me that the government is breaking business's legs with these trade agreements? They're breaking business's legs in a number of different ways. We have an adversarial relationship that's destroying jobs and sending them overseas while we have the finest workers in the world.

Keep in mind the factory worker has nothing to do with anything except putting it together on the factory floor. It's our obligation to make sure that we give him the finest products in the world to put together and we don't break his legs in the process.

MODERATOR: Governor Clinton, one minute.

CLINTON: I really can't believe Mr. Bush is still trying to make trust an issue after "Read my lips" and 15 million new jobs and embracing what he called voodoo economics and embracing an export enhancement program for farmers he threatened to veto and going all around the country giving out money in programs that he once opposed.

But the main thing is he still didn't get it from what he said the other night to that fine woman on our program, that the 209 people in Richmond—they don't want us to keep talking about each other, they want us to talk about the problems of this country.

I don't think he'll be reelected, because trickle-down economics is a failure, and he's offering more of it. And what he's saying about my program is just not true. Look at the Republicans that have endorsed me—high-tech executives in Northern California. Look at the twenty-four generals and admirals retired who have endorsed me, including the deputy commander of Desert Storm. Look at Sarah Brady, Jim Brady's wife—President Reagan's press secretary who endorsed me because he knuckled under to the NRA and wouldn't fight for the Brady Bill.

We've got a broad-based coalition that goes beyond party, because I am going to change this country and make it better with the help of the American people.

Closing Statements

MODERATOR: All right. Now that—that was the final, that was the final question and answer, and we now go to the closing statements. Each candidate will have up to two minutes. The order was determined by a drawing. Governor Clinton you are first. Governor.

CLINTON: First, I'd like to thank the commission and my opponents for participating in these debates and making them possible. I think the real winners of the debates were the American people. I was especially moved in Richmond a few days ago when 209 of our fellow citizens got to ask us questions. They went a long way toward reclaiming this election for the American people and taking their country back. I want to say, since this is the last time I'll be on a platform with my opponents, that even though I disagree with Mr. Perot on how fast we can reduce the deficit and how much we can increase taxes on the middle class, I really respect what he's done in this campaign to bring the issue of deficit reduction to our attention. I'd like to say to Mr. Bush, even though I've got profound differences with him, I do honor his service to our country. I appreciate his efforts, and I wish him well. I just believe it's time to change.

I offer a new approach. It's not trickle-down economics. It's been tried for twelve years, and it's failed. More people are working harder for less, 100,000 a month losing their health insurance, unemployment going up, our economy slowing down. We can do better. And it's not tax-and-spend economics. It's invest and grow, put our people first, control health care costs, and provide basic health care to all Americans. Have an education system second to none and revitalize the private economy.

That is my commitment to you. It is the kind of change that can open up a whole new world of opportunities to America as we enter the last decade of this century and move toward the twenty-first century. I want a country where people who work hard and play by the rules are rewarded, not punished. I want a country where people are coming together across the lines of race and region and income. I know we can do better. It won't take miracles and it won't happen overnight, but we can do much, much better if we have the courage to change. Thank you very much.

MODERATOR: President Bush, your closing statement, sir.

BUSH: Three weeks from now—two—two weeks from tomorrow, America goes to the polls, and you're going to have to decide who you want to lead this country to economic recovery. On jobs, that's the Number 1 priority, and I believe my program for stimulating investment, encouraging small business, brand new approach to education, strengthening the American family, and, yes, creating more exports is the way to go.

I don't believe in trickle-down government. I don't believe in larger taxes and larger government spending. On foreign affairs, some think it's irrelevant. I believe it's not. We're living in an interconnected world. The whole world is having economic difficulties. The U.S. is doing better than a lot, but we've got to do even better, and if a crisis comes up, I ask who—who has the judgment and the experience and, yes, the character, to make the right decision.

And lastly, the other night on character, Governor Clinton said it's not the character of the president, but the character of the presidency. I couldn't disagree more. Horace Greeley said the only thing that endures is character. And I think it was Justice Black who talked about great nations like great men must keep their word. And so the question is, who will safeguard this nation? Who will safeguard our people and our children? I need your support. I ask for your vote. And may God bless the United States of America.

MODERATOR: Mr. Perot—Mr. Perot, your closing statement. Mr. Perot, your closing statement, sir.

PEROT: To the millions of fine, decent people who did the unthinkable and took their country back in their own hands and put me on the ballot, let me pledge to you that tonight is just the beginning. These next two weeks, we will be going full steam ahead to make sure that you get a voice and that you get your country back. This Thursday night on ABC from 8:30 to 9:00, Friday night on NBC from 8:00 to 8:30, and Saturday night on CBS from 8:00 to 8:30, we'll be down in the trenches, under the hood, working on fixing the old car to get it back on the road. Now, question is: can we win? Absolutely we can win, 'cause it's your country. Question is—really is: who do you want in the White House? It's that simple. Now you got to stop letting these people tell you who to vote for, you got to stop letting these folks in the press tell you you're throwing your vote away. You got to start using your own head.

Then the question is: can we govern? That—I love that one. The "we" is you and me. You bet your hat we can govern, because we will be in there together, and we will figure out what to do, and you won't tolerate gridlock, you won't tolerate endless meandering and wandering around, and you won't tolerate nonperformance. And believe me, anybody that knows me understands I have a very low tolerance for nonperformance also. Together we can get anything done. The president mentioned that you need the right person in a crisis. Well, folks, we got one. And that crisis is a financial crisis.

Pretty simply—who's the best qualified person up here on the stage to create jobs? Make your decision and vote on November 3. I suggest you might consider somebody who's created jobs. Second, who's the best person to manage money? I suggest you pick a person who's successfully managed money. Who's the best person to get results and not talk? Look at the record and make your decision. And finally, who would you give your pension fund and your savings account to—to manage? And last one—who would you ask to be the trustee of your estate and take care of your children if something happened to you? Finally, to you students up there, God bless you. I'm doing this for you. I want you to have the American dream. All right. And to the American people, to the American people, I'm doing this because I love you. That's it. Thank you very much.

Appendix 1
Procedures Employed in the Study

This study used a computer program for qualitative research to facilitate analysis of the debates: The Ethnograph. This program requires computer text files for the discourse being studied, and these files must be formatted into a particular format. Computer files of the transcripts of the three 1992 presidential debates were edited to prepare them for this analysis (one file for each debate). First, all questions and comments by the moderators were eliminated: only the utterances by the candidates were coded (of course, transcripts of both questions and answers were kept to help interpret and code the candidates' responses where necessary). Ethnograph does not require this procedure, but the computer files for each of the three debates were fairly long. Because we were coding only the candidates' utterances, and not the questions, we decided to delete all other comments to shorten the three files.

Second, in order for the computer program to be able to process the transcript files, margins were changed. Each candidate's turn at talk was formatted into a hanging indent, with the beginning of each utterance flush left, and the remainder of the turn indented. A right margin of forty left room for Ethnograph to number each line of the transcript. This margin also provided space for Ethnograph to insert coding symbols into the file on each numbered line.

Furthermore, symbols were inserted to identify the beginning of discrete segments of the transcripts (i.e., the beginning of a candidate's turn). Ethnograph uses a plus sign (+) to identify the beginning of a turn at talk. We provided two bits of information for each turn at talk. We labeled each turn as D1, D2, or D3, depending upon whether the transcript belonged to the first, second, or third debate. Also, we identified the candidate who was speaking in each utterance as B(ush), C(linton), or P(erot). We could have added codes to provide other information (e.g., we could have consecutively numbered each turn at talk for the candidate), but we chose not to do so.

Next, the Ethnograph produced a printed transcript with numbers for each line. We used these numbered transcripts to perform the initial coding of the debates as discussed in chapter 2. Transcripts produced by Ethnograph were coded (see, e.g., Holsti, 1969; or Weber, 1985) as instances of the strategies of persuasive attack and defense. Three steps were involved in the coding process. First, we identified each example of persuasive attack or persuasive defense in the three debates. The coding unit employed here was the theme, a coherent utterance that could be a paragraph, a sentence, or even part of a sentence. Berelson defined a theme as "an assertion about a subject matter" (1952, p. 18). In the case of persuasive attack, the subject matter was one of the candidate's opponents (Bush, Clinton, Perot) and the assertion concerned an offensive action or characteristic in the utterance linked to that opponent. In the case of persuasive defense, the subject is the candidate him- or herself, and the assertion rejects the offensiveness of the alleged action (or characteristic) and/or the candidate's responsibility for that action (or characteristic).

Once themes of persuasive attack and of persuasive defense had been identified, each instance of attack or defense was coded utilizing the strategies of persuasive attack and defense discussed above and summarized in tables 1 and 2 (one category of persuasive defense, attacking accuser, was omitted because this analysis codes persuasive attack separately). These codes consisted of three letters: the first letter designated an utterance as either attack (A) or defense (D), and the second and third letters uniquely identified one of the specific attacking or defending categories. Third, we identified the line numbers containing the beginning and end of the utterance (of course, a particular line of the transcript often contained the end of one strategy and the beginning of the next, which is not a problem for this program). Each utterance was coded into only one category (although the program permits multiple codings). One author performed the preliminary coding for two debates, and the other author did the initial coding for the remaining debate.

We employed the notion of context unit in our content analysis to help in the interpretation of themes. This is important because, as Krippendorff explains, we assume "that symbols codetermine their interpretation and that they derive their meanings in part from the immediate environment in which they occur" (1980, p. 59).[1] We used three aspects of the context to interpret the message: utterances by the speaker that occurred prior to the theme being coded, the question prompting the theme being coded (opening statements and closing remarks, of course, did not have specific prompting questions), and statements by the speaker's opponent(s) (especially persuasive attacks) that appeared to us to have prompted the theme being coded.

At this point the author who had not performed the initial coding of a given debate examined each coding decision, to check for agreement on (1) whether the utterance should be considered an example of persuasive attack and defense (and which of these two possibilities it was) and (2) whether the utterance had been coded into the proper category. Disagreements on both of these issues were resolved through discussion, and the authors reached agreement for the coding of every example of persuasive attack and defense for all three debates (hence, no intercoder reliability calculation was needed, because the authors reached 100 percent agreement on all coding decisions for all utterances coded from each of the three candidates in all of the debates).

Third, we identified the issues addressed by each of the candidates in their persuasive attack and defense in the three debates. Each instance of persuasive attack and each instance of persuasive defense identified in step 1 was classified according to the issue addressed (the same theme and context unit were used in this analysis).[2] Here the categories (of issues) were taken from a public opinion poll conducted prior to the debates. Table 11 reports the categories used in this analysis.[3] As with the coding for strategies of persuasive attack and defense in step 2, one author did the initial coding of issues addressed for two debates, and the other author performed the initial coding on the remaining debate. Then each author checked the coding of the issues addressed in the other debate(s). Disagreements were again resolved by discussing individual examples, and both authors reached agreement for all of the coding of the issues concerned in each instance of persuasive attack and defense in the three debates.

Inspection of the issues included in this table indicates that there is some overlap between them, which is not surprising, because the pollsters were not attempting to generate mutually exclusive categories. Accordingly, after we coded the three debates, several categories were combined to simplify the table (i.e., federal deficit, government spending, and taxation were all combined, as were poverty, welfare, and homelessness). Furthermore, because we were using as our categories issues rated by the public as important for the candidates to address—rather than trying to comprehensively describe the debates—some utterances were not coded for topic.[4]

The coding information was then entered into The Ethnograph. The computer program was used to print out every instance of persuasive attack and defense in each of the debates, grouped by category (first, all instances of persuasive attack were printed, grouped by attack strategy; then all instances of persuasive defense were printed, grouped by defense strategy). We used these printouts (one for each debate) to check the other author's initial coding of the strategies, discussed in chapter 2.

After we reached agreement on the coding of each instance of persuasive attack and defense, the codes were edited to reflect our final coding decision. The Ethnograph then printed every example of persuasive attack and defense, again grouped by strategy. We used this to write the results of our analysis.

An example of part of one debate edited into proper form and coded is presented in appendix 2. The Ethnograph has other features, such as the ability to select text using multiple codes. Although getting the text into the proper format and entering the codes were time-consuming tasks, we found it convenient that The Ethnograph would sort and print out all instances of a given strategy together rather than making us flip back and forth through many pages of text to compare examples.

Table 11. "What ONE ISSUE do you wish the Presidential candidates would talk about MOST?" (percent)

Issue	Response (%)
Economy	34
Unemployment	13
Federal deficit	10
Health care	7
Education	4
Taxes	4
Domestic policy	3
Abortion	3
Environment	2
National defense, military	1
Government spending	1
Foreign policy	1
Elderly	1
Honesty/integrity	1
Poverty	1
Welfare	1
Family values	—
Rebuilding of inner cities	—
Homelessness	—
Race relations	—
AIDS	—
Crime	—
Child care	—

Source: New York Times/CBS News, October 2, 1992, p. 8.

If we were to do this study again, we would probably number each of the candidates' utterances consecutively and add the numbers to the codes at the beginning of each turn at talk (i.e., after the plus sign, the identification of the debate, and identification of candidate). It would then be easier to move back and forth between the excerpts printed by The Ethnograph and the original transcripts (with questions and contextual information).

For those who are interested in learning more about the computer program used in this analysis, "The Ethnograph" is available from Qualis Research Associates, P.O. Box 2070, Amherst, MA 01004, Tel. (413) 256-8835.

Notes

1. We would argue that meanings are supplied by the audience and do not reside in symbols. Thus we would phrase this point as "auditors develop their interpretations from the interaction of symbols" (rather than "symbols co-determine their interpretation"), and "auditors ascribe meaning in part from the immediate environment of the symbols" (rather than "they derive their meaning in part from the immediate context"). We don't see this approach as necessarily inconsistent with Krippendorff's point, though, about the importance of other symbols and of the immediate environment.

2. Use of this procedure meant that utterances that addressed one of these issues but had not been coded as persuasive attack or defense were not included in our analysis of issues addressed. However, given the purpose of this study—to display the use of persuasive attack and defense in the 1992 presidential debates—we are not concerned by this limitation, although we acknowledge it. Furthermore, we coded the bulk of their utterances as either persuasive attack or defense, and so only a relatively small portion of the candidates' utterances remained uncoded.

3. Generally similar results were obtained in a Harris Poll (Taylor, 1992, p. 3) that asked: "What two issues do you think will be of most importance to you in determining who you will support" in the election?

4. Two topics that occurred in the debates but were not coded because they were not part of the coding scheme seem worth mentioning: foreign lobbyists and the role of women in the Bush administration.

Appendix 2
Sample Coded Transcript: Excerpts from Debate 1

PEROT:

The	021 \
thing that separates my candidacy and	022 |
makes it unique is that this came from	023 |
millions of people in fifty states all	024 |
over this country who wanted a	025 | D: Bolstering
candidate that worked and belonged to	026 |
nobody but them. I go into this race	027 |
as their servant. And I belong to	028 |
them. So this comes from the people.	029 /

CLINTON:

I believe that experience counts, but	072 \
it's not everything. Values,	073 |
judgment, and the record that I have	074 | D: Bolstering
amassed in my state also should count	075 |
for something. I've worked hard to	076 <
create good jobs and to educate	077 |
people. My state now ranks first in	078 |
the country in job growth this year,	079 |
fourth in income growth, fourth in the	080 | D: Bolstering
reduction of poverty, third in overall	081 |
economic performance, according to a	082 |
major newsmagazine. That's because we	083 |
believe in investing in education and	084 |
in jobs.	085 /

And we have to change this country.	086 \	
You know, my wife, Hillary, gave me a	087 |	
book about a year ago in which the	088 |	A: Neg. Gen.
author defined insanity as just doing	089 |	
the same old thing over and over again	090 |	
and expecting a different result. We	091 <	
have got to have the courage to	092 |	
change. Experience is important, yes.	093 |	
I've gotten a lot of good experience	094 |	
in dealing with ordinary people over	095 |	D: Bolstering
the last year, month. I've touched	096 |	
more people's lives and seen more	097 |	
heartbreak and hope, more pain and	098 |	
more promise, than anybody else who's	099 |	
run for president this year. And I	100 <	
think the American people deserve	101 |	A: Eff. on Aud.
better than they're getting.	102 <	
We have gone from first to thirteenth in the	103 |	
world in wages in the last twelve years,	104 |	A: Severity
since Mr. Bush and Mr. Reagan have	105 |	
been in. Personal income has dropped	106 <	A: Eff. on Aud.
while people have worked harder. In	107 <	
the last four years there have been	108 |	A: Severity
twice as many bankruptcies as new jobs	109 |	
created. We need a new approach. This	110 <	
same old experience is not relevant.	111 |	
We're living in a new world after the	112 |	
cold war, and what works in this new	113 |	A: Neg. Gen.
world is not trickle-down, not	114 |	
government for the benefit of the	115 |	
privileged few, not tax and spend, but	116 <	
a commitment to invest in American	117 |	
jobs and American education,	118 |	D: Corr. Act.
controlling American health care costs	119 |	
and bringing the American people	120 |	
together.	121 /	

BUSH:

But this	137 \	
country's not coming apart at the	138 |	
seams, for heaven's sakes. We're the	139 |	D: Simple Denial
United States of America. We—in	140 |	
spite of the economic problems, we are	141 <	
the most respected economy around	142 |	D: Bolstering
the world. Many would trade for it.	143 /	
We've been caught up in a global	144 \	D: Defeasibility
slowdown. We can do much much	145 /	
better, but we ought not try to	146 \	

convince the American people that   147 |
America is a country that's coming   148 |
apart at the seams. I would hate to be   149 | A: Neg. Gen.
running for president and think that   150 |
the only way I could win would be to   151 |
convince everybody how horrible things   152 |
are. Yes, there are big problems. And   153 /
yes, people are hurting. But I believe   154 \
that this agenda for American renewal   155 | D: Corr. Act.
I have is the answer to do it, and I   156 |
believe we can get it done now, whereas   157 <
we didn't in the past, because you're   158 |
going to have a whole brand new bunch   159 | A: Shift Blame
of people in the Congress that are   160 |
going to have to listen to the same   161 |
American people I'm listening to.   162 /

PEROT:

Well, they got a point. I don't   163 \
have any experience in running up a $4   164 | A: Severity
trillion debt. I don't have any   165 <
experience in gridlock government,   166 |
where nobody takes responsibility for   167 | A: Neg. Gen.
anything and everybody blames   168 |
everybody else. I don't have any   169 <
experience in creating the worst   170 |
public school system in the   171 | A: Severity
industrialized world, the most violent   172 |
crime-ridden society in the   173 |
industrialized world. But I do have a   174 <
lot of experience in getting things   175 |
done. So if we're at a point in   176 |
history where we want to stop talking   177 |
about it and do it, I've got a lot of   178 | D: Bolstering
experience in figuring out how to   179 |
solve problems, making the solutions   180 |
work, and then moving on to the next.   181 /

References

ABC Television. (1992, November 3). "Election Eve Coverage: Report of the Michigan Exit Poll."

Abramowitz, A. (1978). "The Impact of a Presidential Debate on Voter Rationality." *American Journal of Political Science* 22:680–90.

"Accused Levee Saboteur Did It for Party, Witness Says." (1994, November 1). *Columbia Daily Tribune:*1A.

"After the Debates." (1992, October 21). *Washington Post:*A18.

"The Aftermath of Round Three." (1992, October 24). *Congressional Quarterly Weekly Report* 50:3336.

Alberts, J. K. (1988). "An Analysis of Couples' Conversational Complaints." *Communication Monographs* 55:184–97.

———. (1989). "A Descriptive Taxonomy of Couples' Complaint Interactions." *Southern Speech Communication Journal* 54:125–43.

Alexander, H. E., and Margolis, J. (1980). "The Making of the Debates." In *Presidential Debates: Media, Electoral, and Policy Perspectives,* edited by G. F. Bishop, R. G. Meadow, and M. Jackson-Beeck, 18–32. New York: Praeger.

Allen, R. E. (1993, September 23). "Apologies Are Not Enough." *New York Times:*C3.

Andersen, K., and Clevenger, T. (1963). "A Summary of Experimental Research in Ethos." *Speech Monographs* 39:59–78.

Apple, R. W. (1992, October 12). "First of Three Debates: Bush and Clinton Tangle over Anti-War Roles—Perot Adds Color." *New York Times:*A1, A12.

Aristotle. (1954). *Rhetoric.* Translated by W. R. Roberts. New York: Random House.

Auer, J. J. (1962). "The Counterfeit Debates." In *The Great Debates: Back-*

ground, Perspective, Effects, edited by S. Kraus, 142–50. Bloomington: Indiana University Press.

Baker, R. W. (1989, June 14). "Critics Fault Exxon's 'PR Campaign.' " *Christian Science Monitor:*8.

Balz, D. (1992a, October 11). "Debate Marathon Opens Tonight: Bush Is Seen with the Most at Stake." *Washington Post:*A1, A33.

———. (1992b, October 11). "A Big Win Eludes Bush in Debate." *Washington Post:*A1, A14.

Balz, D., and Devroy, A. (1992, October 20). "President Comes Out Slugging in Final Debate: Clinton and Perot Accuse Bush of Mishandling Iraq, Economy." *Washington Post:*A1, A35.

"BASS and Its Founder Hit with Lawsuit." (1992, February 23). *Columbia Daily Tribune:*8B.

Beatty, M. J., and Adams, W. C. (1977). "Dogmatism, Need for Social Approval, and Resistance to Persuasion." *Communication Monographs* 44:321–25.

Becker, L. B., Sobowale, I. A., Cobbey, R. E., and Eyal, C. H. (1978). "Debates' Effects on Voters' Understanding of Candidates and Issues." In *The Presidential Debates: Media, Electoral, and Policy Perspectives,* edited by G. F. Bishop, R. G. Meadow, and M. Jackson-Beeck, 126–39. New York: Praeger.

Becker, S. L., and Kraus, S. (1978). "The Study of Campaign '76: An Overview." *Communication Monographs* 45:265–67.

Benoit, W. L. (1982). "Richard M. Nixon's Rhetorical Strategies in His Public Statements on Watergate." *Southern Speech Communication Journal* 47:192–211.

———. (1988). "Senator Edward M. Kennedy and the Chappaquiddick Tragedy." In *Oratorical Encounters: Selected Studies and Sources of Twentieth-Century Political Accusations and Apologies,* edited by H. R. Ryan, 187–99. Westport, CT: Greenwood Press.

———. (1991a). "A Cognitive Response Analysis of Source Credibility." In *Progress in Communication Sciences,* edited by B. Dervin and M. J. Voigt, vol. 10, pp. 1–19. Norwood, NJ: Ablex.

———. (1991b). "Two Tests of the Mechanism of Inoculation Theory." *Southern Communication Journal* 56:219–29.

———. (1995). *Accounts, Excuses, Apologies: A Theory of Image Restoration Strategies.* Albany: State University of New York Press.

———. (in press). "Sears' Repair of Its Auto Service Image: Image Restoration Discourse in the Corporate Sector." *Communication Studies.*

Benoit, W. L., and Anderson, K. K. (under review). "Blending Politics and Entertainment: Dan Quayle Versus Murphy Brown."

Benoit, W. L., and Brinson, S. (1994). "AT&T: Apologies Are Not Enough." *Communication Quarterly* 42:75–88.

Benoit, W. L., and Dorries, B. (in press). "*Dateline NBC*'s Persuasive Attack of Wal-Mart."

Benoit, W. L., Gullifor, P., and Panici, D. A. (1991). "President Reagan's Defensive Discourse on the Iran-Contra Affair." *Communication Studies* 42:272–94.

Benoit, W. L., and Hanczor, R. (1994). "The Tonya Harding Controversy: An Analysis of Image Restoration Strategies." *Communication Quarterly* 42:416–33.

Benoit, W. L., and Lindsey, J. J. (1987a). "Argument Fields and Forms of Inference in Natural Language." In *Argumentation: Perspectives and Approaches*, edited by F. H. van Eemeren, R. Grootendorst, J. A. Blair, and C. A. Willard, 215–24. Dordrecht, Holland: Foris.

———. (1987b). "Argument Strategies: Antidote to Tylenol's Poisoned Image." *Journal of the American Forensic Association* 23:136–46.

Benoit, W. L., and Nill, D. (under review). "Oliver Stone's Defense of *JFK*."

Berelson, B. (1952). *Content Analysis in Communication Research*. New York: Free Press of Glencoe.

Berke, R. L. (1992, October 19). "On the Eve of Last Presidential Debate, Bush Aide Predicts 'Tough' Race." *New York Times*:A1, A10.

Berquist, G. F. (1994). "The 1976 Carter-Ford Presidential Debates." In *Rhetorical Studies of National Political Debates, 1960–1992*, edited by R. F. Friedenberg, 29–44. 2nd ed. New York: Praeger.

Berquist, G. F., and Golden, J. L. (1981). "Media Rhetoric, Criticism, and the Public Perception of the 1980 Presidential Debates." *Quarterly Journal of Speech* 67:125–37.

Bishop, G. F., Oldendick, R. W., and Tuchfarber, A. J. (1978). "The Presidential Debates as a Device for Increasing the 'Rationality' of Electoral Behavior." In *The Presidential Debates: Media, Electoral, and Policy Perspectives*, edited by G. F. Bishop, R. G. Meadow, and M. Jackson-Beeck, 179–96. New York: Praeger.

Bitzer, L., and Rueter, T. (1980). *Carter versus Ford: The Counterfeit Debates of 1976*. Madison: University of Wisconsin Press.

Bowes, J. E., and Strentz, H. (1978). "Candidate Images: Stereotyping and the 1976 Debates." In *Communication Yearbook 2*, edited by B. Rubin, 391–406. New Brunswick, NJ: Transaction.

Brennen, E. (1992, June 14). "An Open Letter to Sears' Customers." *New York Times*:A56.

Brinson, S. L., and Benoit, W. L. (in press). "Image Repair Strategies in Dow Corning's Breast Implant Crisis." *Communication Quarterly*.

Broder, D. S. (1992, October 20). "President Comes Out Slugging in Final Debate: Strong Show by Bush May Change Little." *Washington Post*:A1, A35.

Broder, D. S., and Marcus, R. (1992, October 16). "Clinton, Bush, and Perot Stick to Issues in Debate." *Washington Post*:A1, A37.

Brown, P., and Levinson, S. (1978). "Universals in Language Usage: Politeness Phenomena." In *Questions and Politeness*, edited by E. Goody, 56–310. Cambridge: Cambridge University Press.

Brydon, S. R. (1985a, November). *Reagan versus Reagan: The Incumbency Factor in the 1984 Presidential Debates*. Paper presented at the annual meeting of the Speech Communication Association, Denver, CO.

Brydon, S. R. (1985b). "The Two Faces of Jimmy Carter: The Transformation of a Presidential Debater, 1976 and 1980." *Central States Speech Journal* 36:138–51.

Burgoon, M., Burgoon, J. K., Riess, M., Butler, J., Montgomery, C. L., Stinnett, W. D., Miller, M., Long, M., Vaughn, D., and Caine, B. (1976). "Propensity of Persuasive Attack and Intensity of Pretreatment Messages as Predictors of Resistance to Persuasion." *Journal of Psychology* 92:123–29.

Burgoon, M., and Chase, L. J. (1973). "The Effects of Differential Linguistic Patterns in Messages Attempting to Induce Resistance to Persuasion." *Speech Monographs* 40:1–7.

Burgoon, M., Cohen, M., Miller, M. D., and Montgomery, C. L. (1978). "An Empirical Test of a Model of Resistance to Persuasion." *Human Communication Research* 5:27–39.

Burgoon, M., and King, L. B. (1974). "The Mediation of Resistance to Persuasion Strategies by Language Variables and Active-Passive Participation." *Human Communication Research* 1:30–41.

Burke, K. (1970). *Rhetoric of Religion.* Berkeley: University of California Press.

———. (1973). *The Philosophy of Literary Form,* 3/e. Berkeley: University of California Press.

"Bush's Motive in Pardons Questioned: President Might be Avoiding Witness Stand." (1992, December 27). *Columbia Daily Tribune:*1A.

Carlin, D. P. (1989). "A Defense of the 'Debate' in Presidential Debates." *Journal of the American Forensic Association* 25:208–13.

———. (1992). "Presidential Debates as Focal Points for Campaign Arguments." *Political Communication* 9:251–65.

Carlin, D. P. (1994). "A Rationale for a Focus Group Study." In *The 1992 Presidential Debates in Focus,* edited by D. B. Carlin and M. S. McKinney, 3–19. Westport, CT: Praeger.

Carlin, D. P., Howard, C., Stanfield, S., and Reynolds, L. (1991). "The Effects of Presidential Debate Formats on Clash: A Comparative Analysis." *Argumentation and Advocacy* 27:126–36.

Chaffee, S. H. (1978). "Presidential Debates—Are They Helpful to Voters?" *Communication Monographs* 45:330–46.

———. (1979). "Approaches of U.S. Scholars to the Study of Televised Political Debates." *Political Communication Review* 4:19–33.

Clark, R. A., and Delia, J. G. (1979). "*Topoi* and Rhetorical Competence." *Quarterly Journal of Speech* 65:187–206.

Condit, C. M. (1989). "Feminized Power and Adversarial Advocacy: Levelling Arguments or Analyzing Them?" *Journal of the American Forensic Association* 25:226–30.

"Congressman Paid Self for Office Space: Report: Rostenkowski Used Campaign Funds." (1992, December 14). *Columbia Daily Tribune:*5A.

Conrad, C. (1993). "Political Debates as Televisual Form." *Argumentation and Advocacy* 30:62–76.

Cook, R. (1992, November 7). "Clinton Picks the GOP Lock on the Electoral College: He Was Favored by the Youngest and Oldest, the Best- and the Least-Educated, the Suburbs and Cities." *Congressional Quarterly* 50:3548–53.

Cragan, J. F., and Cutbirth, C. W. (1984). "A Revisionist Perspective on Political Ad Hominem Argument: A Case Study." *Central States Speech Journal* 35:228–37.

Crane, E. (1962). "Immunization—With and Without Use of Counterarguments." *Journalism Quarterly* 39:445–50.

Cupach, W. R., and Metts, S. (1990). "Remedial Processes in Embarrassing Predicaments." In *Communication Yearbook 13*, edited by J. A. Anderson, 323–52. Newbury Park: Sage.

———. (1992). "The Effects of Type of Predicament and Embarrassability on Remedial Responses to Embarrassing Situations." *Communication Quarterly* 40:149–61.

Davis, D. K. (1979). "Influence on Vote Decisions." In *The Great Debates: Carter versus Ford, 1976*, edited by S. Kraus, 331–47. Bloomington: Indiana University Press.

Davis, M. H. (1982). "Voting Intentions and the 1980 Carter-Reagan Debate." *Journal of Applied Social Psychology* 12:481–92.

Denton, R. E., and Woodward, G. C. (1990). *Political Communication in America*, 2/e. New York: Praeger.

Depoe, S. P., and Short-Thompson, C. (1994). "Let the People Speak: The Emergence of Public Space in the Richmond Presidential Debate." In *The 1992 Presidential Debates in Focus*, edited by D. B. Carlin and M. S. McKinney, 85–98. Westport, CT: Praeger.

Desmond, R. J., and Donohue, T. R. (1981). "The Role of the 1976 Televised Presidential Debates in the Political Socialization of Adolescents." *Communication Quarterly* 29:302–308.

Dowd, M. (1992, October 16). "A No-Nonsense Sort of Talk Show: Audience Puts Stop to Mud Wrestling." *New York Times*:A1.

Drew, D., and Weaver, D. (1991). "Voter Learning in the 1988 Presidential Election: Did the Debates and the Media Matter?" *Journalism Quarterly* 68:27–37.

Drucker, S. J., and Hunold, J. P. (1987). "The Debating Game." *Critical Studies in Mass Communication* 4:202–207.

Ellsworth, J. W. (1965). "Rationality and Campaigning: A Content Analysis of the 1960 Presidential Campaign Debates." *Western Political Quarterly* 18:794–802.

"EPA Officials Criticized for Driving Gas-Guzzlers." (1992, June 16). *Columbia Daily Tribune*:9A.

Estrich, S. (1992, October 15). "Stay Cool, Clinton." *New York Times*:A27.

Eveland, W. P., McLeod, D. M., and Natanson, A. I. (1994). "Reporters versus Undecided Voters: An Analysis of the Questions Asked During the 1992 Presidential Debates." *Communication Quarterly* 42:390–406.

Fisher, W. R. (1970). "A Motive View of Communication." *Quarterly Journal of Speech* 56:131–39.

"Flashy Beer Commercials Draw Children, Study Finds." (1994, February 11). *Columbia Daily Tribune*:12A.

"Flight 427 Flew Shorter Routes to Avoid Overhaul: Jet Was Part of Cost-Cutting Effort, Source Says." (1994, September 21). *Columbia Daily Tribune*:3A.

Frankovic, K. A. (1993). "Public Opinion in the 1992 Campaign." In *The Election of 1992: Reports and Interpretations*, edited by G. M. Pomper, F. C. Arterton, R. K. Baker, W. D. Burnham, K. A. Frankovic, M. R. Hershey, and W. C. McWilliams, 110–31. Chatham, NJ: Chatham House.

Freedman, J. L., and Steinbruner, J. D. (1964). "Perceived Choice and Resistance to Persuasion." *Journal of Abnormal and Social Psychology* 68:678–81.

Frenette, C. A. (1991, April 28). "Open Letter." *Nation's Restaurant News*:24.

Friedenberg, R. V. (1979). " 'We are Present Today for the Purpose of Having a Joint Discussion': The Conditions Requisite for Political Debates." *Journal of the American Forensic Association* 16:1–9.

———. (1981). " 'Selfish Interests'; or, The Prerequisites for Political Debate: An Analysis of the 1980 Presidential Debate and its Implications for Future Campaigns. *Journal of the American Forensic Association* 18:91–98.

———. (1994a). "Patterns and Trends in National Political Debates, 1960–1988." In *Rhetorical Studies of National Political Debates, 1960–1992*, edited by R. F. Friedenberg, 191–299. 2d ed. New York: Praeger.

———. (1994b). "The 1992 Presidential Debates." In *The 1992 Presidential Campaign: A Communication Perspective*, edited by R. E. Denton, 89–110. Westport, CT: Praeger.

———, ed. (1994c). *Rhetorical Studies of National Political Debates, 1960–1992*. 2d ed. New York: Praeger.

Gallup, G. (1987). "The Impact of Presidential Debates on the Vote and Turnout." In *Presidential Debates: 1988 and Beyond*, edited by J. L. Swerdlow, 34–42. Washington, DC: Congressional Quarterly.

Gallup Opinion Polls. (1994a, October 12). *Roper Center at University of Connecticut: Public Opinion Online*.

———. (1994b, October 16–18). *Roper Center at University of Connecticut: Public Opinion Online*.

———. (1994c, October 19). *Roper Center at University of Connecticut: Public Opinion Online*.

Geer, J. G. (1988). "The Effects on Presidential Debates on the Electorate's Preference on Candidates." *American Politics Quarterly* 16:486–501.

Gill, M. M. (1986). "Presidential Debates: Political Tool or Voter Information?" *Speaker and Gavel* 24:36–40.

Gladwell, M. (1992, February 11). "Documents Tell Risk of Implants: Dow Corning Corp. Releases Memos, Replaces Chairman." *Washington Post*:A1, A4.

Goffman, E. (1967). "On Face-Work." *Interaction Ritual*, 5–46. New York: Anchor Books.

———. (1971). "Remedial Interchanges." *Relations in Public: Microstudies of the Public Order*, 95–187. New York: Harper and Row.

Goodman, E. (1992, March 14). "Old Joe Camel Might have Met His Match." *Columbia Daily Tribune*:4A.

Graber, D. A., and Kim, Y. Y. (1978). "Why John Q. Voter Did Not Learn Much from the 1976 Presidential Debates." In *Communication Yearbook 2*, edited by B. Rubin, 407–21. New Brunswick, NJ: Transaction.

Gronbeck, B. E. (1992). "Negative Narrative in 1988 Presidential Campaign Ads." *Quarterly Journal of Speech*, 78:333–46.

Hagner, P. R., and Rieselbach, L. N. (1978). "The Impact of the 1976 Presidential Debates: Conversion or Reinforcement?" In *The Presidential Debates: Media, Electoral, and Policy Perspectives*, edited by G. F. Bishop, R. G. Meadow, and M. Jackson-Beeck, 157–78. New York: Praeger.

Hahn, D. F. (1994). "The 1992 Clinton-Bush-Perot Presidential Debate." In *Rhetorical Studies of National Political Debates, 1960–1992*, edited by R. V. Friedenberg, 187–210. 2d ed. Westport, CT: Praeger.

Hahn, D. F., and Gustainis, J. J. (1987). "Defensive Tactics in Presidential Rhetoric: Contemporary *Topoi*." In *Essays in Presidential Rhetoric*, edited by T. Windt and B. Ingold, 43–75. Dubuque: Kendall-Hunt.

Hample, D. (1992). "Writing Mindlessly." *Communication Monographs* 59:315–23.

Hart, R. P. (1984). *Verbal Style and the Presidency: A Computer-Based Analysis*. Orlando: Academic Press.

Harvey, J. H., and Weary, G. (1984). "Current Issues in Attribution Theory and Research." *Annual Review of Psychology* 35:427–59.

Hellweg, S. A., Pfau, M., and Brydon, S. R. (1992). *Televised Presidential Debates: Advocacy in Contemporary America*. New York: Praeger.

Hellweg, S. A., and Phillips, S. L. (1981a). "Form and Substance: A Comparative Analysis of Five Formats Used in the 1980 Presidential Debates." *Speaker and Gavel* 18:67–76.

——. (1981b). "A Verbal and Visual Analysis of the 1980 Houston Republican Presidential Primary Debate." *Southern Speech Communication Journal* 47:23–38.

Hellweg, S. A., and Stevens, M. D. (1990, November). *Argumentative Strategies in the Vice-Presidential Debates: 1976, 1984, and 1988*. Paper presented at the annual meeting of the Speech Communication Association, Chicago.

Hellweg, S. A., and Verhoye, A. M. (1989, November). *A Comparative Verbal Analysis of the two 1988 Bush-Dukakis Presidential Debates*. Paper presented at the annual meeting of the Speech Communication Association, San Francisco.

Hilts, P. J. (1989, March 31). "Environment May Show Spill's Effects for Decade." *Washington Post*:A6.

Hinck, E. A. (1993). *Enacting the Presidency: Political Argument, Presidential Debates, and Presidential Character*. Westport, CT: Praeger.

Hogan, J. M. (1989). "Media Nihilism and the Presidential Debates." *Journal of the American Forensic Association* 25:220–25.

Holsti, O. R. (1969). *Content Analysis for the Social Sciences and Humanities*. Reading, MA: Addison-Wesley.

Houston, P. (1991, March 14). " 'Outlandish' Billings by Stanford Alleged: The University May Have Overcharged the U.S. $160 Million in the Last Decade, an Auditor Tells a Congressional Hearing." *Los Angeles Times*:A3.

Ifill, G. (1992, October 9). "Clinton's Four-Point Plan to Win the First Debate." *New York Times*:A21.

Infante, D. (1975). "Effects of Opinionated Language on Communicator Image and in Conferring Resistance to Persuasion." *Western Speech Communication* 39:112–19.

"Interim Secretary of State Sworn In: Impeached Moriarty Awaits Court Edict." (1994, October 7). *Columbia Daily Tribune:*1A.

Isocrates. (1976). "Antidosis." *Isocrates*. Vol. 1. Translated by G. Norlin. Loeb Classical Library. Cambridge, MA: Harvard University Press.

Jackson-Beeck, M., and Meadow, R. G. (1979a). "Content Analysis of Televised Communication Events: The Presidential Debates." *Communication Research* 6:321–44.

———. (1979b). "The Triple Agenda of Presidential Debates." *Public Opinion Quarterly* 43:173–80.

Jacoby, J., Troutman, T. R., and Whittler, T. E. (1986). "Viewer Miscomprehension of the 1980 Presidential Debate: A Research Note." *Political Psychology* 7:297–308.

Jamieson, K. H. (1987). "Television, Presidential Campaigns, and Debates." In *Presidential Debates 1988 and Beyond*, edited by J. L. Swerdlow, 27–33. Washington, DC: Congressional Quarterly.

———. (1992). *Dirty Politics: Deception, Distraction, and Democracy*. New York: Oxford University Press.

Jamieson, K. H., and Birdsell, D. S. (1988). *Presidential Debates: The Challenge of Creating an Informed Electorate*. New York: Oxford University Press.

Jamieson, K. H., and Campbell, K. K. (1982). "Rhetorical Hybrids: Fusions of Generic Elements." *Quarterly Journal of Speech* 68:146–57.

"Justice Department Reprimands FBI Chief for Lapses in Ethics." (1993, January 20). *Columbia Daily Tribune:*7A.

Katz, E., and Feldman, J. J. (1977). "The Debates in Light of Research: A Survey of Surveys." In *The Great Debates: Kennedy versus Nixon, 1960*, edited by S. Kraus, 173–223. Bloomington: Indiana University Press.

Kellermann, K. (1992). "Communication: Inherently Strategic and Primarily Automatic." *Communication Monographs* 59:288–300.

Kelley, H. H. (1967). "Attribution Theory in Social Psychology." In *Nebraska Symposium on Motivation*, edited by D. L. Vine, 15:192–238.

Kelley, H. H., and Michela, J. L. (1980). "Attribution Theory and Research." *Annual Review of Psychology* 31:457–501.

Kelley, M. (1992, October 18). "The Matter of Trust: Clinton's Big Burden." *New York Times:*A24.

Kelley, S. (1962). "Campaign Debates: Some Facts and Issues." *Public Opinion Quarterly* 26:351–66.

———. (1983). *Interpreting Elections*. Princeton, NJ: Princeton University Press.

Kirk, Paul. (1995, October 28). "Presidential Debates and Democracy." C-SPAN.

Kraus, S., ed. (1979). *The Great Debates: Carter versus Ford, 1976*. Bloomington: Indiana University Press.

———. (1987). "Voters Win." *Critical Studies in Mass Communication* 4:214–16.

———. (1988). *Televised Presidential Debates and Public Policy*. Hillsdale, NJ: Lawrence Erlbaum.

Kraus, S., and Davis, D. K. (1981). "Political Debates." In *Handbook of Political Communication*, edited by D. Nimmo and K. R. Sanders, 273–96. Beverly Hills, CA: Sage.

Krippendorff, D. (1980). *Content Analysis: An Introduction to Its Methodology*. Beverly Hills, CA: Sage.

Lamoureaux, E. R., Entrekin, H. S., and McKinney, M. S. (1994). "Debating the Debates." In *The 1992 Presidential Debates in Focus*, edited by D. B. Carlin and M. S. McKinney, 55–67. Westport, CT: Praeger.

"Landmark Breast Cancer Data Faked." (1994, March 13). *Columbia Daily Tribune:*6A.

Lang, G. E. (1987). "Still Seeking Answers." *Critical Studies in Mass Communication* 4:211–14.

Lang, G. E., and Lang, K. (1978). "The Formation of Public Opinion: Direct and Mediated Effects of the First Debate." In *The Presidential Debates: Media, Electoral, and Policy Perspectives*, edited by G. F. Bishop, R. G. Meadow, and M. Jackson-Beeck, 61–80. New York: Praeger.

Lang, K., and Lang, G. E. (1977). "Reactions of Viewers." In *The Great Debates: Carter versus Ford, 1976*, edited by S. Kraus, 313–30. Bloomington: Indiana University Press.

Lanoue, D. J. (1991). "The 'Turning Point': Viewers' Reactions to the Second 1988 Presidential Debate." *American Politics Quarterly* 19:80–95.

Lanoue, D. J., and Schrott, P. R. (1989). "Voter's Reactions to Televised Presidential Debates: Measurement of the Source and Magnitude of Opinion Change." *Political Psychology* 10:275–85.

Leff, M. C., and Mohrmann, G. P. (1974). "Lincoln at Cooper Union: A Rhetorical Analysis of the Text." *Quarterly Journal of Speech* 60:346–58.

Lemert, J. B. (1993). "Do Televised Presidential Debates Help Inform Voters?" *Journal of Broadcasting and Electronic Media* 37:83–94.

Lemert, J. B., Elliott, W. R., Bernstein, J. M., Rosenberg, W. L., and Nestvold, K. J. (1991). *News Verdicts, the Debates, and Presidential Campaigns*. New York: Praeger.

Leon, M. (1993). "Revealing Character and Addressing Voters' Needs in the 1992 Presidential Debates: A Content Analysis." *Argumentation and Advocacy* 30:88–105.

Leuthold, D. A., and Valentine, D. C. (1981). "How Reagan 'Won' the Cleveland Debate: Audience Predispositions and Presidential Debate 'Winners.' " *Speaker and Gavel* 18:60–66.

Limbaugh, R. H. (1992, October 15). "Get Angry, Bush." *New York Times:*A27.

Littlejohn, S. W. (1971). "A Bibliography of Studies Related to Variables of Source Credibility." *Bibliographic Annual in Speech Communication* 2:1–40.

Lubell, S. (1977). "Personalities versus Issues." In *The Great Debates: Carter versus Ford, 1976*, edited by S. Kraus, 151–62. Bloomington: Indiana University Press.

Madsen, A. (1991). "Partisan Commentary and the First 1988 Presidential Debate." *Argumentation and Advocacy* 27:100–13.

Martel, M. (1981). "Debate Preparations in the Reagan Camp: An Insider's View." *Speaker and Gavel* 18:34–46.

———. (1983). *Political Campaign Debates: Images, Strategies, and Tactics.* New York: Longmans.

Mathews, J., and Peterson, C. (1989, March 31). "Oil Tanker Captain Fired after Failing Alcohol Test; Exxon Blames Government for Cleanup Delay." *Washington Post:*A1, 6.

Mayer, M. A., and Carlin, D. B. (1994). "Debates as an Educational Tool." In *The 1992 Presidential Debates in Focus,* edited by D. B. Carlin and M. S. McKinney, 127–38. Westport, CT: Praeger.

McClain, T. B. (1989). "Secondary School Debate Pedagogy." *Journal of the American Forensic Association* 25:203–204.

McCroskey, J. C. (1970). "The Effects of Evidence as an Inhibitor of Counter-Persuasion." *Speech Monographs* 38:188–94.

McCroskey, J. C., Young, T. J., and Scott, M. D. (1972). "The Effects of Message Sidedness and Evidence on Inoculation Against Counterpersuasion in Small Group Communication." *Speech Monographs* 39:205–12.

McFadden, R. D. (1984, December 10). "India Disaster: Chronicle of a Nightmare." *New York Times:*A1, A6.

McGuire, W. J. (1961). "The Effectiveness of Supportive and Refutational Defenses in Immunizing and Restoring Beliefs Against Persuasion." *Sociometry* 24:184–97.

———. (1964). "Inducing Resistance to Persuasion: Some Contemporary Approaches." In *Advances in Experimental Social Psychology,* edited by L. Berkowitz, vol. 1, pp. 191–229. New York: Academic Press.

McKinnon, L. M., Tedesco, J. C., and Kaid, L. L. (1993). "The Third 1992 Presidential Debate: Channel and Commentary Effects." *Argumentation and Advocacy* 30:106–18.

McLaughlin, M. L., Cody, M. J., and O'Hair, H. D. (1983). "The Management of Failure Events: Some Contextual Determinants of Accounting Behavior." *Human Communication Research* 9:208–24.

McLaughlin, M. L., Cody, M. J., and Rosenstein, N. E. (1983). "Account Sequences in Conversations Between Strangers." *Communication Monographs* 50:102–25.

McLeod, J. M., Bybee, C. R., and Durall, J. A. (1979). "Equivalence of Informed Political Participation: The 1976 Presidential Debates as a Source of Influence." *Communication Research* 6:463–87.

McLeod, J., Durall, J., Ziemke, D., and Bybee, C. (1979). "Reactions of Young and Older Voters: Expanding the Context of Effects." In *The Great Debates: Carter versus Ford, 1976,* edited by S. Kraus, 348–67. Bloomington: Indiana University Press.

Meadow, R. G. (1987). "A Speech by Any Other Name." *Critical Studies in Mass Communication* 4:207–10.

Meadow, R. G., and Jackson-Beeck, M. (1978a). "A Comparative Perspective on Presidential Debates: Issue Evolution in 1960 and 1976." In *The Presidential Debates: Media, Electoral, and Policy Perspectives,* edited by G. F. Bishop, R. G. Meadow, and M. Jackson-Beeck, 33–58. New York: Praeger.

———. (1978b). "Issue Evolution: A New Perspective on Presidential Debates." *Journal of Communication* 28:84–92.

Mehrabian, A. (1967). "Substitute for Apology: Manipulation of Cognitions to Reduce Negative Attitude Toward Self." *Psychological Reports* 20:687–92.

Metts, S., and Cupach, W. R. (1989). "Situational Influence on the Use of Remedial Strategies in Embarrassing Predicaments." *Communication Monographs* 56:151–62.

Middleton, R. (1962). "National TV Debates and Presidential Voting Decisions." *Public Opinion Quarterly* 26:426–29.

Milic, L. T. (1979). "Grilling the Pols: Q and A at the Debates." In *The Great Debates: Carter versus Ford, 1976,* edited by S. Kraus, 187–208. Bloomington: Indiana University Press.

Miller, A. H., and MacKuen, M. (1979). "Learning About the Candidates: The 1976 Presidential Debates." *Public Opinion Quarterly* 43:326–46.

Miller, M. D., and Burgoon, M. (1979). "The Relationship Between Violations of Expectations and the Induction of Resistance to Persuasion." *Human Communication Research* 5:301–13.

Modigliani, A. (1971). "Embarrassment, Facework, and Eye Contact: Testing a Theory of Embarrassment." *Journal of Personality and Social Psychology* 17:15–24.

Morello, J. T. (1988a). "Argument and Visual Structuring in the 1984 Mondale-Reagan Debates: The Medium's Influence on the Perception of Clash." *Western Journal of Speech Communication* 52:277–90.

———. (1988b). "Visual Structuring of the 1976 and 1984 Nationally Televised Presidential Debates: Implications." *Central States Speech Journal* 39:233–43.

———. (1990, November). *Argument and Visual Structuring in the 1988 Bush-Dukakis Presidential Campaign Debates.* Paper presented at the annual meeting of the Speech Communication Association, Chicago, IL.

———. (1992). "The 'Look' and Language of Clash: Visual Structuring of Argument in the 1988 Bush-Dukakis Debates." *Southern Communication Journal* 57:205–18.

Morris, G. H. (1988). "Finding Fault." *Journal of Language and Social Psychology* 7:1–25.

"Mr. Bush's Campaign Mode: Nasty." (1992, October 9). *New York Times:*A32.

Murphy, J. M. (1992). "Presidential Debates and Campaign Rhetoric: Text Within Context." *Southern Communication Journal* 57:219–28.

Nielson Media Research. (1993). *Nielson Tunes into Politics: Tracking the Presidential Election Years, 1960–1992.* New York: Nielson Media Research.

Nimmo, D. (1974). *Popular Images of Politics.* Englewood Cliffs, NJ: Prentice-Hall.

Nimmo, D., Mansfield, M., and Curry, J. (1978). "Persistence and Change in Candidate Images." In *The Presidential Debates: Media, Electoral, and Policy Perspectives,* edited by G. F. Bishop, R. G. Meadow, and M. Jackson-Beeck, 140–56. New York: Praeger.

Nixon, R. N. (1970). "Cambodia: A Difficult Decision." *Vital Speeches of the Day* 37:450–52.

O'Keefe, B. J., and Delia, J. G. (1982). "Impression Formation and Message Production." In *Social Cognition and Communication*, edited by M. E. Roloff and C. R. Berger, 33–72. Beverly Hills, CA: Sage.

O'Keefe, D. J. (1992). *Persuasion: Theory and Research.* Newbury Park, CA: Sage.

Owen, D. (1995). "The Debate Challenge: Candidate Strategies in the New Media Age." In *Presidential Campaign Discourse: Strategic Communication Problems*, edited by K. E. Kendall, 135–55. Albany: State University of New York Press.

Payne, J. G., Golden, J. L., Marlier, J., and Ratzan, S. C. (1989). "Perceptions of the 1988 Presidential and Vice-Presidential Debates." *American Behavioral Scientist* 32:425–35.

Pepsi-Cola. (1991, March 11). "Accounts Payable/Receivable." *Nation's Restaurant News*:34.

Peterson, C. (1989, April 3). "Coast Guard Faults Plans to Contain Spill." *Washington Post*:A17.

Pfau, M. (1988). "Intra-Party Political Debate and Issue Learning." *Journal of Applied Communication Research* 16:99–112.

Pfau, M., and Burgoon, M. (1988). "Inoculation in Political Campaign Communication." *Human Communication Research* 15:91–111.

———. (1989). "The Efficacy of Issue and Character Attack Message Strategies in Political Campaign Communication." *Communication Reports* 1:53–61.

Pfau, M., Diedrich, T., Larson, K. M., and Van Winkle, K. M. (1993). "Relational and Competence Perceptions of Presidential Candidates During Primary Election Campaigns." *Journal of Broadcasting and Electronic Media* 26:275–92.

Pfau, M., and Eveland, W. P. (1994). "Debates Versus Other Communication Sources: The Pattern of Information and Influence." In *The 1992 Presidential Debates in Focus*, edited by D. B. Carlin and M. S. McKinney, 155–73. Westport, CT: Praeger.

Pfau, M., and Kang, J. G. (1991). "The Impact of Relational Messages on Candidate Influence in Televised Political Debates." *Communication Studies* 42:114–28.

Pfau, M., and Kenski, H. C. (1990). *Attack Politics: Strategy and Defense.* New York: Praeger.

Pfau, M., Kenski, H. C., Nitz, N., and Sorenson, J. (1990). "Efficacy of Inoculation Strategies in Promoting Resistance to Political Attack Messages: Application to Direct Mail." *Communication Monographs* 57:25–43.

Pfau, M., and Van Bockern, S. (1994). "The Persistence of Inoculation in Conferring Resistance to Smoking Initiation Among Adolescents: The Second Year." *Human Communication Research* 20:413–30.

Pfau, M., Van Bockern, S., and Kang, J. G. (1992). "Use of Inoculation to Promote Resistance to Smoking Initiation Among Adolescents." *Communication Monographs* 59:213–30.

Pomerantz, A. (1987). "Attributions of Responsibility: Blamings." *Sociology* 12:266–74.

"Prominent Cardinal Accused of Sex Abuse." (1993, November 12). *Columbia Daily Tribune*:12A.

"Prostitution Sting Nets St. Louis City Prosecutor." (1992, March 13). *Columbia Daily Tribune*:3A.

Pryor B., and Steinfatt, T. M. (1978). "The Effects of Initial Belief Level on Inoculation Theory and Its Proposed Mechanisms." *Human Communication Research* 4:217–30.

Rawl, L. G. (1989, April 3). An Open Letter to the Public. *New York Times*:A12.

"Rebuffed Moviegoers Get Apology." (1992, March 31). *Columbia Daily Tribune*:3A.

Reinhold, R. (1976, September 22). "Large Group of Undecided Voters Found Looking to Debates for Aid." *New York Times*:11.

Rensberger, B. (1992, November 3). "Breast Implant Records Were 'Faked': Dow Corning Acknowledges That Technicians Changed Some Charts." *Washington Post*:A3.

Reusch, J., and Bateson, G. (1951). *Communication: The Social Matrix of Psychiatry*. New York: Norton.

"Riders Lament Inadequacies of Bus Service." (1994, February 5). *Columbia Daily Tribune*:1A.

Riley, P., and Hollihan, T. A. (1981). "The 1980 Presidential Debates: A Content Analysis of the Issues and Arguments." *Speaker and Gavel* 18:47–59.

Riley, P., Hollihan, T., and Cooley, D. (1980, November). *The 1976 Presidential Debates: An Analysis of the Issues and Arguments*. Paper presented at the annual meeting of the Central States Speech Association, Chicago, IL.

Ritter, K., and Henry, D. (1994). "The 1980 Reagan-Carter Presidential Debate." In *Rhetorical Studies of National Political Debates, 1960–1992*, edited by R. F. Friedenberg, 69–93. 2d ed. New York: Praeger.

Roper, E. (1960, November). "Polling Post-Mortem." *Saturday Review*:10–13.

Rosenfield, L. W. (1968). "A Case Study in Speech Criticism: The Nixon-Truman Analog." *Speech Monographs* 35:435–50.

Rosenthal, P. I. (1966). "The Concept of Ethos and the Structure of Persuasion." *Speech Monographs* 33:11–26.

Rouner, D., and Perloff, R. M. (1988). "Selective Perception of Outcome of First 1984 Presidential Debate." *Journalism Quarterly* 65:141–47, 240.

Rowland, R. (1986). "The Substance of the 1980 Carter-Reagan Debate." *Southern Speech Communication Journal* 51:142–65.

Ryan, H. R. (1982). "*Kategoria* and *Apologia*: On Their Rhetorical Criticism as a Speech Set." *Quarterly Journal of Speech* 68:256–61.

———, ed. (1988). *Oratorical Encounters: Selected Studies and Sources of Twentieth-Century Political Accusations and Apologies*. Westport, CT: Greenwood.

———. (1994). "The 1988 Bush-Dukakis Presidential Debates." In *Rhetorical Studies of National Political Debates, 1960–1992*, edited by R. F. Friedenberg, 145–66. 2d ed. New York: Praeger.

"Safer Cigarette Developed, Not Marketed." (1992, September 9). *Columbia Daily Tribune:*4A.

Safire, W. (1992, October 12). "Clinton Doesn't Lose: The Debate Had Its Moments." *New York Times:*A19.

"Same Drugs Cost Far More in U.S. than in Britain." (1994, February 2). *Columbia Daily Tribune:*7A.

Samovar, L. A. (1962). "Ambiguity and Unequivocation in the Kennedy-Nixon Television Debates." *Quarterly Journal of Speech* 48:277–79.

———. (1965). "Ambiguity and Unequivocation in the Kennedy-Nixon Debates: A Rhetorical Analysis." *Western Speech* 29:211–18.

Sawyer, A. G. (1973). "The Effects of Repetition of Refutational and Supportive Advertising Appeals." *Journal of Marketing Research* 10:23–33.

Schlenker, B. R. (1980). *Impression Management: The Self-Concept, Social Identity, and Interpersonal Relations.* Monterey, CA: Brooks/Cole.

Schneider, W., and Shiffrin, R. M. (1977). "Controlled and Automatic Human Information Processing: I. Detection, Search, and Attention." *Psychological Review* 84:1–66.

Schonbach, P. (1980). "A Category System for Account Phases." *European Journal of Social Psychology* 10:195–200.

———. (1990). *Account Episodes: The Management or Escalation of Conflict.* Cambridge: Cambridge University Press.

Scott, M. H., and Lyman, S. M. (1968). "Accounts." *American Sociological Review* 33:46–62.

"Scouts Files Suggest Group Is 'Magnet for Pedophiles.' " (1993, October 14). *Columbia Daily Tribune:*12A.

"Sears to Drop Incentives in Auto Service Centers." (1992, June 23). *Columbia Daily Tribune:*5B.

"Security for President's Haircut Costs $1,800." (1993, May 26). *Columbia Daily Tribune:*1A.

Semin, G. R., and Manstead, A. S. R. (1983). *Accountability of Conduct: A Social Psychological Analysis.* New York: Academic Press.

Sharkey, W. F. (1992). "Use and Responses to Intentional Embarrassment." *Communication Studies* 43:257–75.

Sharkey, W. F., and Stafford, L. (1990). "Responses to Embarrassment." *Human Communication Research* 17:315–42.

Shiffrin, R. M., and Schneider, W. (1977). "Controlled and Automatic Human Information Processing: II. Perceptual Learning, Automatic Attending, and a General Theory." *Psychological Review* 84:127–90.

Sigelman, L., and Sigelman, C. K. (1984). "Judgments of the Carter-Reagan Debate: The Eyes of the Beholders." *Public Opinion Quarterly* 48:624–28.

Simons, H. W., and Leibowitz, K. (1979). "Shifts in Candidate Images." In *The Great Debates: Carter versus Ford, 1976,* edited by S. Kraus, 398–404. Bloomington: Indiana University Press.

Smith, C. A., and Smith, K. B. (1994). "The 1984 Reagan-Mondale Presidential Debates." In *Rhetorical Studies of National Political Debates, 1960–1992,* edited by R. F. Friedenberg, 95–119. 2d ed. New York: Praeger.

Snyder, C. R., Higgins, R. L., and Stucky, R. J. (1983). *Excuses: Masquerades in Search of Grace.* New York: John Wiley and Sons.

"Stealth Job by CIA Draws Fire: Congress Angry Over $310 Million Project." (1994, August 9). *Columbia Daily Tribune*:1A.

Stokes, D. E., and DiIulio, J. J. (1993). "The Setting: Valence Politics in Modern Elections." In *The Elections of 1992*, edited by M. Nelson, 1–20. Washington, DC: Congressional Quarterly Press.

Stuckey, M. E., and Antczak, F. J. (1995). "The Battle of Issues and Images: Establishing Interpretive Dominance." In *Presidential Campaign Discourse: Strategic Communication Problems*, edited by K. E. Kendall, 117–34. Albany: State University of New York Press.

Swerdlow, J. L. (1984). *Beyond Debate: A Paper on Televised Presidential Debates*. New York: Twentieth Century Fund.

———. (1987). "The Strange—and Sometimes Surprising—History of Presidential Debates in America." In *Presidential Debates 1988 and Beyond*, edited by J. L. Swerdlow, 3–16. Washington, DC: Congressional Quarterly.

Sykes, G. M., and Matza, D. (1957). "Techniques of Neutralization: A Theory of Delinquency." *American Sociological Review* 22:664–70.

Tannenbaum, P. H., Maccaulay, J. R., and Norris, E. L. (1966). "Principle of Congruity and Reduction of Persuasion." *Journal of Personality and Social Psychology* 3:233–38.

Tate, E., and Miller, G. R. (1973). *Resistance to Persuasion Following Counter-Attitudinal Advocacy: Some Preliminary Thoughts*. Paper presented at the annual meeting of the International Communication Association, Montreal, Canada.

Taylor, H. (1992, October 11). "Most Americans Think 'It is Time for a New Generation of Leadership' and That's Bad News for President Bush." *Harris Poll* 63:1–5.

Tedeschi, J. T., and Reiss, M. (1981). "Verbal Strategies in Impression Management." In *The Psychology of Ordinary Explanations of Social Behavior*, edited by C. Antaki, 271–326. London: Academic Press.

Thistlethwaite, D. L., Kemenetsky, J., and Schmidt, H. (1956). "Factors Influencing Attitude Change Through Refutative Communications." *Speech Monographs* 23:14–25.

Tiemens, R. K. (1978). "Television's Portrayal of the 1976 Presidential Debates: An Analysis of Visual Content." *Communication Monographs* 45:362–70.

Tiemens, R. K., Hellweg, S. A., Kipper, P., and Phillips, S. L. (1985). "An Integrative Verbal and Visual Analysis of the Carter-Reagan Debate." *Communication Quarterly* 33:34–42.

Times Mirror Center for the People and the Press. (1992, November 15). "The People, The Press, and Politics: Campaign '92." News release, Times Mirror Center, New York.

Toner, R. (1992a, October 15). "Clinton, Fending Off Assaults, Retains Sizable Lead, Poll Finds: Tonight's Debate Grows in Importance for Bush." *New York Times*:A1, A22.

———. (1992b, October 16). "Focus on Economy: Few Chances for Bush to Score Needed Points on Character Issue." *New York Times*:A1, A10.

———. (1992c, October 18). "Democrats' Hopes Soar, Republicans' Grow Heavy." *New York Times*:A1, A24.

Tracy, K. (1990). "The Many Faces of Facework." In *Handbook of Language and Social Psychology,* edited by H. Giles and W. P. Robinson, 209–26. Chichester, England: John Wiley.

"Transcript of the First TV Debate Among the Presidential Candidates." (1992, October 12). *New York Times:*A14–17.

"Transcript of Second TV Debate Between Bush, Clinton, and Perot." (1992, October 16). *New York Times:*A11–14.

"Transcript of Third TV Debate Between Bush, Clinton, and Perot." (1992, October 20). *New York Times:*A20–23.

Trent, J. D., and Trent, J. S. (1995). "The Incumbent and His Challengers: The Problem of Adapting to Prevailing Conditions." In *Presidential Campaign Discourse: Strategic Communication Problems,* edited by K. E. Kendall, 69–92. Albany: State University of New York Press.

Trent, J. S., and Friedenberg, R. V. (1983). *Political Campaign Communication: Principles and Practices.* New York: Praeger.

"TV Ministry to Seek Return of $9.3 Million from Bakkers." (1988, January 2). *New York Times:*A9.

Ullman, W. R., and Bodaken, E. M. (1975). "Inducing Resistance to Persuasive Attack: A Test of Two Strategies of Communication." *Western Speech Communication* 39:240–48.

Vancil, D. L., and Pendell, S. D. (1984). "Winning Presidential Debates: An Analysis of Criteria Influencing Audience Response." *Western Journal of Speech Communication* 48:62–74.

Vangelisti, A. L., Daly, J. A., and Rudnick, J. R. (1991). "Making People Feel Guilty in Conversations: Techniques and Correlates." *Human Communication Research* 18:3–39.

Von Wright, G. H. (1971). *Explanation and Understanding.* London: Routledge and Kegan Paul.

Wall, V., Golden, J. L., and James, H. (1988). "Perceptions of the 1984 Presidential Debates and a Select 1988 Presidential Primary Debate." *Presidential Studies Quarterly* 18:541–63.

Ware, B. L., and Linkugel, W. A. (1973). "They Spoke in Defense of Themselves: On the Generic Criticism of *Apologia.*" *Quarterly Journal of Speech* 59:273–83.

Watzlawik, P., Beavin, J. H., and Jackson, D. D. (1967). *Pragmatics of Human Communication.* New York: Norton.

Wayne, S. J. (1992). *The Road to the White House 1992: The Politics of Presidential Elections.* New York: St. Martin's Press.

Weber, R. P. (1985). *Basic Content Analysis.* Newbury Park, CA: Sage.

"Webster Guilty of Corruption." (1993, June 3). *Columbia Daily Tribune:*1A.

Weiler, M. (1989). "The 1988 Electoral Debates and Debate Theory." *Journal of the American Forensic Association* 25:214–19.

Weiss, R. O. (1981). "The Presidential Debates in Their Political Context: The Issue-Image Interface in the 1980 Campaign." *Speaker and Gavel* 18:22–27.

Windt, T. (1987). "Different Realities: Three Presidential Attacks on the

News Media." In *Essays on Presidential Rhetoric*, edited by T. Windt and B. Ingold, 76–91. Dubuque, IA: Kendall-Hunt.

———. (1994). "The 1960 Kennedy-Nixon Presidential Debates." In *Rhetorical Studies of National Political Debates, 1960–1992*, edited by R. F. Friedenberg, 1–27. 2d ed. New York: Praeger.

Winkler, C. K., and Black, C. F. (1993). "Assessing the 1992 Presidential and Vice Presidential Debates: The Public Rationale." *Argumentation and Advocacy* 30:77–87.

Wright, L. (1993, November 26). "Retailer Hit with Ad Violations: Attorney General Cites Show-Me Furniture." *Columbia Daily Tribune:*1A.

Zakahi, W. R., and Hacker, K. L. (1995). "Televised Presidential Debates and Candidates Images." In *Candidate Images in Presidential Elections*, edited by K. L. Hacker, 99–122. Westport, CT: Praeger.

Zarefsky, D. (1992). "Spectator Politics and the Revival of Public Argument." *Communication Monographs* 59:411–14.

Zhu, J., Milavasky, J. R., and Biswas, R. (1994). "Do Televised Debates Affect Image Perception More than Issue Knowledge? A Study of the First 1992 Presidential Debate." *Human Communication Research* 20:302–33.

Index

About the Authors

William L. Benoit is Associate Professor of Communication, University of Missouri-Columbia. He received his bachelor's degree from Ball State University, his master's from Central Michigan University, and his doctorate from Wayne State University. His publications include *Accounts, Excuses, and Apologies: A Theory of Image Restoration* (1995).

William T. Wells is currently a Ph. D. candidate in the Department of Communication at the University of Missouri-Columbia. He received his bachelor's and master's degrees from Southwest Missouri State University. He is preparing a dissertation titled "An Analysis of Persuasive Attack and Defense Strategies Used by Incumbents and Challengers in the 1976, 1980, and 1984 Presidential Debates."

About the Series

STUDIES IN RHETORIC AND COMMUNICATION
General Editors:
E. Culpepper Clark, Raymie E. McKerrow, and David Zarefsky

The University of Alabama Press has established this series to publish major new works in the general area of rhetoric and communication, including books treating the symbolic manifestations of political discourse, argument as social knowledge, the impact of machine technology on patterns of communication behavior, and other topics related to the nature or impact of symbolic communication. We actively solicit studies involving historical, critical, or theoretical analyses of human discourse.